Early Project Appraisal

# Early Project Appraisal

## Making the Initial Choices

Knut Samset

palgrave
macmillan

First published 2010 by
PALGRAVE MACMILLAN

Palgrave Macmillan in the UK is an imprint of Macmillan Publishers Limited, registered in England, company number 785998, of Houndmills, Basingstoke, Hampshire RG21 6XS.

Palgrave Macmillan in the US is a division of St Martin's Press LLC, 175 Fifth Avenue, New York, NY 10010.

Palgrave Macmillan is the global academic imprint of the above companies and has companies and representatives throughout the world.

Palgrave® and Macmillan® are registered trademarks in the United States, the United Kingdom, Europe and other countries.

ISBN 978–0–230–27324–5 hardback

This book is printed on paper suitable for recycling and made from fully managed and sustained forest sources. Logging, pulping and manufacturing processes are expected to conform to the environmental regulations of the country of origin.

A catalogue record for this book is available from the British Library.

A catalog record for this book is available from the Library of Congress.

10 9 8 7 6 5 4 3 2 1
19 18 17 16 15 14 13 12 11 10

Printed and bound in Great Britain by
CPI Antony Rowe, Chippenham and Eastbourne

# Contents


*List of Figures* ix

*List of Tables* xiii

*Preface* xiv

*Acknowledgements* xv

**Part I Front-End Assessment of Projects** 1

1 Attributes of a Project 3
- 1.1 The project as a means to achieve an aim 3
- 1.2 What this book is about 5

2 Successful Projects 10
- 2.1 Strategic and tactical performance 10
- 2.2 Two project cases 12
- 2.3 Analyses and decisions 18

3 Three Perspectives on a Project 20
- 3.1 The project's main stakeholders 20
- 3.2 The stakeholders' interests in the project 22
- 3.3 A broad planning perspective 24
- 3.4 The project concept 26
- 3.5 Projects in a life-cycle perspective 29

4 Three Main Phases in a Project 32
- 4.1 Processes and project phases 32
- 4.2 The possibilities to make amendments 35
- 4.3 The costs and benefits of front-end assessment 36

5 Uncertainty, Risk and Opportunities 38
- 5.1 Uncertainty in decisions 38
- 5.2 Uncertainty and information 43
- 5.3 Uncertainty as a metric in projects 45

6 Possibilities of Foreseeing 51
- 6.1 The desire to foresee 51
- 6.2 Predictions in projects 52
- 6.3 Predicting simple events 54
- 6.4 Predicting complex events 55
- 6.5 Trends and discontinuities 56

6.6 Predictable surprises 58
6.7 Predictability and information 60
6.8 Scenario planning 61
6.9 Costs and benefits of information 62

7 Strategic Guidance and Tactical Flexibility 66
7.1 Strategic guidance 66
7.2 Tactical flexibility 68
7.3 Limits to strategic planning and management 71

8 The Problem of Cost 76
8.1 Benefit versus cost overrun 76
8.2 Systematic underestimation of cost 78

9 The Problem of Utility 83
9.1 Overestimation of utility 84
9.2 Effects and impacts of projects 86

10 What is a Concept? 90
10.1 Concepts and strategic choice 90
10.2 Identifying a concept 94
10.3 Requirements and choice of concept 97
10.4 The choice of concept 100

11 Project Alignment: Needs, Objectives and Effects 104
11.1 Alignment of needs, objectives and effects 104
11.2 Stakeholder analysis 106

12 Objectives and Their Formulation 113
12.1 Using objectives in projects 113
12.2 Linked and parallel objectives 116
12.3 Identifying objectives: Four cases 119
12.4 Causality and probability assessment 126

13 Methods and Analyses in the Front-End Phase 130
13.1 Simple methods, facts and judgemental data 130
13.2 Four types of analyses 131
13.3 The half-life of information 136

14 Quality of Information 138
14.1 Qualitative versus quantitative information 138
14.2 Information and validity 141
14.3 Judgemental, probabilistic assessment of utility 143
14.4 Precision – clarity and unambiguity 145
14.5 Rational choice, causality and probability 146
14.6 Constructing valid information hierarchies 147

15 Front-End Assessment and the Decision to Finance a Project 149
15.1 Reason and experience 149
15.2 Information processes up front 151
15.3 Quality assurance of the bases for decisions 154

16 Three Steps in Front-End Assessment: Definition, Development and Appraisal of Concept 158
16.1 Tools in front-end assessment 159
16.2 Identifying the concept 162
16.3 Developing the concept 163
16.4 Appraisal of the concept 165

**Part II Tools and Techniques** **167**

17 Systems Analysis 169
17.1 An open-ended systematic process 169
17.2 Example: Choice of energy system 173

18 SWOT Analysis 182
18.1 A review of pros and cons 182
18.2 Example: Assessing sites for a housing development 186

19 Strategy Analysis – Logical Framework 188
19.1 Evaluating project strategies 188
19.2 Basis for the LogFrame 192
19.3 Expert judgement 194
19.4 Example: Building a tunnel for coastal ship traffic 195

20 Rough Analysis of Uncertainty 200
20.1 Probability and effects 200
20.2 Example: Building a tunnel for coastal ship traffic 203

21 Strategic Frames for Implementation 209
21.1 Strategic guidance and tactical flexibility 209
21.2 Contractual assignment of risk 210
21.3 Strategic frames 211
21.4 Example: Building a university complex 213

22 Top-Down Probability-Based Cost Estimation 215
22.1 Resources and precision 215
22.2 Example: Building a shopping centre 218

23 Assessing Profitability 225
23.1 Expressions of costs and benefits 225

24 Risk Analysis 230
24.1 Quantified expressions of expected value 230
24.2 Risk matrix 231
24.3 Identifying risk factors 232
24.4 Classifying risk 233
24.5 Risk policy 233
24.6 Example: Developing and implementing an IT system 235

25 Probability-Based Progress Analysis 239
25.1 Improved network analysis 239
25.2 Example: Linking a town to the mainland 242

26 Evaluating Projects 248
26.1 The moment of truth 248
26.2 Types of evaluation 249
26.3 An evaluation model 251
26.4 Ex ante evaluation 253

27 Boondoggles and White Elephants 257
27.1 Some project cases 257
27.2 Analysis and decision to improve quality at entry 260

*Notes* 264

*Reference List* 270

*Bibliography* 274

*Index* 279

# List of Figures


1.1 The project – a means to achieve a goal by applying a certain amount of resources 5

2.1 Measures of success – tactical and strategic performance 12

2.2 The indicators of success applied in this textbook 16

2.3 Measures of success as seen in relation to the management of the project, the project as such, and the business case, which defined the project 17

2.4 Indicators of success associated with the project's various outputs and outcome as time passes 18

3.1 Assessing projects in view of time and uncertainty 25

3.2 The project hierarchy as seen in the project's context 28

3.3 The project considered in a societal perspective 29

4.1 The project management view of a project during implementation 33

4.2 The effect of information on uncertainty up front 35

4.3 Economic effects of improved planning up front 36

5.1 Uncertainty, risks and opportunities 40

5.2 Outcome space for decisions to invest 41

5.3 Outcome space constrained according to an adopted risk policy 42

5.4 Potential to reduce uncertainty up from and during implementation 43

5.5 Operational and contextual uncertainty through the project phases 46

5.6 Uncertainty and risk versus the size, complexity and nature of a project 48

6.1 Continues trends as basis for prediction and prescription 57

6.2 Discontinuous change or trend breaks 58

6.3 Predictable discontinuities 59

6.4 Cost/information ratio and quality of information in a project 63
7.1 Strategic and tactical performance – four project categories 72
7.2 The project goal in view of the impact of a project 74
8.1 Cost estimates at four times in the front-end phase 79
8.2 Development of cost estimates in three projects 80
8.3 Strategic underestimation of cost 81
9.1 Unrealistic forecasting of passenger volume an inter-city train line 84
9.2 Strategic overestimation of benefit 86
9.3 Cause-effect chain including expected effects and side effects 87
10.1 The project in relation to the investment case 91
10.2 The Eiffel Tower – one of the most successful construction projects ever 92
10.3 Two persistent problems in defining alternative concepts 93
10.4 SpaceShipOne – an unconventional approach to solve major obstacles in space travel 95
10.5 The concept as an intervention in a cause-effect chain 97
10.6 A problem – not the absence of a specific solution, but an undesired condition 98
11.1 Alignment of needs, goals and effects 105
11.2 Deficient alignment of needs, goals and effects 106
11.3 Example of stakeholders in a project 107
11.4 Example – building project location map 108
11.5 Stakeholder analysis. The Influence versus Interest grid 111
12.1 Campus project: Hierarchy of objectives 121
12.2 Cause-effect chain for a combat aircraft acquisition project 123
12.3 Final cause-effect chain 123
12.4 Shipping tunnel cause-effect chain 124
12.5 Formally agreed road project cause-effect chain 125
12.6 Goal structure – requirements 127

13.1 Four types of assessments – from statistical analyses of facts to subjective judgement 132
13.2 Half-life of information 137
14.1 Qualitative and quantitative information by level of scale 139
14.2 Qualitative expressions of subjective probability 140
14.3 Validity as an expression of the quality of information 141
14.4 Validity and reliability, focus versus precision 143
15.1 Information during the front-end phase 152
15.2 A technocratic decision model 155
15.3 An anarchistic type decision model 155
15.4 External quality assurance for major public investment projects 156
16.1 Overview of tools for systematic front-end phase appraisal 161
17.1 General view of a system 170
17.2 Production system described as an input-output-model 171
17.3 Energy consumption in countries at different stages of development 173
17.4 Energy system showing the input-output parameters 174
17.5 Hydrogen as an energy carrier 179
17.6 Hydrogen-based energy system 180
18.1 SWOT matrix 183
18.2 Example of a building project: Three alternative concepts displayed 185
19.1 A logical framework for appraisal of projects 189
19.2 Example of a shipping tunnel: Initial layout in a logical framework 197
20.1 The first round crude review of uncertainties 201
20.2 More detailed classification of risks 203
20.3 Example of a shipping tunnel: A crude analysis of risk factors 205
20.4 Procedure for assessing uncertainties 206
21.1 Two types of contract: Reimbursement and fixed-price contracts 211

| | | |
|---|---|---|
| 21.2 | Strategic framework for project implementation | 212 |
| 22.1 | Probability distributions for input and output data in stochastic cost estimation | 217 |
| 22.2 | Splitting up a project into its constituent items | 219 |
| 22.3 | The cost estimation input values | 220 |
| 22.4 | Prioritization list (tornado diagram) | 221 |
| 22.5 | S-curve showing the cumulative probability for total cost | 224 |
| 23.1 | Cash flow over the lifetime of a project | 226 |
| 23.2 | Undiscounted and discounted cash flow in a project | 227 |
| 23.3 | Discounting – calculating the net present value (NPV) of an investment | 228 |
| 24.1 | Risk matrix | 232 |
| 24.2 | As Low As Reasonable Possible (ALARP) principle as a basis for risk policy | 234 |
| 24.3 | The risk matrix as used to provide an overview of the risk profile of a project | 235 |
| 24.4 | The influence diagram shows links between various risk elements | 237 |
| 24.5 | Example of an IT project: Risk matrix | 237 |
| 25.1 | Diagram for network analysis | 241 |
| 25.2 | Road connection to a town at the mouth of a fjord | 243 |
| 25.3 | Simple network diagram for deterministic calculation of implementation time | 244 |
| 25.4 | A tornado diagram to illustrate the uncertainties of estimates | 246 |
| 25.5 | Probability distribution for a project's total implementation time | 246 |
| 26.1 | Evaluation at different stages of a project | 250 |
| 26.2 | Evaluation criteria in a goal-oriented evaluation according to a Log-frame model | 251 |
| 26.3 | Evaluation criteria in relation to project strategy and cross-cutting issues | 253 |
| 26.4 | Summary evaluation of two projects | 256 |
| 27.1 | Decision tree with possible outcomes in a project | 261 |

# List of Tables


| | | |
|---|---|---|
| 3.1 | Three main stakeholders in a project | 21 |
| 3.2 | Examples of stakeholder perspectives and corresponding focus on objectives in two types of projects | 23 |
| 3.3 | Preferences of the two main stakeholders during preparation and implementation of a project | 31 |
| 11.1 | Effects of the new building on neighbours | 109 |
| 14.1 | Selected indicators of user satisfaction in assessing an office building project | 144 |
| 17.1 | Identification of needs | 175 |
| 17.2 | Requirement specification | 176 |
| 17.3 | Characteristics of energy systems | 177 |
| 17.4 | Evaluation of energy systems | 178 |
| 22.1 | Two types of costs estimation | 216 |
| 22.2 | Rough estimates and corresponding output values | 221 |
| 22.3 | Detailing of estimates, Step 2 and corresponding output values | 222 |
| 22.4 | Detailing of estimates, Step 3 and corresponding output values | 223 |
| 24.1 | Estimated risks of 13 anticipated events | 236 |
| 25.1 | Estimated durations: Input values from expert review | 245 |
| 25.2 | Estimated durations: Output values from simulation | 245 |

# Preface

This book is about what happens up front before a project is agreed upon and designed. It is about appraisal, analysis and decision making during the earliest stages when information is limited – but the decisions that will have the largest impact on the project's success or failure nevertheless have to be taken.

One current trend in society is that major tasks are increasingly carried out as designated projects, regardless of sector and size. Tasks that were carried out by specialized institutions in the past are now organized independently as projects across sectors, involving several institutions. There are numerous such examples, such as in infrastructure development, information technology and exploration and development of energy resources.

Experience in the field of project management clearly indicates the importance of systematic assessment of uncertainty and strategic choices in the earliest phase. This is when uncertainty is greatest, but at the same time when the possibilities for influencing development are strongest. Research indicates that a number of the major problems that occur in projects were apparent and could have been identified already at the earliest phase before the project was planned. Selecting the wrong type of concept incurs enormous additional costs in society, both during implementation and after projects have been completed. Uncertainty assessment and concept development in the front-end phase of projects is a neglected field. This is despite the fact that major improvements can be made in the front-end phase using relatively simple methodology and at reasonable cost that together can subsequently improve the chance of success significantly.

This book is aimed at university students, planners, advisors and decision makers in industry and the public administration. The first part of the book provides an overview of essential terms and principles necessary to understand the underlying pathology and what it takes to design healthy projects. The second part describes tools and techniques that can be used to this end, to manipulate key parameters in a consistent way. A number of examples are used throughout the book to illustrate principles and methods, which make the text accessible to non-experts as well.

# Acknowledgements

This book draws upon experience and findings from almost ten years of research on front-end management of major investment projects within the 'Concept Research Program' at the Norwegian University of Science and Technology in Trondheim, Norway. For more information see www.concept.ntnu.no. Good friends and colleagues in the research community have shared their ideas, suggestions and comments at various stages of the process, in particular Bjørn Andersen, Bjørn Otto Elvenes, Kjell Austeng, Frode Drevland, Tore Haavaldsen, Ole Jonny Klakegg, Ola Lædre, Ole Morten Magnussen, Nils Olsson, Carl Christian Røstad and Olav Torp. Many thanks also to Peder Berg of the Norwegian Ministry of Finance and other very capable professionals assigned to the ministry's Quality Assurance Scheme. Special thanks to Terry Williams at the University of Southampton's School of Management for thorough comments and suggestions in the final round of editing. Finally, I am thankful to my wife, Kristin Ingstad Sandberg, a highly accomplished researcher in her own right, who has offered her ideas, comments and patience.

Knut Samset
February 2010

# Part I Front-End Assessment of Projects

1. Attributes of a Project
2. Successful Projects
3. Three Perspectives on Projects
4. Three Main Phases in a Project
5. Uncertainty, Risk and Opportunities
6. Possibilities of Foreseeing
7. Strategic Guidance and Tactical Flexibility
8. The Problem of Cost
9. The Problem of Utility
10. What is a Concept?
11. Project Alignment
12. Objectives and their Formulation
13. Methods and Analysis in the Front-End Phase
14. Quality of Information
15. Front-End Assessment and the Decision to Finance a Project
16. Three Steps in Front-End Assessment

# 1
# Attributes of a Project

*Introduction to the nature of projects and to some characteristics and issues of their design and implementation. This chapter also provides an overview of the contents and organization of this book.*

*Plans are worthless, but planning is everything.*
*—Dwight D. Eisenhower*

## 1.1 The project as a means to achieve an aim

The project is a relatively recent mode of work. In times gone by, dedicated, permanent organizations handled most public- and private-sector undertakings, such as the construction of bridges and roads, the arrangement of cultural and sports events, the development of new industrial products, the solving of research problems or the testing of new drugs.[1]

However, over the past few decades, projects have become an increasingly important way to organize work. More than ever before, projects are used to handle major corporate and public works. They operate across organizations, and are terminated when a planned task is completed. The number of such major projects has increased dramatically, not least in sectors such as offshore, infrastructure and information technology. But projects are also organized within individual organizations. This means that an organization's value added and profitability increasingly depend on successful projects.

Work performed by organizations generally involves either operations or projects, although the two may overlap. Operations and projects share many characteristics; for example, both are performed by people, and both are planned, executed and controlled. They differ primarily in that

> A project is a temporary endeavour undertaken to create a unique product or service.
>
> (Project Management Institute, PMI)

operations are ongoing and repetitive while projects are temporary and unique. Temporary means that every project has a definite beginning and a definite end. Unique means that the product or service involved differs in some distinguishing way from all similar products or services.

Projects are undertaken at all levels of the organization. A project may involve an individual or thousands of people. A project may be completed in less than 100 hours or may require several million hours of work. A project may involve a single unit of an organization or may cross organizational boundaries, as in joint ventures and partnering. Projects are often critical components of the performing organization's business strategy. Examples of projects include:

- developing a new product or service
- effecting a change in structure, staffing or style of an organization
- designing a new transport vehicle
- developing or acquiring a new or modified information system
- constructing a building or facility
- managing a campaign for political office
- implementing a new business procedure or process

The tasks that projects are assigned to execute are defined in terms of more or less precise and realistic goals, see Figure 1.1. A project is a temporary arrangement and comprises a more or less unique undertaking, so the uncertainty of it is often greater than what is commonplace in permanent organizations. Because planning and implementation entail uncertainty, the extent to which the project will attain its goal is also uncertain. This is one reason why advanced know-how and tools that can improve the planning and management of projects have considerable, ever-greater economic impact. It is also one of the reasons why there has been an upswing in evaluating ongoing and completed projects.

There are innumerable examples of projects that have incurred high additional costs, both during and after they have been implemented.

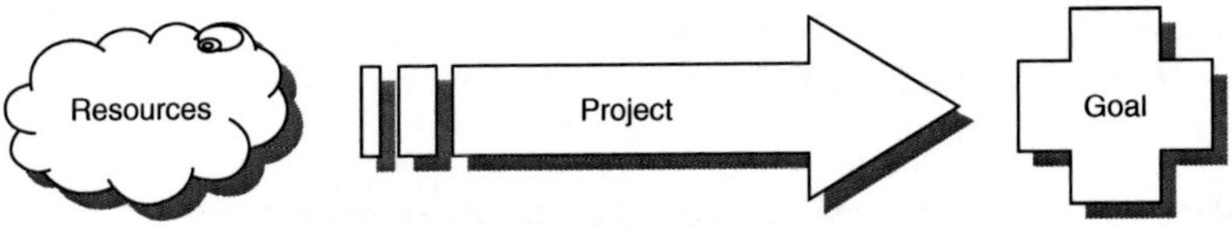


*Figure 1.1* A project is a means to achieve a goal by applying a certain amount of resources. Somewhere along the line there might be a need to undertake an evaluation in order to ascertain whether the project will be or has been successful

A comprehensive study of major projects[2] (Morris and Hough 1991) concluded that the track records of projects, particularly large and complex projects, are fundamentally poor. Overruns are common. Many projects are seen as failures, particularly by the public. Consequently the increasing use of projects seems inconsistent with the recurring problems of their overrunning budgets and overreaching set limits.

That said, most projects attain their immediate objectives in one way or another, even if many are inordinately expensive or delayed. Cost overruns and delays may have serious consequences in some projects, though in many cases their impacts may be less severe, such as when seen in a long-term perspective. Often a cost overrun is minor if viewed in relation to life-cycle costs and revenue. Another issue is whether a cost overrun is caused by an unrealistic budget or by poor project management. In other words: could an overly costly project realistically have been cheaper, or was the result attained as good as possible?[3]

Projects are increasingly used for several reasons. First and foremost, many tasks are so large and complex that individual organizations lack the expertise or capacity to carry them out alone. This is particularly the case in small countries. Another reason is that a project focuses and visualizes the task and consequently has a motivating effect on all stakeholders. In projects, responsibilities are clarified, and the different parties are made accountable. Moreover, the project affords an expedient means for transferring risk from the financing to the implementing party. The project also is an advantageous way to organize activities, which lets participants pool resources and cooperate towards a common goal.

## 1.2 What this book is about

The focus in this book is on the success of projects. More specifically, it delineates how we, in the early stages of a project, can improve the choice of concept through systematic assessment of the problems, needs and requirements to be met, as well as the uncertainty that may affect the project in the future.

To succeed, we need to identify the different stakeholders that are involved or may be affected by the project. A project is a meeting place for project owners, contractors, users and the public. Different stakeholders may have common interests, conflicting interests, or both. Their interests will reflect their perspective on the project. An overall societal perspective is usually broader than that of a bank, an entrepreneur or the users. Much of the discussion involving projects in the media is constrained to their implementation, to the delivery of their outputs or to attention-grabbing aspects, such as cost overruns and delays. This perspective is short sighted, principally because it assesses immediate results that can be expressed in quantitative terms. In a more long-term perspective, the project's effectiveness or its utility is measured against its more complex objectives that can be verified only at a later stage. However, during the front-end phase, it is essential to have a broad perspective on an intended project and its features that are relevant for different stakeholders. These matters are discussed in Chapters 1–4.

Why do some projects fail to realize their objectives? The keyword is uniqueness. All projects are unique. A particular type of project may have been repeatedly implemented under similar conditions, but in fact, each such project has never been undertaken before. That said, it is essential to draw on experience from similar projects, not least because doing so may significantly improve the chances of success. But even with a solid foundation of prior experience, results may be elusive. For instance, foundation works have been completed thousands of times in similar construction projects, yet cost overruns for excavation works are commonplace. We can devote considerable resources to defining objectives, strategies and designs up front, yet can be fairly certain that changes will have to be made and that many of the assumptions of planning and estimation will not hold true. This is particularly true of projects that are really unique, large or complex, or apply new technologies. The time span may be considerable when decision makers must determine the project concept. The decision is needed as early as possible, but will have consequences well into the future. To make long-term strategic choices is important. The lack of information and our limited ability to predict under various circumstances are central problems. These issues are discussed in Chapters 5 and 6.

This book highlights the distinction between the strategic and long-term perspective on a project, and the tactical perspective, that is the short-term and problem-solving approach. The merits of detailed strategic planning are disputed. Several authors (Mintzberg 1994; Slevin and Pinto 1989; Christensen and Kreiner 1991) have discussed the limitations of strategic planning. Obviously, long-term plans are less likely to be implemented without major changes than are short-term plans.[4] Detailed planning is therefore less meaningful if the target is well in the future. It is equally essential to be sufficiently flexible to respond to situations that may arise as we progress.[5] This is what is called tactical performance. In a speech to the National Defence Reserve Conference held 14 November 1957 in Washington DC, President Dwight D. Eisenhower remarked that 'plans are worthless, but planning is everything.' One interpretation of the statement is that planning is useful in deciding on the direction and the strategic framework for a project and in attempting to foresee difficulties that may arise, so as to prepare for and eventually make the right tactical choices. This book elaborates the steps to be taken to ensure that the strategic perspective is right at an early stage. The limitations that follow are discussed in Chapter 7.

Uncertainty is inherent in all projects and consequently should be taken into account in a project's objectives and strategic framework. Not all organizations have a relevant established practice for so doing. One reason might be that the organization lacks the expertise for systematic identification and follow-up of uncertainty. Another reason is that the organization lacks the culture or policy to generate and apply stochastic estimates. This is particularly the case in public projects where decision makers have a tradition of using only deterministic estimates. For instance, politicians would not have been able to approve a budget frame for an infrastructure project if it had been expressed in terms of a cost range, for instance between 4.5 and 10 million Euro, even if this was the closest they could get to a realistic cost estimate up front. The problem with such a wide cost range is that it cannot be used for cost control – it would be an excuse to allow cost increases. The cost estimate must be defined in narrower terms, and with an expected value that allows realistic flexibility to manage uncertainty when the project is implemented. Such estimates must be based on systematic judgement of uncertainty at an early stage.

Failure to assess uncertainty in relation to cost estimation is one of the reasons why many projects are initiated with unrealistic budgets.[6] Project managers are then confronted with a difficult, often impossible task. There is loss of credibility vis-a-vis authorities, decision makers and the public. However, experience also clearly indicates that systematic underestimation of cost occurs frequently, most often to ensure that a particular project concept is chosen. Discrepancies can be considerable, so that the final budget ends up ten times the original estimate or more. Also, utility is often overestimated up front. The effect of this type of miscalculations can be severe, since it might affect the choice of concept. Realistic budgeting could help weed out bad project ideas. This is discussed in Chapters 8 and 9.

The front-end phase takes place when the project is only a concept or a construction of thought that has yet to be planned and implemented. It includes all activities from deciding on the initial concept to the final decision to finance the project. It is a precursor in which the main premises are decided, when the consequences of the decisions made are greatest, and when information available is lowest. It also is the time at which the cost incurred in making major changes is minimal. This implies that it pays to do a proper job before the concept is chosen and the project is planned in detail. It is therefore a paradox that most of the curriculum and textbooks for students in the profession termed Project Management focus on how to manage a project during the implementation phase, while the problem of how to systematically arrive at better project concepts up front is largely neglected. The concept is a solution to a specific problem that is expressed in sufficiently generic terms to allow different alternative technical solutions to be considered. Issues related to the definition and choice of concepts is discussed in Chapters 10–12.

One of the main problems in strategic planning is the lack of exact information. The time and energy we are willing to expend to generate relevant information is restricted. Also, our ability to predict the future is limited, even in cases when all conceivable information is available. Therefore, to a greater degree, our decisions will be based on judgement.[7] Given the uncertainty in the information basis, it often is senseless to use sophisticated analytical tools. The precision of findings depends entirely on the precision of the relevant data. Consequently, the finding will not be more credible if weak or judgemental data are processed for instance in a simulation model or one that produces stochastic information. This is what is commonly termed GIGO, or garbage in–garbage out. However, there is considerable evidence that much can be achieved up front by applying simple methods and intuitive judgement, provided we are willing to use resources to collect relevant information from similar projects, to systematically analyze and to assess uncertainty. The value of detailed planning at an early stage will have to be judged against the complexity in the subsequent decision-making process, which commonly involves various stakeholders with differing, often conflicting interests. So, the outcome can therefore be difficult to foresee as well as divergent from the advice of the analysts. This is discussed in Chapters 13–15.

This book presents suggestions for systematic front-end assessment of projects. A distinction is made between three phases: Concept Definition, Concept Development and Concept Assessment. Chapter 16 provides a brief description of this process, the parameters that are applied and how these parameters are used in different analyses.

Part 2 of the book comprises a more detailed presentation of these analytical tools. These are methods that can be used on the way from the initial idea until the final choice of project concept, where due consideration must be made of relevant alternatives, uncertainties and the strategic framework that will subsequently be the point of departure for detailed planning and engineering. The methods are presented in separate chapters and illustrated by examples.

# 2
# Successful Projects

*There is no single definition for the term success, and opinion varies on the characteristics of a successful project. The chapter aims to discuss these matters, illustrated with examples from some major public investment projects.*

> *Murphy's Law: If it can go wrong, it will.*
> *O'Mally's Law: If it can't possibly go wrong, it will.*
> *Sod's Law: It will go wrong in the worst possible way.*

## 2.1 Strategic and tactical performance

News about projects occasionally hits the headlines, usually when costs exceed budgets or when projects are significantly delayed. This is in itself a paradox, as the public as well as the media seem more concerned about the immediate outputs of a project than about the long-term outcome of the investment. Cost overrun and timeliness of delivering the outputs are restricted, premature measures of a project's success. In a broader perspective, a successful project is one that significantly contributes to the fulfillment of its agreed objectives. Moreover, it should have only minor negative unintentional effects; its objectives should be consistent with needs and priorities in society, and it should be viable in the sense that the intended long-term benefits are realized. These requirements were first formulated in the 1960s to be applied by the United States Agency for International Development (USAID). They were subsequently endorsed by the United Nations (UN), the Organization for Economic Co-Operation and Development (OECD) and finally the European Commission (EC). They are summarized in terms of five requirements or success factors that should be fulfilled: *efficiency*, *effectiveness*, *relevance*, *impact* and *sustainability*.

These are tough requirements that go well beyond the issues usually covered by the media or apparently the main concern of many planners and decision makers (Samset 2003). What is termed efficiency here represents only the immediate indications of a project's success in delivering its outputs. Clearly, there are many examples of projects that failed to pass the efficiency test yet still proved to be tremendously successful, both in the short and the long run. The leaning tower in Pisa might serve as a prominent example. As problems became apparent, construction was halted for decades twice and completion delayed with more than a century. Subsequently, it was the failures that made the tower such a tremendous tourist magnet and put an insignificant little town named Pisa on the world map.

Also, many projects have scored high on efficiency, but subsequently have proven disastrous in terms of their impact and utility.

> The concept of project success has remained ambiguously defined, both in the project management literature and, indeed, often within the psyche of project managers. Projects are often rated as successful because they have come in on or near budget and schedule and achieved an acceptable level of performance. Other project organisations have begun to include the client satisfaction variable in their assessment of project success. Until project management can arrive at a generally agreed upon determinant of success, our attempts to accurately monitor and anticipate project outcomes will be severely restricted.
>
> (Pinto and Slevin 1988)

In applying the success criteria above, we distinguish between the projects' *tactical* and *strategic* performance. Success in tactical terms typically means meeting short-term performance targets, such as producing agreed outputs within budget and on time. These are essentially *project management* issues. Strategic performance, however, includes the broader and longer-term considerations of whether the project would have a sustainable impact and remain relevant and effective over its lifespan. This is essentially a question of getting the *business case* right, or, in short, of choosing the most viable project *concept*. This is depicted in Figure 2.1. On the one hand, there is the project management perspective of doing things right. On the other hand the societal perspective of doing the right thing. Two project cases, discussed in Section 2.2 below, illustrate the distinction between the two types of performance.

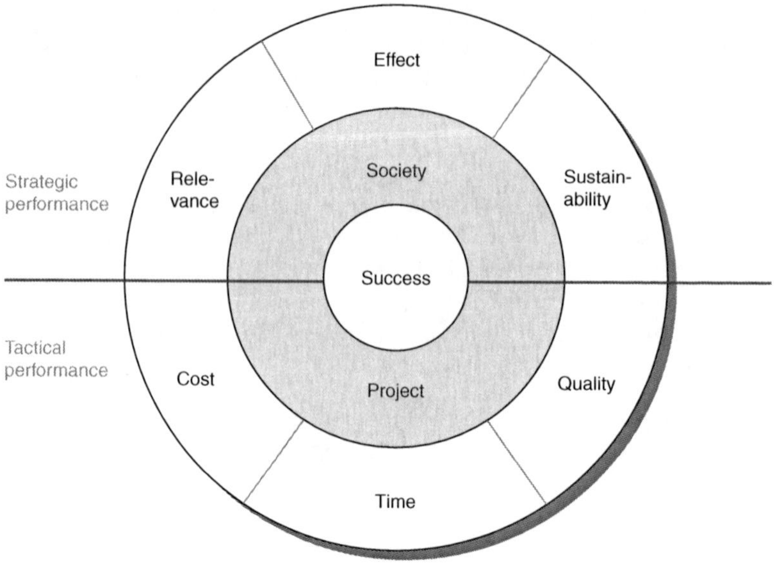


*Figure 2.1* Successful projects. Tactical performance is a question of delivering the project outputs as planned, while strategic performance is the worth or utility of the project as seen in a long-term perspective

## 2.2 Two project cases

The first project case that involved the building of the new University Hospital in Oslo, Norway was regarded to be viable in strategic terms but inefficient tactically. It was completed in 2000, one year behind schedule and at a considerable cost overrun. Newspapers comprehensively covered developments during the construction phase, and a public inquiry was subsequently commissioned to ascertain the reasons for the problems. Clearly, the cost overrun was considerable in absolute terms. But in relative terms, it was equivalent to just a few months of operational costs for the entire hospital and therefore insignificant when seen in a lifetime perspective. The overall conclusion after a few years of operation was that the University Hospital was a highly successful project.

It is far more serious when a project fails in strategic terms, even if it successfully produces intended outputs. Strategic failure means that the choice of concept is proved wrong. It could be the wrong solution or just a partial solution to the problem at hand. In some cases, the project may create more new problems than it solves, so problems outweigh benefits. In some cases the initial problem no longer exists when the project is completed.

The second project case, an on-shore torpedo battery built in rock on the northern coast of Norway in 2004 is an example of this sort of flaw. The facility is huge and complex and was designed to accommodate as many as 150 military personnel for up to three months at a time. It was officially opened as planned and without cost overrun. However, just one week later it was closed down by Parliamentary resolution. The reason was obvious: no potential enemy would be inclined to expose its ships to so obvious a risk. The concept of permanent torpedo batteries was a leftover from the Second World War and had long since been made obsolete by political, technological and military developments when the decision to build was made in 1997. What was remarkable was that this flawed investment, which can only be characterised as a strategic failure, was hardly mentioned in the media, perhaps because the project did not fail in tactical terms.

The torpedo battery project evolved out of a front-end phase that lasted for more than a decade. The effect of such a facility could be measured in terms of its defence capability or ability to deter. Clearly the torpedo battery could have no such effect, as the facility never became operational. The reason, of course, is that the project is no longer *relevant*, because the political scenario and warfare technology have changed over the last decades, and the anticipated military threat no longer exists. On the positive side, the project had some short-term *impact* in terms of local enterprise and employment, but its long-term effects are negligible. The project is not *sustainable* because the government is unwilling to pay for operations. It is unlikely that facilities can be sold at a price that covers investment costs, or utilized in a way that generates adequate income.

How could such a project be approved for funding? In retrospect, the key question is whether the problem could have been foreseen. The essential issue at that time was to prove that the torpedo battery was relevant. In this case, the assessment of relevance is essentially one of establishing a realistic military scenario. But the military scenario has changed since the Second World War. However, there's no doubt that sufficient information was available more than a decade before the final decision to go ahead was made. The Cold War had ended. Missile technologies have rendered permanent installations like the torpedo battery obsolete. If these facts were not entered into the equation up front, they should at any rate have been entered later had reviews of the project's relevance been made at regular intervals, especially in view of political developments such as the downfall of the Soviet Union. In this case, the conclusion is wobvious: there are no excuses. In view of developments in military technology and the political scenario, the concept should have been abandoned.

**Success factors**

| | |
|---|---|
| 1. Efficiency | The degree to which project outputs have been delivered as planned and in accordance with budget. Whether it could have been done cheaper, more quickly and with better quality. |
| 2. Effectiveness | The extent to which the objective has been achieved, that is the first order effect of the project for the users, in the market, in terms of production, etc. |
| 3. Impact | All other positive and negative changes and effects of the project, both in the short and the long term. |
| 4. Relevance | Whether the objectives are aligned with needs and priorities of users and the society. |
| 5. Sustainability | Whether the positive effects of the project will be sustained after the project has been concluded. |

The National University Hospital project incurred a considerable cost overrun during construction and was delayed by one year. *Efficiency* was therefore less than expected. However, there is no doubt that the project was relevant. It is the main national hospital, which provides highly specialized, state-of-the-art expertise not found elsewhere in the country, and it also is a key educational institution. It has proved to operate effectively. One of its secondary effects was to allow for urban development in the city centre on the old hospital grounds after the new hospital was built on the periphery of the downtown area. The project therefore scores highly on *effectiveness, relevance* and *impact*. In terms of its *sustainability*, there is no doubt about the commitment of the government to provide operational funding in the future. The additional cost incurred in construction is marginal in a broader-time perspective and has little impact on the future economic viability. On this basis, the conclusion is that the project is highly successful.

Could the problems encountered have been foreseen in this case? It was evident at an early stage that the project was *relevant* and would be *sustainable,* and would be so throughout the front-end phase and beyond. This provided a solid foundation for further planning and decision making. With this type of certainty up front, most projects would probably succeed in the long term. A retrospective view elicits a different answer. What went wrong had to do with emerging new technologies and added responsibilities after the budget was set. These problems became evident during the engineering phase and required additional funding and time. These are minor issues, and it would be unjust to expect that initial planning should have been able to capture problems at this level of precision.

Peoples' perception of success or failure in projects is commonly affected by personal preferences. This is why different people tend to assess the success of the same project differently, depending on their experiences and values. The need for common evaluation criteria, such as those presented above, is therefore needed. The primary advantage would be to improve consistency in evaluation procedures and judgement, and project-to-project transferability of lessons learned.

However, success is a highly aggregated parameter. There are large variations in how it is defined and interpreted. Success tends to be measured differently in different types of projects, depending of the nature of their immediate output and more long-term outcome. A hospital is assessed in terms of its health benefits, an industrial project might be judged essentially in financial terms, and an infrastructure project in term of its utility. Success can also be measured in different perspectives: more narrowly in terms of production output or more widely in terms of the market response or utility. It can be measured at different stages and may vary with time.

To illustrate how success is affected by time, take the track-record of the Empire State Building in New York as an example. The building was commissioned by General Motors, who wanted to exceed the height of the rival car manufacturer Chrysler's building, still under construction when the plans were released in 1929. Despite a very tight schedule, the building was completed more than one year ahead of schedule, almost 50 per cent below budget (the onset of the depression halved the anticipated cost) and was designed as per the specifications. In the narrow project management perspective the project would therefore be a complete success. However, considering the rented space it was a meager 20 per cent at the building's opening, so it was nicknamed the Empty State Building. In this respect the project was a failure. It took 17 years for the building to have enough tenants to turn a profit. Today it is again the tallest building in New York, it is an icon for the city and as of 2002 it was 97 per cent occupied.

But the assessment can also be in absolute or relative terms – that is in relation to what was agreed versus what was realistic. The project's ambition is expressed in terms of its agreed objectives. Project performance is a direct measure of what has been actually achieved. Clearly success measured in absolute terms may give a misleading conclusion if objectives are unrealistic. By measuring in relative terms, that is in relation to what could reasonably be expected as compared with experiences in similar projects – the projects might possibly be considered a success.

Success as a generic term means to gain advantage, superiority, accomplishment, achievement or added value. One interpretation of project success is that the stakeholders who are part of or affected by the project are satisfied. This is discussed in chapter 11.

Being such a compound measure, success will have to be translated into a hierarchy of indicators that would enable measuring. The five

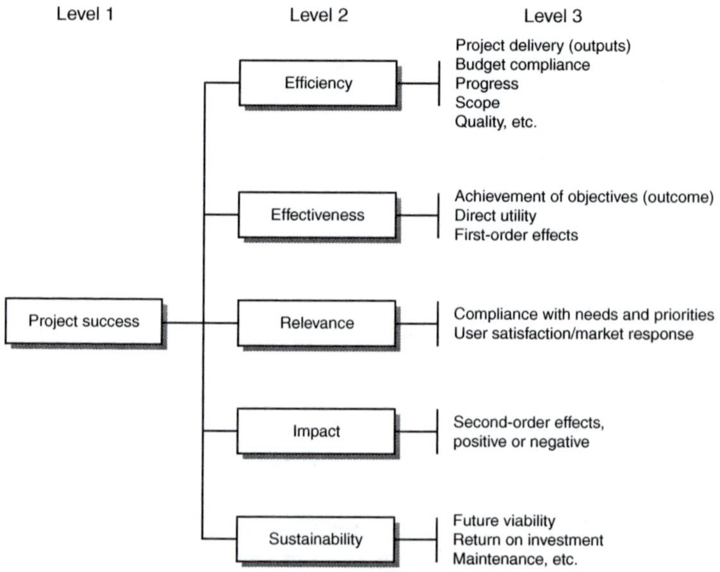


*Figure 2.2* The indicators of success applied in this textbook. The five overall indicators would provide a comprehensive assessment provided they are substantiated with sufficient evidence at level 3 in the hierarchy of information

success criteria presented above are shown in Figure 2.2. Examples of other such sets of indicators are presented in Figures 2.3 and 2.4. What the three have in common is that they intend to embrace a variety of types of projects, seen in the wide and the long-term perspective. At the top of the hierarchy (to the left) the indicators are generic and suitable for all types of projects. Further down in the hierarchy (to the right) the indicators become more 'detailed' and sector specific. The requirement would be that the success measure at the same time should be comprehensive and sufficiently detailed to provide a valid and reliable representation of what we intend to measure, in this case the success of a project. This is further discussed in Chapter 14. The success measures in Figure 2.2 are applied as general evaluation criteria in Chapter 26.

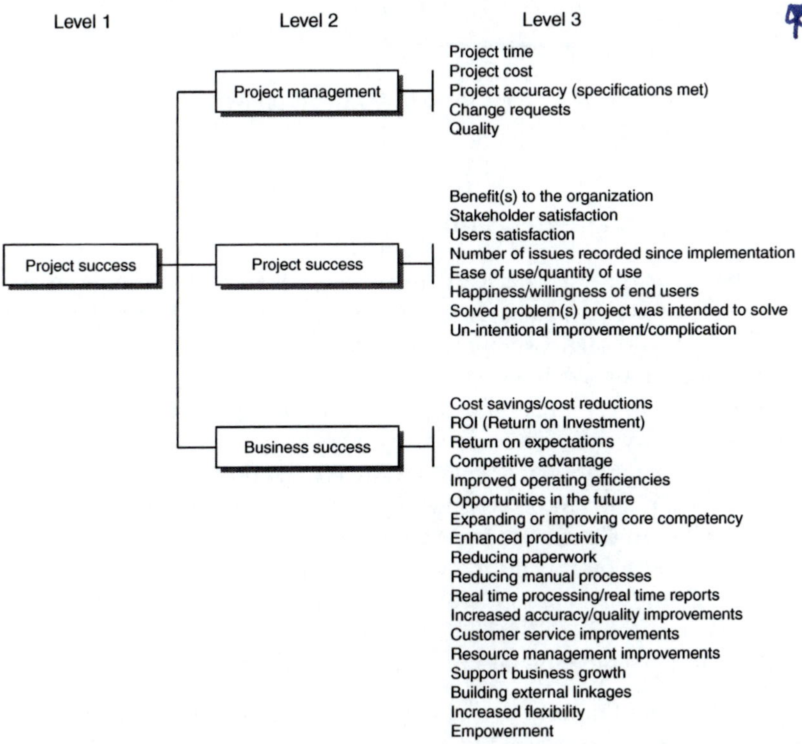


*Figure 2.3* Measures of success as seen in relation to the management of the project, the project as such, and the business case, which defined the project

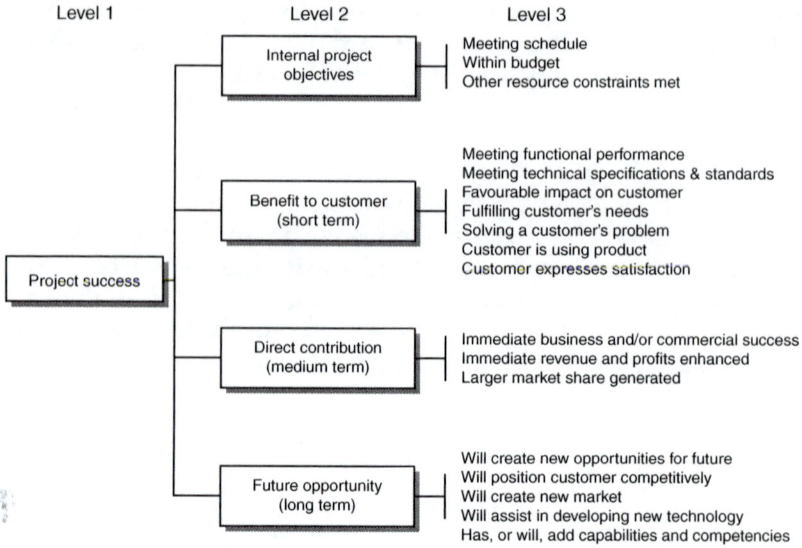


*Figure 2.4* Indicators of success associated with the project's various outputs and outcome as time passes

## 2.3 Analyses and decisions

This book focuses on what is required in analyses and planning in the front-end phase to ensure better projects. This is commonly termed rationalism. Although we appreciate the rational-decision model as an ideal, we are fully aware of the limitations facing planners and decision makers in real life: Time is limited, information is sparse, and stakeholder preferences vary and often conflict. But above all, we all live in a political reality that is not rational or even reasonable and only to a limited degree predictable. What can be achieved by rational analysis and planning is accordingly limited. In the front-end phase of a project, the main challenge is to develop a realistic overall understanding of the situation in order to identify an appropriate strategy, and then to identify the major requirements that must be fulfilled to solve the initiating problem, which will eventually guide the selection of project concept.

The bounded rationality model (Simon 1979) holds that problems and decisions should be reduced to a level at which they will be understood. In other words, the model suggests that we should interpret information and extract essential features and then make rational decisions within these boundaries. We can hope not for a perfect solution but for one that is 'good enough' based on the limited abilities of the analysts to handle the complexity of the situation, ambiguity and information.

To further complicate matters, we must take into account whether or not the analysts' advice is applied by decision makers. In the ideal model for decision making, decision and analysis follow in a logical, chronological sequence that eventually leads to the selection and go-ahead of the preferred project without unforeseen interventions or conflicts. In reality, the process is complex, less structured, and affected by chance. Analysis may be biased or inadequate. Decisions may be affected more by political priorities than by rational analysis. Political priorities may change over time. Alliances and pressures from individuals or groups of stakeholders may change. Information may be interpreted and used differently by different parties. The possibility for disinformation is considerable, etc.

This more complex type of decision making is what we typically expect in a democratic society. In major investment projects, the front-end phase may last for many years and include several parliamentary election periods with changes of government. In such cases, the outcome of a decision process is difficult to foresee. This might seem to be an intractable problem. On the other hand, it permits ideas and decisions to mature, objectives to be aligned with policy and political preferences, stakeholders to be involved, the public to be informed, etc. Democratic decisions take time.

Under any circumstances, starting with a well-formulated strategy may be an advantage, but is no guarantee for the best choice when the final decision is made. In some cases, the result may be entirely different from the initial choice. In other cases, the lengthy and unpredictable decision process may result in an optimal decision, even though the initial choice was entirely wrong. What the two projects discussed in this chapter had in common was that their success versus failure originated in the earliest phase when the choice of concept was made. The difference between the two was that the University Hospital was successful in strategic terms but less so tactically. The torpedo battery was an utter failure in strategic terms. When that happens, satisfactory tactical performance is irrelevant.

# 3
# Three Perspectives on a Project

*The most general criterion against which a project is assessed is the degree to which it is considered successful. Different stakeholders will have different perspectives and interests and often conclude differently in assessing the same project. This chapter discusses three main perspectives associated with the three main stakeholders: the contractors, the users and the commissioners.*

> *Too few people on a project can't solve the problems – too many create more problems than they can solve.*
>
> —*Anon*

## 3.1 The project's main stakeholders

Project stakeholders are individuals, groups and organizations who are actively involved in the project, or whose interests may be positively or negatively affected as a consequence of project execution or project completion. Usually many groups of stakeholders, external and internal, are associated with a project, ranging from those directly involved to those indirectly affected. Government agencies may be involved as initiators, commissioners or regulators. Owners and funders will have a major stake in the project; contractors and suppliers are responsible for carrying out what is agreed; there is a market and users who will use the product of the project; and there are the media outlets, individual citizens, lobbying organizations and society at large concerned about the outcome and impact of the project. That said, in this chapter, we will focus on three main stakeholders: the commissioner, the contractor and the users.

Projects are implemented by project managers or contractors in accordance with a given budget and schedule. What is commonly termed the *project perspective* is often the perspective of the contractor. This term is misleading, as usually several stakeholders are parties to a project. Assessment of the success of a project will reflect the interests of the project's different stakeholders.

The key direct stakeholders are the *commissioner*; the *contractor* and the *users*, see Table 3.1. Their roles and interests are described in section 3.2. The outline is simplified and does not take into account that in many cases there may be no clear-cut distinction between the three groups. The commissioner can, for instance, represent the society's perspective in a public project to construct a power plant, or could also represent the users directly in a residential housing project initiated by a housing association. In many cases, there is no distinction between the commissioner and the contractor, for example in a project which is internal to an organization. In other cases the contractor may also be the key user of the project's outputs.[1] The role of stakeholders is discussed further in section 11.2.

The contractor will not automatically be concerned with the project's possible impact on users and the society, unless explicitly so obliged by his contract. The contractor is not likely to follow up on such aspects on his own initiative, particularly if a follow-up might adversely affect cost, progress or other key management concerns. Also, usage and effect criteria might not be amenable to direct follow-up when the implementation is underway, because one can only measure the true impact after the result of the project is in use.

As discussed in Chapter 1, a project might not be successful in a broad societal perspective, even if it is implemented successfully from the

*Table 3.1* Three main stakeholders in a project

| **Key stakeholders** | **Role** | **Focus** | **Commonplace terms** |
|---|---|---|---|
| Commissioner | The initiating party with an interest in the long-term effect of the project. The party that provides resources and direction for the project. | Project purpose | Developer, project owner, project sponsor, initiating or financing party |
| User | Primary user of the (first-order) results or services of the project. The party that articulates priorities and needs, and ultimately approves deliverables. | Project goal | Target group, customer, beneficiary |
| Contractor | The party that is directly responsible to the commissioning party for delivering the outputs or product of the project. | Project outputs | Implementing party, Contractor, project manager |

perspectives of both the contractor (in terms of time, cost and quality) and the user. Also, we cannot unthinkingly assume that a project with significant time and cost overruns and with crucial quality flaws will be seen as a failure when viewed from the users' or the society's perspectives. Many projects that have failed in the implementation phase subsequently have proven successful, when assessed in a wider perspective. One example is Sydney Opera House, which started out with a six-year time frame and a budget of 7.2 million Australian dollars. In reality, it took more than 16 years to complete at a total cost of 102 million Australian dollars. Afterwards, the building became an international attraction, has triggered considerable direct and indirect financial gains and has put Sydney on the world map.

A basic lesson gleaned from project management studies is that to succeed, establishing the bigger picture is essential and to strike a reasonable balance between narrow and broad perspectives, in other words, the interests of the commissioner, the contractor and the user. Too often, the main focus is on the contractor's perspective. This might be one reason why some projects fail to meet overall needs and expectations of the public.[2]

## 3.2 The stakeholders' interests in the project

### The contractor's perspective

The project contractor is often also called the project manager or the implementing party, and is the one that is directly responsible for delivering the product of the project. The attention of project contractors is first and foremost directed at the production of project outputs, focusing on the cost, time frame and quality produced. In other words: the concern is the *tactical* completion of the project within the *strategic frames* which are laid down by the commissioner.

This is the most restricted and short-sighted perspective one can use in assessing projects. It refers to the lowest level in the project's hierarchy of objectives, as shown in Figure 3.2. For example, in a road project, the focus is narrowed down to the construction of the road itself and the extent to which it is built according to the agreed quality standard, budget and schedule. The project outputs for a school construction project might correspondingly be restricted to constructing and outfitting the school buildings.

A focus on the contractor's perspective alone can lead to a number of problems. Excessive emphasis on the agreed time schedule, budget and

*Table 3.2* Examples of stakeholder perspectives and corresponding focus on objectives in two types of projects

| Perspective | Focus | Road case | University case |
|---|---|---|---|
| Owner/Commissioner perspective | Purpose (second-order effects) | Economic effects of more efficient transportation | Long-term economic effects caused by graduates when employed |
| User perspective | Goal (first-order effects) | Traffic efficiency | Education |
| Contractor perspective | Outputs | Road constructed | University buildings completed and equipped |

so forth might divert attention away from possible adverse side effects of the project, which can, in the long run, bring about considerable negative reactions in society. Paradoxically this can result in a far more costly solution or can reduce the long-term economic benefits resulting from the project.

### The user's perspective

Users are also called clients, or the market in commercial projects. They are the ones that receive the product of the project, approve deliverables and state requirements. From their points of view, users are more concerned with the utility of the project and less concerned with its actual implementation. They tend to assess the project from a broader perspective, with reference to the *project goal.* The parameters used to assess the extent of success are associated with the project's first-order effects. Consequently assessment focuses on how the project's application and financial aspects affect the user. In a road construction project, assessment partly concerns the technical quality of the road but principally is concerned with whether the road makes it easier and faster to travel from A to B, in other words the distance and the flow of traffic. For a school construction project, the user's interests go beyond the suitability of the school buildings and are concerned with the learning and teaching that take place in the buildings. Such matters obviously fall outside the contractor's responsibility. The user's concern is that the project's goal is fulfilled, as illustrated in Figure 3.3. This is a first-order effect of the project that can only be achieved after the outputs have been produced. Hence, it is more ambitious, its fulfilment is more uncertain and the chance of success is more restricted as compared with producing the outputs which are the contractor's responsibility.

### The commissioner's perspective

The commissioner, also called the project owner or the project sponsor, is an individual, a group of investors or a government agency in public projects, who initiates the project and provides direction and resources for its implementation. The commissioner establishes the contract defining the work of the project and normally has a perspective beyond that of a user. In general, a society has a perspective that comprises the combined impact of the project on society as a whole. This is what is termed the project's *purpose*, which is the highest-level objective and expresses the long-term consequences of the project. Private investors normally place greater emphasis on the value added or profitability, while public investors will emphasize public utility.

In a road construction project, one is concerned not so much about the traffic flow, but with the positive economic effects it can have in terms of reducing travel time, by bringing about more productive time, by attracting new settlements and new enterprises near the road, and so on. In a school construction project, the long-term perspective might be to focus on the effect of education in terms of employment, the economic effect of provision of goods and services, and so on. In principle, the assessment is similar to that of the user, but now related not only to the primary 'user-group' but also to the interests of other parties that are affected by the project, directly or indirectly. Such assessments are ambitious; as the time horizon is extended and uncertainty is higher than is the case in the other perspectives (see Figure 3.1).

## 3.3 A broad planning perspective

One may distinguish between the project itself and two levels of spin-off effects that inevitably occur later and entail much uncertainty, as illustrated in Figure 3.3. The uncertainty associated with attaining the project's outputs is the lesser of the two, so the chances of success are greater. The uncertainty associated with achieving the goal is considerable, because it presupposes attainment of outputs. So the chance of success is correspondingly less. The greatest uncertainty is associated with accomplishing an overall objective, here termed the project's purpose, which assumes that both outputs and goals are attained. This is the longest-term perspective.

Experience from project activities indicates that success is in part contingent upon an early attempt to capture the entirety and find a sensible

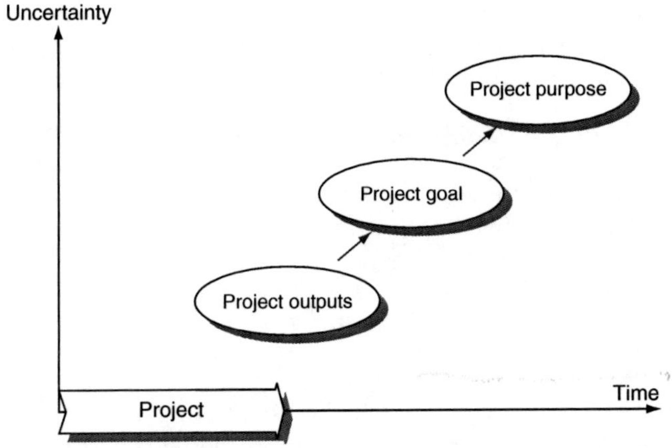


*Figure 3.1* Assessing projects from different perspectives as regards time and uncertainty

balance of perspective between narrow and broad well before the project is planned. In the activity traditionally called project management, the focus has principally been on the project perspective. Consequently projects often lack paramount goals or may have formally agreed goals that are unattainable compared to resource allocation. In many projects, the overview of uncertainty is inadequate, so the chances of realizing goals are further weakened. An early, systematic appraisal of projects in a broad perspective is necessary for a realistic design, that is, one in which the likelihood of success is acceptably high.

Market analyses, user analyses and quality assurance are usually used to expand the perspective to include user assessment. Impact assessment is the greater society's formal instrument for attending to the societal perspective in larger projects and developments. Experience also indicates that the owners of smaller projects often would be well served by an overall assessment of a project made before its planning and inception.

This is principally because the choice of a broader perspective automatically raises questions about the choice of concept itself. Concepts taken for granted, from the project perspective, as being most logical or most profitable can be less viable than differing concepts evaluated from the user perspective or the societal perspective.

Hence, the front-end phase should include consideration of which perspective should be used in evaluating a project concept. Today, there's tradition for the front-end phase assessments to build more on downstream analyses of the consequences of project choice and not on upstream assessments of alternative concepts in relation to goals and priorities.

That's what should be addressed in front-end phase assessments. It's about attaining the best possible strategic comprehension on a project as early as possible. It presupposes that a concept is evaluated with respect to an overall perspective, that is, the user and societal perspectives, and is not limited to the project perspective.

## 3.4 The project concept

The layout of a project concept, which is the starting point for the project plan, should set forth both the principal components of the project and the key contextual uncertainty components that might affect implementation (see Figure 3.2). It should include the three planning perspectives. It should have an overall objective or purpose that provides the reason for conducting the project and a goal that clearly and concretely states the condition to which the project is intended to contribute. For instance, as set forth in Box 3.1, a road project should contribute to solving a traffic problem. In turn, it should reduce accident incidence and cut travel time, so people may devote time to more valuable pursuits, such as work and leisure. Building of a school should contribute to education. In turn, that should contribute to improving production and services in society. Roads and schools are outputs; traffic flow and education are goals; and more productive uses of time and improved services are purposes.

Outputs should be tangible in the sense that the project is expected to be likely to achieve them. The goals and purposes are hypothetical in the sense that the project is but one of several conditions to be fulfilled before they are realized. The likelihood of that happening is accordingly less.

A good concept design builds upon a cause-effect chain that starts with a quantity of inputs to be used in the project to realize a number of outputs. Resources, of course, must be adequate to ensure that it happens. Consequently outputs must be defined so they are regarded as nearly a 100 per cent attainable. In practice, formal plan documents occasionally delineate outputs that are hypothetical because they lie outside the scope of the mandate and the resources of the project. Hence, the chances of success within the framework conditions of the project are formally absent.

**Example:**

Projects are often designed without an adequate analysis of the key stakeholders' interests and needs: a sub-sea road tunnel was built in order to connect a community on a small island with another island in the area. The project was part of a vague overall strategy to promote economic development in remote areas. Important aspects such as the users' ability and willingness to pay for the new infrastructure, or its usefulness for local industry were not properly assessed.

The project was successful from the contractor's perspective, being built on time and with costs considerably below budget estimates. However, because of the island's small population, it became apparent that the financial basis was inadequate and that user toll was unacceptably high. Also, it was obvious that a road connection to the mainland was not decisive for the industry. The size of the investment, combined with low revenue from toll fees made this seemingly successful project a heavy burden for local district authorities.

An analysis of how to interpret 'regional development' in this case could have restricted the project to meet the priorities of local industry and revealed that the real need was not for a road connection with the mainland, but for improved harbour facilities. In economic terms a much smaller project would therefore have been economically viable.

In the design of a project, the goal should not be more ambitious than what is realistically attainable within the time schedule for the goal. It's the same for the purpose. These objectives should be set forth as precisely as possible. It's also important that there be only one goal. That will help focusing planning, apportioning resources, project management and control. Often, projects have several independent goals, usually cause-effect chains at differing levels of ambition. In some cases, a single project can have several goals that work against each other. This results in vague management signals in the allocation of resources. It allows leeway for interpretation, so various parties can see the objectives of a project differently. Consequently good concept formulation of a project identifies a unifying goal; see the hierarchy of objectives in Figure 3.2.

The structure of objectives comprises the information essential for an overriding, unified description of the project. Such a description, devoid of detail, will be demonstrative for all parties affected by the project as well as a good starting point for evaluating the whole with regard to realism and design. This is in contradistinction to the delimited but detailed picture of a project usually presented using common project management software, in which assessment essentially is limited to attaining outputs on the basis of a detailed underlying activity plan.

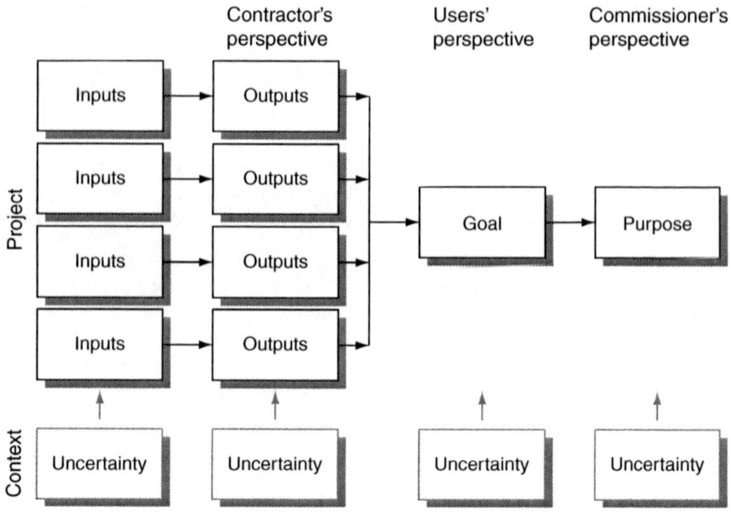


*Figure 3.2* The project hierarchy or structure of objectives, as seen in the project's context. The hierarchy depicts the logical linkage between resources and the project's outputs, as well as objectives that the project is intended to contribute to. In a realistically designed project, the probability of fulfilment of objectives at each level must be acceptable, conditional on the combined probability of fulfilling underlying objectives as well as the effect of contextual uncertainty external to the project

It's obviously wise to establish and analyse such an overriding structure before details are described and regulated by contract. The level of ambition must be clarified on the basis of systemic assessment of the likelihood of realization. This often is neglected. Projects are planned without appropriate prior assessment of prioritization seen from the user perspective. The societal perspective is probed probably only in projects that are so extensive as to evoke legal requirements of impact assessment.

However, many projects are the results of thorough needs appraisal or political proceedings in which various aspects of a project are assessed. Nonetheless systematic assessment of conditional probability of attaining objectives at various levels sometimes is avoided. In many cases, such an assessment can provide clarification that reflects back upon the formulation of the project and in some cases may trigger a complete redesign to make the project more realistic or to improve its long-term effect.

## 3.5 Projects in a life-cycle perspective

As discussed above, the perspectives people may have are related to their roles and responsibilities. The commissioner usually has a broader perspective than that of the contractor, which in turn is broader than the subcontractor's perspective. If there is no broad perspective at the highest level, one cannot expect that it will appear at lower levels. However, all parties need a comprehensive, precise picture of the project strategy that explains in accurate terms what is expected to be achieved by realizing the project outputs. This makes it easier for all concerned parties to help produce relevant information for managers at higher levels.

Figure 3.3 illustrates the project over time as seen in relation to the three planning perspectives outlined above. The project is a focussed undertaking where the primary objective is to produce a number of agreed outputs within a specified time frame. Commonly the project can be seen as a time-constrained part of a *process* with a wider purpose and a time perspective beyond that of the project. This process can be characterized by what is termed the project goal. In turn, the process contributes to a broader and more long-term societal process, which in this context is characterized by what is termed the project purpose. This objective gives a concerted strategic perspective both for the project and the process that the project is part of. It is often the case that the process presupposes the running of several projects concurrently or in sequence. In turn, the process will be one of many

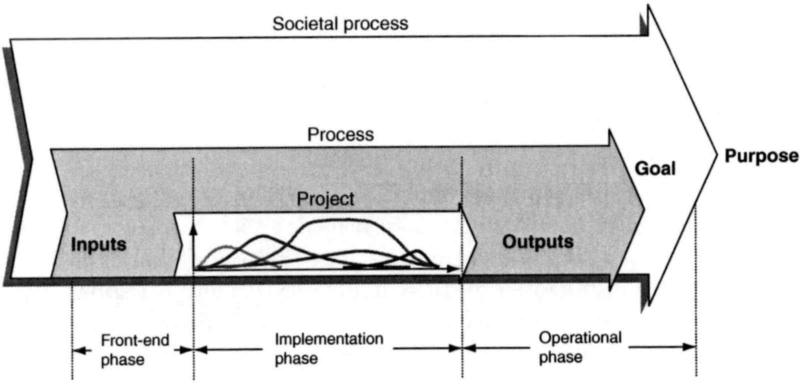


*Figure 3.3* The project as a part of a larger process, considered in a societal perspective

processes that contribute to the long-term objective, here called the project purpose.

The project is formulated in a *front-end phase*, which ends when the final decision is made to appropriate the relevant funds. It is planned and executed in the *implementation phase*, which ends when the project outputs are realized. Finally, there is an *operational phase* that follows when the project outputs are realized, that is when the building is built, the road is constructed, etc. As shown in Figure 3.3, it may be more appropriate to view this phase as a part of the process that defines the project. As discussed above, it is essential to distinguish between the project and the process, since both the objectives and the implementing responsibilities usually will differ in the two cases.

It follows from Figure 3.3 that time perspectives differ for the various parties. The contractor may have a time perspective of three to four years, and would wish to delimit his commitments to the period of the guarantee. The commissioner may have a broader time perspective equal to the payback period or beyond, and will seek to restrict his obligations to this period. For large infrastructure projects, the period could be 15–20 years. The lifespan of a construction can be far longer. A society can accordingly be obliged to maintain the built object for generations.

Economically the front-end phase deals, to a greater extent, with the organization of who bears the uncertainty and risk involved in the project. When the commissioner has established the strategic framework for the project, defined the main terms that should guide planning and implementation, and identified a qualified party to take on the responsibility for implementation, then it is implicit in the arrangement that he does not wish to manage the project in detail but hand the responsibility for implementation and the associated risk over to the contractor. This is summarized in Table 3.3.

His concern may rather be to ensure that the project moves in the right direction. He should monitor the project and detect as early as possible which amendments may be necessary to ensure that the project has the desired effect in a strategic perspective. The division of responsibilities between the commissioner and the contractor usually is regulated by contracts to ensure flexibility for the contractor within the strategic framework laid down by the commissioner.

In the front-end phase, the contractor will be concerned first and foremost with estimating a price that permits carrying out the work to a

*Table 3.3* Preferences of the two main stakeholders during preparation and implementation of a project

| | **Commissioners' main interest** | **Contractors' main interest** |
|---|---|---|
| Front-end phase | Ensure positive long-term effects | Establish a reasonable price |
| Implementation phase | Transfer responsibilities and risk | Secure efficient implementation and profitability |
| Operational phase | Secure return on investment | None |

satisfactory level without excessive risk and, at the same time, realizing a profit. This transaction is viable because the transfer of risk comes at a price. A core part of the contract between the two parties implicitly concerns how to share and price the risk. This forms the basis for the sharing of responsibility, such that both parties can fully or partly attain their goals.

This suggests a need to ensure all processes essential for project success, not only those active during the implementation phase. This is termed *project governance*. Experience indicates that many major failures could have been avoided, and return on investments could have been considerably higher, had the strategic alignment and design of projects been improved up front. This is because even major failures often result from surprisingly obvious or predictable causes, such as in the case of the torpedo battery in Chapter 2. A common problem is inadequate management and analysis in the front-end phase resulting in unrealistic assessments of the perceived project in a broad societal or user perspective. It may be assumed that in quite a few of such cases efforts to improve the choice of concept and design of project up front would pay off. This is what is termed *quality at entry*.

# 4
# Three Main Phases in a Project

*Experience suggests that our possibility to make major amendments is at its highest in the earliest stages of a project while at the same time the cost of making the right decisions is low. The cost of making major amendments will rapidly increase as the project enters its implementation phase. In other words, our chance to increase return on investments at a relatively reasonable cost is at its highest up front.*

*Time passes – even when you are sitting still.*
*—Danish humorist Robert Storm Pedersen*

## 4.1 Processes and project phases

*Quality at entry* (QaE) is an indicator used by The World Bank to assess the viability of project proposals before they are approved. QaE is considered a prime determinant of successful project outcomes. The assessment focuses on three main questions:

- Are the project objectives worthwhile and the risks commensurate with potential rewards?
- Is the project likely to achieve its objectives?
- Is the underlying logic clearly articulated?

Procedures are in operation to use this metric on all projects supported by The World Bank and annual reviews are carried out to determine how the organization is performing on what is perceived as an essential indicator of future performance when projects are implemented. The reason is the strong correlation between QaE and the success of projects that the Bank has documented, see section 7.1.

The *entry phase* here is synonymous with what is termed the front-end phase in this book, which ends with the final decision to appropriate funds for the project. The front-end phase is easily defined from the commissioner's point of view, not necessarily the project manager's perspective.

Seen in a project management perspective, the project is a sequential series of overlapping processes as illustrated in Figure 4.1, from the time it is commissioned until its outputs have been delivered. The planning and execution processes dominate. The project starts when funding is secured and the decision to go-ahead is finalized. It starts with initiating processes that essentially are concerned with committing the various parties to planning and execution. It proceeds with planning and detailed engineering, while at the same time the execution processes are phased in. Planning continues well into the execution phase. The project will be finalized in a short but intense phase of closing processes involving approval, accounting, documentation, training etc. In combination, this is termed project management and is described in textbooks such as Project Management Institute's 'Body of Knowledge' (PMI 2006).

However, this book focuses on the processes that precede the project – pre-studies are made; the concept is identified; alternatives solutions considered; stakeholders get involved; funding is negotiated etc. The contractor may not yet have been selected. At this stage, the project is considered in terms of a black box, an input-output device applied to serve

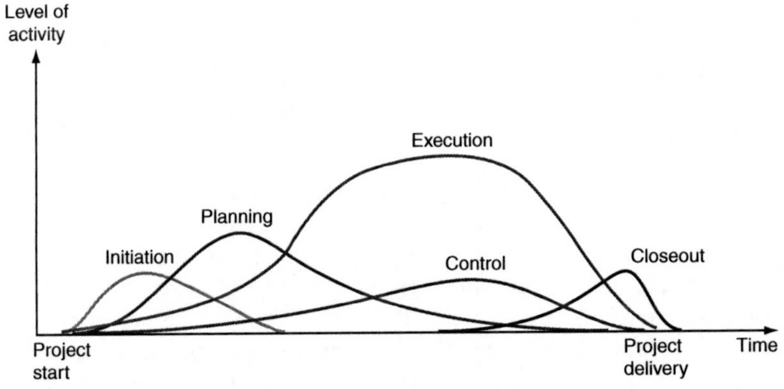


*Figure 4.1* The project management view of a project from agreement to go ahead until outputs are delivered and the project is terminated

**Project phases**

| | |
|---|---|
| Front-end Phase | From the time initial concepts are conceived until funds are appropriated to the project |
| Implementation Phase | From detailed planning until agreed outputs (operational objectives) have been produced |
| Operational Phase | The pay-back period until the results of the project (buildings, roads, software, etc.) are no longer in use |

a purpose. The concern is essentially on the purpose and on how well it will be served by the outputs of the project, than on the project itself. This is illustrated in Figure 3.3.

A project's life cycle may be split into separate phases. What characterizes the different phases may be more or less clearly defined. Phases are defined according to what appears useful, commonly by processes, ownership or responsibilities. One common way to split the life cycle of a project is to distinguish between the identification phase, the definition phase, the pre-appraisal phase, the planning phase, the implementation phase, the operational phase and the termination phase. Since these phases will overlap, the distinction between them may seem unclear. Accordingly, in this book, the picture is simplified by splitting the life cycle into just three phases: the front-end phase, the implementation phase and the operational phase, with the focus on the first of the three. The distinction is made between concept development and detailed planning. Concept development starts out with an overall analysis of needs, problems and requirements in order to identify the most feasible project strategy, the project's main features and its objectives. This process aims to identify the overall generic concept and the different concept alternatives that should be considered.

On the other hand, planning is the detailed design of the project in terms of its budget, activities, scope, time schedule and quality. While the concept development process yields an overall understanding of the project in its context and life-cycle perspective, the project plan provides the terms of reference for how it should be implemented. Consequently, in this book the implementation phase includes all activities subsequent to the final decision is made to finance the project, such as detailed planning and engineering in addition to the implementation of the project itself.

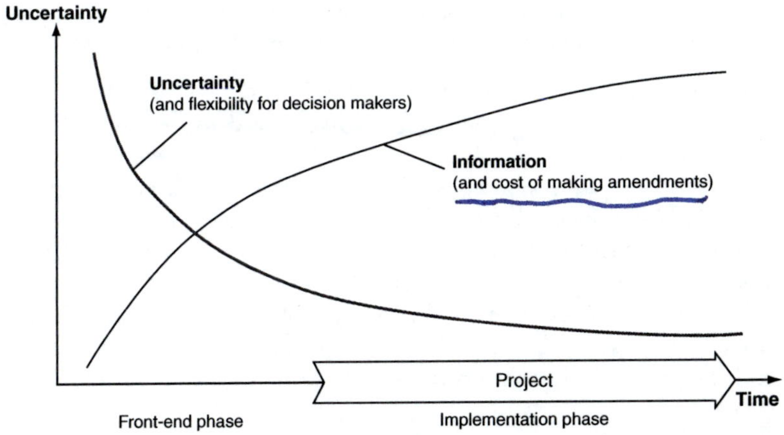


*Figure 4.2* Our possibility to influence is highest up front, and the cost of major amendments in the project increases rapidly as time approaches detailed planning and project execution

## 4.2 The possibilities to make amendments

Terms for the project are defined in the front-end phase. At that stage, our possibilities to influence are greatest and the knowledge of what lies ahead is least. The influence possibilities diminish little by little as decisions are made, alternatives chosen, strategies determined, contracts entered and work begun and finished out in the project phase. This is illustrated in Figure 4.2.

Early on, before the realization of a project starts through binding agreements, the project's goal and constraints can be changed without unduly affecting costs. Consequently it's vital that the uncertainty of the project be charted early, so that knowledge of it can be used to shape the project by exploiting the positive consequences of uncertainty and reducing the negative.

In principle, the later substantial changes are made in the course of a project, the greater excess costs they incur, as they may involve changes in existing plans, work in progress or contractual commitments. Such changes introduced in the implementation phase can considerably affect costs. In general, it's increasingly difficult to introduce change as a project nears completion, and the effects of changes diminish as work draws to a close. This underscores the importance of a total picture of a project's uncertainty with possibilities and risks, as failing to handle uncertainty early in a project may trigger inconvenient changes later on.

As we will read later, uncertainty customarily is defined as a lack of relevant information for valid decision making. This definition is useful but has its limits. Clearly, uncertainty cannot be eliminated merely by acquiring information. Information is a necessary but insufficient means for mastering and reducing uncertainty. The assumption that uncertainty is greatest in the front-end phase when the wealth of information is least is nonetheless a strong incentive for acquiring as much relevant information as possible early on in order to reduce uncertainty. The central questions then are: What sorts of information are available? What type of information is needed? Are there limits to using information? And so on?

## 4.3 The costs and benefits of front-end assessment

The significance of improving quality at entry can be illustrated by a cash-flow analysis that extends over the lifetime of the project, as

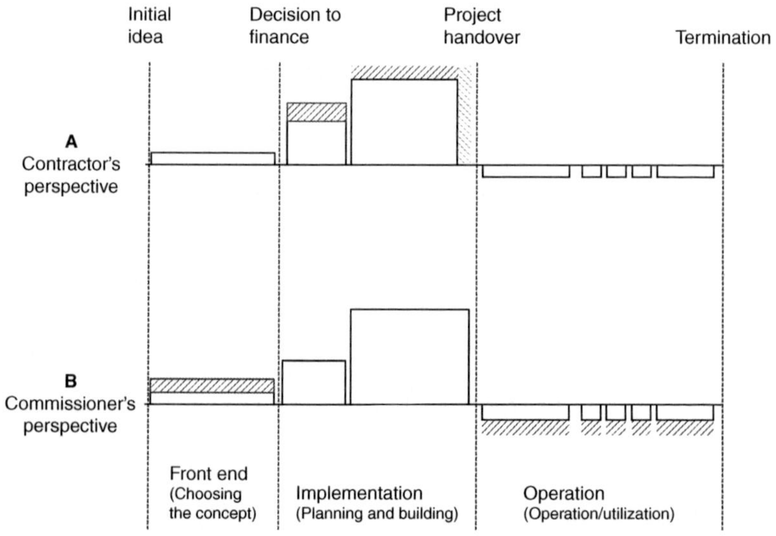


*Figure 4.3* Cash flow analysis – improving a project's economic viability. Diagram A: An increase in resources during the planning and engineering phase might help improve progress and cost control when the project is built. Diagram B: More resources up front might be a better proposition if it results in a better strategy and choice of concept, and ultimately increased utility and benefits during the payback period

In the West, uncertainty is a powerful motivation to start as early as possible to avoid delay. In the East, the corresponding response might be to defer as long as possible in order to consolidate the process and avoid substantial consequences of uncertainty. The rationale clearly is: the cost of delays for a project not yet started are most likely relatively small compared to the costs of correcting flaws on the way.

illustrated in Figure 4.3. The white rectangles in diagrams A and B illustrate the average cash flow during the phases of a project: the graph suggests that relatively small resources are used up front to develop the project concept, significantly more on planning and engineering, while the bulk of resources are spent when the project is built. A subsequent operational phase will yield an annual net income. The project is viable in financial terms when the (discounted) sum of annual income exceeds the sum of investments.

The amount of initial investments varies, depending on the nature of the project. In some cases, where of the project concept is chosen without prior analysis, the cost may be negligible. However, in the long-term perspective, this may prove to be an expensive proposition.

The shaded areas in Figure 4.3 illustrate the possible effect of increasing the use of resources in detailed planning and engineering (diagram A) and the front-end phase (diagram B). What is commonly done is to spend resources on planning and engineering with the likely effect to reduce implementation cost and duration. This is what is termed the contractor's perspective in Figure 4.3, which means, in other words, to improve tactical performance.

Diagram B illustrates the commissioner's perspective, which is essentially a strategic one. The shaded area suggests that more resources up front, to identify alternative concepts and choose the most viable one, can have a positive long-term effect on utility and annual payback. At the same time, there's reason to believe that the threshold for improvements at the earliest stage is low in terms of costs, while the potential for improvements may be considerable. In terms of the benefit/cost factor of such efforts, it could be very high in cases where one succeeds.

In conclusion, this is of course not a question of either–or. It goes without saying that both approaches are essential to success.

# 5
# Uncertainty, Risk and Opportunities

*A project is an ad hoc organization that shall address a specific task, to be completed by a target date, meet a specified budget and have a stipulated quality. Attention is first and foremost focused on the parameters of time, cost and quality. Projects often involve extensive, costly, unique and/or high-risk operations. A project model often is chosen just to handle uncertainty and risk. Employing uncertainty and risk as principal steering parameters then is vital for improving the project result.*

*Probability is the language of uncertainty.*

—*Bruce F. Baird*

## 5.1 Uncertainty in decisions

Risk customarily is defined as the product of the *probability* that an uncertain event will occur, and its *consequence*, that is, the potential effect of the event. Probability is commonly stated in percentages, so that 0.1 is a probability of 10 per cent that an event occurs and 1.0 indicates certainty of occurrence. Consequence may be expressed in monetary units, so risk, then, expresses expected value. It also may be expressed in other units, such as number of people killed or injured. Both risk and consequence may be precisely stated in quantitative terms by the ratio level, be graded at the ordinal level or possibly expressed qualitatively at the nominal level. For example, the comparison may be between two events, one of which not very likely but has major consequences, while the other is highly probable but has small consequences. This way of expressing risk comprises a simple, useful aid for comparing the significance of various events or decisions.

However, equating risk to the product of likelihood and impact can also be fundamentally misguided, particularly if it is used to rank risks. Clearly, risk is a multidimensional phenomenon and people are more averse to certain risks than to others. By producing such quantitative aggregates, the qualitative aspect of risk disappears and comparison and ranking might become meaningless. This is illustrated in Chapter 24.

Most people associate risk with the adverse outcome of an uncertain event. However, the fact that a situation is uncertain implies that it also may offer opportunities. The concepts of uncertainty, risk and opportunity are alike in that the outcomes of all may be either negative loss or positive reward. So viewed, they are interchangeable. That said, the concept of uncertainty sometimes is used to describe a condition in which probability and consequence are not quantified. Likewise, the concept of opportunity is reserved by some for a situation that will result in a positive reward and risk for a situation that probably will result in loss.

Why does complexity beget uncertainty? A traditional interpretation holds that complexity increases as the number of elements (objects) of a system increase. This happens both because there are more objects to understand and keep track of and because there are more relationships that might interact. Moreover system theory holds that numerous, differing attributes of objects and their relationships contribute to complexity, while the way they are organized in patterns and the closeness of links can contribute to reducing complexity.

A mechanical clockwork may seem to be a complex system. But according to system theory, it is simple, because its various elements are tightly linked to each other. That is, they are locked into fixed patterns that permit an individual part or relation few or no degrees of freedom in its behaviour. Consequently the future performance of the system may be precisely predicted. But the stiff linking makes the system extremely vulnerable to disturbances. In a clockwork, only one gearwheel need change an attribute, such as a tooth breaking off, to have consequences for the entire system, which can stop or show a completely wrong time.

Even the simplest social system is far more complex due to the diversity of the attributes of objects and the relationships between them. Consequently the system is less predictable but at once less vulnerable.

Projects are started to exploit *opportunities* envisioned for end products. A project is an investment of which success depends on several assumptions falling into place. Customarily, they sort into six groups of cross-cutting issues, as shown in Figure 5.1: financial, technological, socio-cultural,

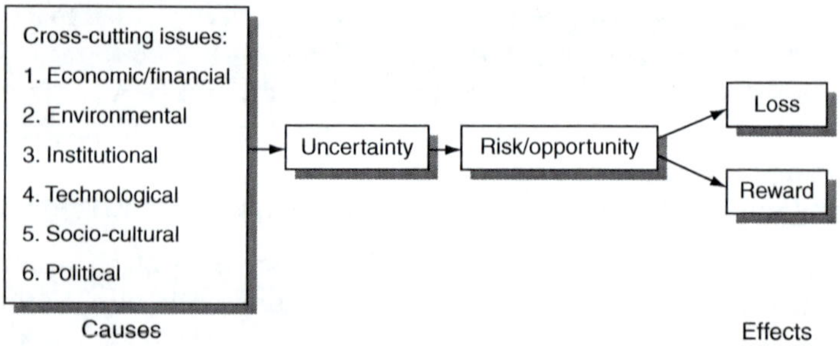


*Figure 5.1* Uncertainty entails risks and opportunities. Realizing opportunities presupposes a willingness to assume risk. The outcome of a choice is either a loss or a reward

political, institutional and environmental.[1] Complexity infuses considerable *uncertainty* in the project. Consequently, the project owner often assumes *risk* in initiating and implementing the project. Opportunity and risk are two aspects of the same thing. The wish to realize opportunity normally presupposes a willingness to assume risk. A major challenge then is to focus on both opportunities and risks in a project throughout its life cycle as well as in the processes of which the project is a part, see Figure 3.3.

The principle of choice in the face of uncertainty is well illustrated by the options that an investor must consider in making a financial investment. Across the board, the *outcome space* for an investor's decision is as illustrated in Figure 5.2. In it, opportunities that offer potential rewards or returns on one side are distinguished from risks that incur potential loss on the other side. A usual risk policy for an investor is that high risk is acceptable only if the potential reward is great. In practice, this means that an investor seeking high return, such as in buying shares rapidly appreciating at the moment, must be willing to assume high risk. In the figure, this is called risk seeking (2). An inclination to assume low risk assumes a willingness to accept low returns, as by depositing money in a bank. The investor's decision then is risk averse (3). Alternative (1) in the Figure is wishful thinking hardly seen as a realistic option. In practice, Alternative (1) involves having luck against better judgement or breaking the law, as by using insider information, which is a punishable offence. The last alternative (4) entails assuming high risk in expectation of a low return. It's of course unacceptable as a decision alternative, even though in practice it is one of the most common outcomes for many investors.

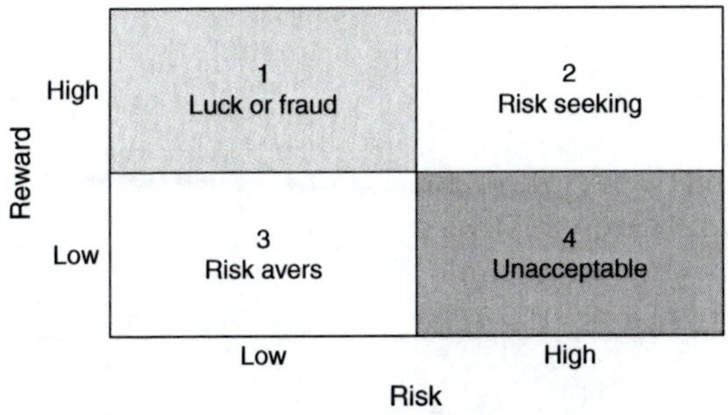


*Figure 5.2* Outcome space for an investment. Real decisions are limited to alternatives 2 and 3; decision 1 is regarded unrealistic, and decision 4 is unacceptable

This means that an investor's *action space* is limited to being risk seeking, that is decision (2), or risk averse, that is decision (3), while alternatives (1) and (4) are not realistic choices.

In principle, this is the same sort of decision that the financing party must make in choosing a project concept. It concerns finding a balance between risk and opportunity that is acceptable as well as realistic. Hence, in the front-end phase it's vital to systematically assess the consequences and the probabilities of various outcomes.

The entire, conceivable outcome space for decisions was illustrated in Figure 5.2. In practice, the outcome space is constrained in hope of excluding poor choices. This constraining is often called risk policy, which comprises guidelines set up for decision makers. The basic principle is illustrated in Figure 5.3. One may, for instance, decide an upper limit for the maximum risk to be assumed, marked with the vertical line. Likewise, there's a lower limit for anticipated return, marked with the horizontal line. The result is that the real action space is limited to the remainders of alternatives (2) and (3) in the figure.

Such a use of risk policy presupposes that alternative actions can be relatively precisely described. This is not a problem for an investor. Units may be quantified at a ratio level expressed in terms of probability and per cent return. For the choice of a project, the alternatives may for the most part depend on qualitative assessments that can be characterized as hazy, such as ranking according to probability and benefit at the ordinal level. The details are set forth more explicitly in Chapter 20.

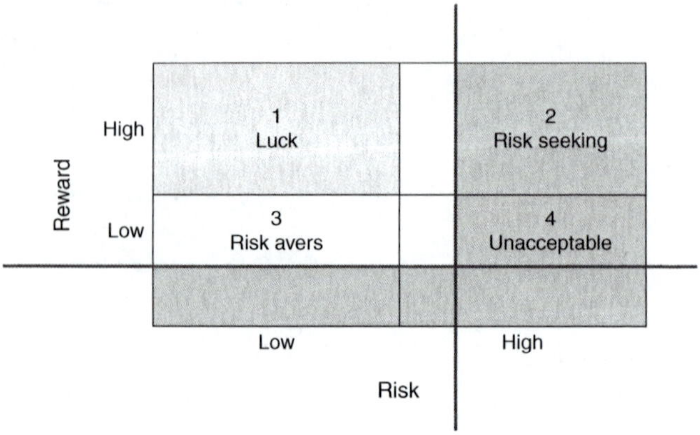


*Figure 5.3* Outcome space for an investment decision constrained according to an adopted risk policy

Many decision makers share the penchant of being more risk averse than risk seeking. Research in decision analysis has shown that most people prefer a certain outcome, even though its profitability is limited, to a more profitable alternative encumbering considerable uncertainty. In other words, to varying degrees, people are *risk averse*. Indeed, the word 'uncertainty' has a negative connotation for most people, as they associate it with risk and not with positive opportunity. This leads to behaviour that not only is risk averse but also *uncertainty averse*.

In turn, this is a drawback that is peremptory, as for the type of information acquired in the front-end phase. For example, a principal emphasis on information on weaknesses and threats augurs a defensive assessment of risk. The result may be that significant opportunities are excluded and that the project focuses on strategies that reduce both risk and uncertainty. Consequently, the overriding guidelines allow no latitude for conscious risk taking that might have contributed to more systematic exploitation of the opportunities afforded by uncertainty.[2] If the information amassed also includes focus on potential strengths and opportunities, the chances are increased for more proactive planning and uncertainty management. Early on, analysis using SWOT (abbreviation for 'Strengths, Weaknesses, Opportunities and Threats') is a useful tool to ensure that both the positive and the negative aspects of a project concept are assessed. The SWOT method is more explicitly described in Chapter 18.

## 5.2 Uncertainty and information

Uncertainty associated with a course of events implies that the actual outputs probably will deviate from those anticipated. Uncertainty manifests itself in the combined impact of all events and processes that cause and influence the output of a project.[3] Each of these events and processes may be predictable to a certain degree. The aggregate impact normally is less predictable. To a degree, uncertainty is determined by the type and scope of such processes and events. In turn, this makes decision making more difficult with increasing uncertainty. But it also causes predictability to increase with increasing inflow of relevant information so that uncertainty is reduced from the viewpoint of the decision maker.

One interpretation of the term uncertainty is that it reflects the extent of the lack of information required to reach a decision that ensures that the anticipated output is realized. One interpretation would then be that if all relevant information is at hand, there is no uncertainty. If the information base is poor, uncertainty is great.

The principle is illustrated in Figure 5.4, in which uncertainty and the compilation of information vary with elapsed time in a project. Uncertainty is greatest at the starting point and thereafter diminishes

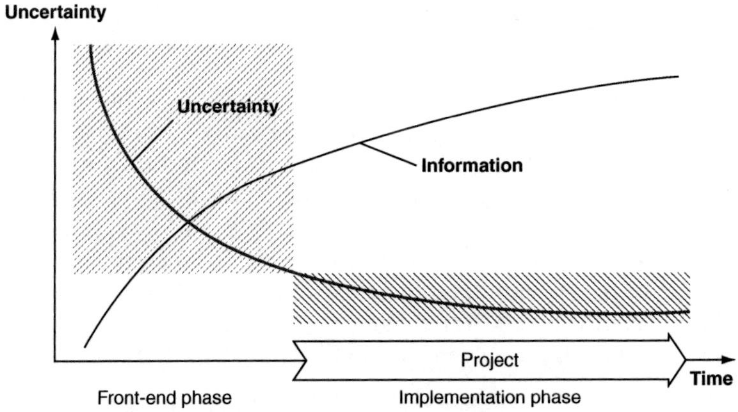


*Figure 5.4* Project life cycle divided into a front-end phase and an implementation phase. Uncertainty is greatest in the front-end phase and diminishes as more and better information is acquired for making decisions. The figure also shows the correlation between uncertainty and available information

as a consequence of gradual acquisition of more information. Accessible information is least at the start. The graph suggests that the potential to reduce uncertainty and risk is largest up front, and decreases substantially when the project is implemented. This illustrates part of a paradox in project studies. The discipline of project management is principally concerned with handling uncertainty in the implementation phase when the possibilities for reducing uncertainty are marginal compared with those in the front-end phase. Most textbooks and teaching in project management focus attention on the implementation phase, while assessment of the front-end phase is cursorily covered in a few pages as if it were an unexplored region on a map.

> The idea of a completely predictable project is utopian. Of course, there's a need for planning, but to believe that planning and other efforts in the front-end phase can eliminate uncertainty and risk is to go on a wild goose chase. Firstly, it's an unattainable utopia in projects that exceed certain degrees of complexity and uniqueness. Moreover it creates a false basis for formulation of plans and other measures. If you believe that risk is eliminated, you need not build in measures for handling unforeseen risk, such as by permitting change. This form of rigidity can itself lead to a considerably less successful project execution. We must plan, but at the same time allow leeway for deviations from plans if necessary or perhaps refrain from planning more than a realistic basis supports. Flexibility, framework plans, self-organization and other approximations are keywords that should be considered.

However, there are limits on how much an increase in information in the front-end phase may reduce project uncertainty. Clearly, uncertainty cannot be eliminated merely by acquiring more information. Equally obvious, not all necessary information will be available early on. This is because projects are dynamic processes that are implemented in societal context, in which the natural dynamics of the process and the influences of the surroundings dictate that much of what happens cannot be foreseen. A good deal of information comes about on the way. In other words, this means that you must always live with uncertainty in a project.[4]

Nonetheless the assumption that uncertainty is greatest in the front-end phase when the compilation of information is least is a powerful incentive to acquire as much relevant information as possible, as early as possible, to reduce uncertainty. Not least, there is consensus that the most important decisions are made in the front-end phase. The principal questions are: What types of information are needed? What sorts of information are available? What are the limits to utilizing information? etc.

## 5.3 Uncertainty as a metric in projects

Projects are exposed to surroundings wherein complexity and dynamics are great, which in turn induces considerable uncertainty in implementation. In project analysis, it's customary to distinguish between *operational* and *contextual* uncertainty (Christensen and Kreiner 1991).

Operational uncertainty is associated principally with the organization and implementation of projects and is regarded to be relatively independent of the context within which the project operates. Operational uncertainty exists both in innovative research and development projects and in routine projects that build upon experience from similar undertakings, in which events are relatively predictable. One characteristic of operational uncertainty is that it declines with time as a project evolves. This happens both because the compilation of information increases and because the project managers acquire a better grasp on the processes they manage. Operational uncertainty in a project can be reduced to some extent through systematic, realistic planning that leads to achievable goals by increasing access to relevant information and by improving project management.

Contextual uncertainty is associated with the surroundings of a project. It is high in innovative projects implemented in unknown conditions. The possibilities of acquiring knowledge of and influencing contextual uncertainty often are limited. This is because contextual uncertainty is associated with aspects outside the project's mandate and sphere of authority, such as political processes or decisions, cooperation with affected institutions, needs and demands in the market, technological development, etc. The possibilities for reducing contextual uncertainty are correspondingly limited. Moreover, in many cases, uncertainty may be understood only retrospectively, after the consequences have become apparent. Contextual uncertainty often is brought about by complex processes, so the information gap persists, despite attempts to acquire relevant information. This is illustrated in Figure 5.5.

Traditionally attention has focused on the internal, operational aspects of projects. Uncertainty associated with the surroundings of projects has

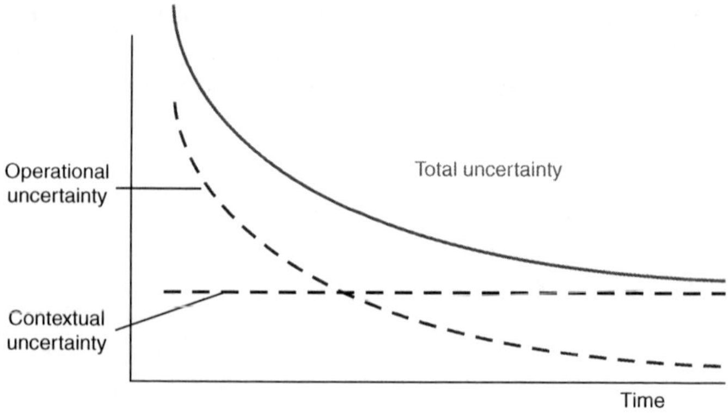


*Figure 5.5* Operational and contextual uncertainty through the project phases

drawn less attention, both theoretical and practical. The challenge here lies first and foremost in understanding the complexity in a project and in its interaction with its surroundings.

> A project often must resort to indirect means to influence contextual uncertainty. Indeed, one definition of surroundings is that they comprise objects and relationships for which the project has no direct control. Few projects are in a situation in which they can dictate a market or a Parliament. On the other hand, they can choose between several influence strategies, they can in part choose the actors with which they have relationships (such as which tasks they accept, which contractors they engage and perhaps which country or legal regime in which the work will be performed). Moreover steps may be taken to protect against unwanted surprises. The steps may include conducting a through analysis of and attaining accountability for the system limits (whether they concern the scope of work, the division of authority or the information flow), controlling the system limits' degrees of openness (areas, cases, time, etc.), building symbiotic relationships between potential sources of uncertainty (so that they uncertainty they create has negative consequences for themselves, such as by entering contracts in which the customers are responsible for acquisition with lead times over several months. A customer's change of mind then makes him liable for the financial consequences associated with an order), build up an 'intelligence service' covering the surroundings, export risks to other actors who are more expert in handling them, etc.

There are considerable differences that depend on the type of project and on its surroundings. Complexity arises in the interplay between technological, market, social, political, environmental and institutional conditions. For example, oil projects are technically complex but involve a lesser degree of institutional risk, because they usually are implemented in remote areas and are socially acceptable because they are high value enterprises. As their products are sold internationally, the financial risk may be ascribed by and large to price variations in the international market and not to local demand. Thermal power plants are less complex, particularly if they are built using standardized solutions and recognized technologies. The financial risk may be reduced through long-term agreements and constant user demand. At the same time, the political risk may be high, as thermal power plants have become a symbol and in part a banner case for all who work to cut emissions of greenhouse gases. Contingent upon changing patterns of power in a society, there may be considerable consequences for such projects, which potentially may be cancelled. Hydroelectric power plants usually are technically less complex, though opposition to them has often arisen because damming watercourses may bring about environmental change. The financial risk usually is low, due to low operating costs combined with stable prices and consistent demand.

The greatest challenge in the front-end phase is to create a set of realistic assumptions for planning a project. Uncertainty is naturally greatest in the beginning, but it doesn't go away before the conclusion of a project. On the way, a project may retain its flexibility, so that goals, frameworks and implementation can adapt to new information as it comes in. The project managers must chart and influence contextual uncertainty from the earliest possible point in time and throughout the entire project's life cycle.[5]

Problems of contextual uncertainty principally are first apparent in the implementation phase. This is why attention first and foremost has focused on uncovering operational uncertainty. An essential question is whether substantial problems can be written back to the formulation of the project and consequently could have been avoided with a better choice of concept. Many research results imply that this is the case. But experience also shows that even with good project management, it's difficult to patch up a project that was inexpediently designed at the outset. The success of a project depends for the most part on the initial choices of strategic guidelines.

Uncertainty is a significant characteristic of all projects. In general, uncertainty is reckoned to increase in step with complexity and with how far a project operates within known domains of technology and the environment as well as in accordance with economic, institutional, political and

**Operational (internal) uncertainty**

- Associated with the organization and implementation of the project
- Assumed to diminish with time as the project progresses
- Can to a degree be reduced by acquiring better information as well as through good planning
- Uncertainty is high in innovative projects and low in routine projects

**Contextual (surroundings-based) uncertainty**

- Associated with aspects external to the project in its surroundings
- Assumed constant, that is, not influenced by the project in its implementation phase
- Outside project management responsibility and authority, with limited susceptibility to influence, even with good information

Uncertainty is high in projects implemented in unknown, untried conditions.

social constraints, as discussed in section 5.1. This is indicated in Figure 5.6. To date, uncertainty usually has not been treated systematically as a steering parameter in projects. This inattention needs to be changed, as consideration of uncertainty in the front-end phase and the implementation phase is essential to improving the results and effects of projects.

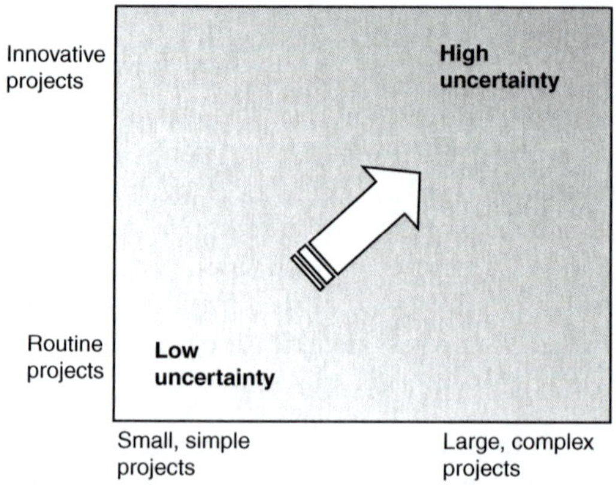


*Figure 5.6* Uncertainty and risk depend to a great degree on the size, complexity and nature of a project

It follows from the above discussion that the handling of uncertainty depends on whether we know how it arises and how it turns out as well as what its outcome may be. Uncertainty may arise and may be classified in many ways. Operational and contextual uncertainties have straightforward definitions (see the Box above). The following discussion focuses on two other ways of characterizing uncertainty of the sort commonplace in projects, particularly in cost estimation.

**Estimate uncertainty vs. event uncertainty**

A typical cost estimate includes assessments of the uncertainties of each of its constituent elements, such as the roads, tunnels, bridges and other works of a transport project, as well as of external influences. As these uncertainties are of estimates, they are known as *estimate uncertainties*. An estimate uncertainty is an expression of the anticipated variation in the time or cost of activities that we know will be carried out, or of recognized, influencing aspects, or of both of these.

Moreover a cost estimate may also include the anticipated effect of an *event uncertainty*. An event uncertainty is expressed as the expected value and probability of occurrence of an event, along with its consequence.

Event uncertainty also arises as a consequence of various events that can influence parts of a project and thereby require contingency funds to deal with the consequences that may arise. Event uncertainty is included in an estimate whenever it is essential to have means to deal with events that may occur. If an event does not occur, the funds will not be used. Such assessments may incorporate several uncertain conditions that will vary with the nature of an event, such as the contingency funds needed to cover various uncertainties as well as when and for how long such allocations may be needed.

**Unsystematic and systematic uncertainty**

The concepts of *unsystematic* and *systematic uncertainty* are used as needed at an overriding level, such as for a portfolio of several projects or a composite project with many contractors. Unsystematic uncertainty designates uncertainty that affects individual projects or is particular to an individual contractor. It concerns the consequences of situations that have no set patterns and may work both ways. The implication then is that unsystematic uncertainty may be ignored whenever there are many constituent parts or the time frame is long. For example, this is the case for governmental agencies that oversee and implement many public projects.

Systematic uncertainty is of the sort that has nearly equal impact on several elements of a project or on several projects in a portfolio. Because it acts in the same way on all projects, it is not nullified by diversification, even in the largest of portfolios, such as those overseen by a government. Consequently systematic uncertainty must be handled explicitly at an overriding level, such as at the portfolio level. The principal examples of it are exchange uncertainty and market uncertainty.

The uncertainty associated with settlement in a foreign currency is a systematic uncertainty. Whenever foreign exchange investments are sufficiently diversified, it's conceivable that a trend of change in one exchange rate will be counterbalanced by the opposite trend of change other exchange rates, with a resultant cancelling of the overall effect of systematic uncertainty.

Systematic and unsystematic certainties are usually associated with questions of diversification. Unsystematic uncertainty will not affect a portfolio that is well diversified. However, for the manager of an individual project, both types of uncertainty often are significant, even though within an individual project there may be cases of uncertainty that can be nullified by diversification. Uncertainty associated with the capabilities of a lone contractor can be problematic if there are no alternatives, but can be handled easily if there are several contractors of comparable capability.

Uncertainty and risk is one area where there are well-established standards for what is termed project risk management, which includes the processes concerned with identifying, analyzing, and responding to risk in projects. It includes maximizing the results of positive events and minimizing the consequences of adverse events. Such standards have been produced by the Project Management Institute in the US in its so-called PM-BOK (PMI 2008) and the UK based Association for Project Management in its PRAM-guide (APM 2004).

# 6
# Possibilities of Foreseeing

*There is a common understanding that we need to have a realistic view of the future situation in order to make successful decisions. Our ability to foresee future events depends on the time perspective, available information, our expertise, the nature of events, etc. Trends can be observed. Some trends are favourable, others need to be discontinued. We make the distinction between prediction and prescription. Indications are that more efforts need to be made by project designers to understand what lies ahead. Many of the problems that occur in unsuccessful projects have been shown to be what is called predictable surprises. They are the result of design flaws that could have been avoided at an early stage.*

> *A prognosis is a means to add credibility to a feeble assumption.*
>
> *—Gudmund Hernes*

## 6.1 The desire to foresee

The human desire to foresee future events is deeply rooted and is reflected in many spheres, not least religion, philosophy, literature, psychology, mathematics, economics and meteorology. The scope of pursuits is enormous, from the speculations in what is known as astrology to precise mathematical modelling in quantum physics and astronomy. The time span also is enormous, from the Delphic oracle of ancient Greece to the present-day, interactive group forecasting method called the Delphi method.

Predictions are made more or less on obscure foundations, positioned somewhere between guessing and constituent fact. In most cases, there is considerable guesswork, even in simple trend projection, as we know that trends can take new courses in the future, even though their histories augur what will happen.

Research in cognitive psychology has shown that as individuals we tend to overestimate our ability to foresee. At the same time, we downgrade the abilities of others to foresee and easily dismiss systematic forecasting, such as future studies, as frivolous. Consequently, we ignore many successful efforts to foresee future events, not only those built on well-documented empirical trends but also those built on scant information. Examples include the numerous Delphi studies that often have been used to assess future technological developments. One of the more exotic studies was conducted at the University of Washington and concerned the emotional responses between spouses. Couples in daily conversations were video filmed in the laboratory. Then the facial expressions of both persons were examined, second by second. The expressions were ranked on an emotional scale from negative to positive, that is, from contempt to admiration. By analysing only these data, it turned out later that the researchers were able, with 95 per cent accuracy, to predict which of the couples would still be married and which would be divorced 15 years later (Gladwell 2005).

## 6.2 Predictions in projects

For a project to be realized one or more decades in the future, the possibility of foreseeing with any degree of precision is severely limited. It is not necessary either. At that point in time the task is to understand the problem and describe realistic strategies for addressing it, as well as identify essential factors that conceivably can influence the realization of the strategies. The problem appears to be contemporary, but of course it often is projected in time in a specific direction. There may be a need to foresee the extent of and changes in anticipated problems with time. This may be done qualitatively or may be quantified with low precision.

By and large, assessments in the initial phase of a project are based on assumptions. The abilities to and possibilities of foreseeing will be decisive for the merit of decisions. The possibilities of foreseeing in part depend on the type of information available, in part on the duration of the time span that to which the assumptions apply, in part to the dynamics and complexity of the constituent processes, in part to the limitations of human imagination and ability to appraise in general and in part to the models and tools used to process and analyze information. Moreover, some situations simply cannot be foreseen. This implies that the initial formidable challenges aggrandize with time as the front-end phase stretches out. In cases when it lasts for decades, the challenges might be found prohibitive.

At the same time, there are examples of many situations that are more predictable than expected. This was examined more closely in a study of 250 research projects (Samset 1998). The study was based on ex-post-evaluation reports that detailed the problems encountered that were decisive for whether or not the project succeeded. Thereafter, the study endeavoured to retrace to the causes of the problems, to the extent that they could have been avoided and the degree to which they could have been foreseen. About two-thirds of the problems were found to have been caused by aspects under the conduct of the project, such as *project management* and *project planning*. Only a third of the problems could be ascribed to contextual factors, such as *market response, environmental conditions*, etc.

Moreover, it was found that in about 70 per cent of the projects, the causes of the problems most likely could have been foreseen. Examples of the causes included *ill-defined division of work between institutions, low prioritization among users* and *poor quality of outputs*. In the remaining 30 per cent of the projects, most of the causes of the problems were considered to be partly predictable. Only in a few cases were they considered unpredictable, due to aspects such as *delayed decisions, poor maintenance, strikes* and *sabotage*.

If the findings of this survey can be more broadly generalized, they dramatically contradict the commonly held belief that the biggest problems in projects are due to external causes that are difficult to predict.

Project strategy in the form of a cause-effect chain of events, as illustrated in Figure 3.2, provides a clue to the extent of the problem faced. The elements of the chain are quantities that essentially are determined on a prescriptive, or normative basis and only to some degree are based on predictions. Goals usually are scaled to the extent of the problem to be solved as foreseen. At the same time, they must be scaled relative to resource allocation of and capacity in the deliverable of the project. The deliverable, designated here by outputs, is in principle predictable, so it is reasonable to assume that it is 100 per cent likely that the project will deliver as agreed.

The external aspects that conceivably can affect strategy appear in the form of events, here designated as uncertainty factors. These must be foreseen. Early on, it's normally sufficient to express uncertainty factors in general in qualitative terms. But it can be helpful to try to foresee when they may occur and the impacts they may have. This entails risk assessment at a relative low level of precision. These matters are explored further in Chapters 12, 19 and 20.

## 6.3 Predicting simple events

Not least, information on similar projects and pertinent experience with them can improve the possibilities of predicting early on. In practice, the difficulty is not so much that such information is not easily accessible. In most cases, relevant information is readily available from many sources. The snag simply is that resources customarily are not allocated to such efforts, so they often are insufficient.

One way of regarding the uncertainty of a decision is to note the deviation between the predicted and actual outcomes. This deviation is a direct expression of the precision of the prediction. However, it can be verified only retrospectively. Prospective assessment must be based on judgement and usually is expressed as the probability that a prediction is correct. In cognitive psychology, many relevant trials have been conducted in which respondents both guess and themselves assess the correctness of their guesses. Some conclusions from such trials are (Wright and Ayton 1987):

1. People often over-estimate low probabilities and under-estimate high ones.
2. Correspondence between probability and actual outcome is usually better for future events than for general knowledge questions.
3. Experts with special knowledge and experience are usually better in assessing the probability that their prediction is correct.
4. Groups can generate better assessments of probabilities by sharing knowledge and experience than can individuals working alone.
5. Training helps in making predictions and most improvements occur early in the training session.
6. Assessment improves when complex events are broken down into more simple events.

On the one hand, such studies confirm that it is difficult to judge the quality of human judgement. There is no such thing as an 'objective' prediction, in the sense of a prediction that depends solely on data. There are always some confounding judgemental effects. Moreover, people do not extract from available data all the information they could, and some people are not disposed to think about uncertainty, so they may not be able to provide good probability assessments. Even the simplest type of prediction is therefore prone to errors, both in terms of weaknesses in data and in human judgement. On the other hand, the type of findings listed above undergird optimism and in practice can have transfer value by supporting sensible decisions through sensible exploitation of available information and constituent resources.

## 6.4 Predicting complex events

The prediction of simple events in experimental situations discussed in the previous section differs from prediction of events in real-life situations, in part because the problem to be addressed is more complex and in part because the assessment process is generative in the sense that people often adapt and change their judgement during the assessment process. In the real world, prediction is a dynamic, social process that builds not only on available information and experience, but also on interaction with other people. Moreover, events seldom may be viewed as having simple cause-effect relationships, but are dynamic processes that are influenced to varying degrees by external factors. This further complicates the picture.

Over the last 30 to 40 years, there have been many attempts to use dynamic simulation models to describe complex systems and foresee events. The approach is highly successful in the natural sciences but has been found little suited to societal problems. Many questionable analyses have been presented as credible and have met harsh professional criticism.[1] Consequently, mathematical simulation increasingly has been recognized as unsuitable to the analysis of self-adjusting, societal processes. The principal difficulty is that as opposed to a physical system, the elements of a societal system can make their own decisions. A physical system is in principle predictable both at the elementary level and at the aggregate level. A societal system can be predictable up to a point at the elementary level but only to a lesser extent at the aggregate level.

## 6.5 Trends and discontinuities

Societal systems, including projects, can be viewed as complex interactions of events. Over time, patterns of causes and effects can be observed. At various points in time, measures may be initiated to influence events in desirable or undesirable directions. The events can be intentional and therefore foreseeable or unintentional and therefore difficult to foresee. It is customary to distinguish between *trends* and *discontinuities*.

A trend expresses a systematic change over time. The change may be decreasing or increasing and depicts an assumed course of future development. Complex situations are described using several parameters, each of which may have its own particular trend. For example, the memory capacity of personal computers has gone up while their prices have gone down, a trend further amplified by general financial inflation in the market.

Trends may be identified retrospectively on empirical bases and be projected to foresee future development; examples include predictions of traffic densities and crime rates. The uncertainty of a prediction increases as it is applied further into the future. Uncertainty also increases with more rapid change as well as with shifts towards conditions that are undesirable, unstable or unthinkable. The explosive increase in the capacity of memory chips is an example. How long can it go on? It is reasonable to assume that it might continue until it meets physical limits at the atomic level but not beyond.

Rapidly increasing trends tend to level off and stabilize, tracing an S-curve, or peak and then decline. For instance, North Sea offshore oil production cannot level off at a high level but will decline as the reservoirs are emptied.

Whenever there is a continuous trend, we principally face two alternative decisions. One is to project the trend and use it as a basis for further planning. This is called trend extrapolation or *prediction*. It presumes that the trend indicates a desirable change. For example, the annual increase in traffic volume has long dictated the planning and building of roads. At the same time, other problems have become increasingly apparent, particularly in large cities. So there is a need for controlled change of the existing trend. This is called *prescription*. We prescribe a condition that is not an extension of the trend but seek means other than road building, such as development of the infrastructure

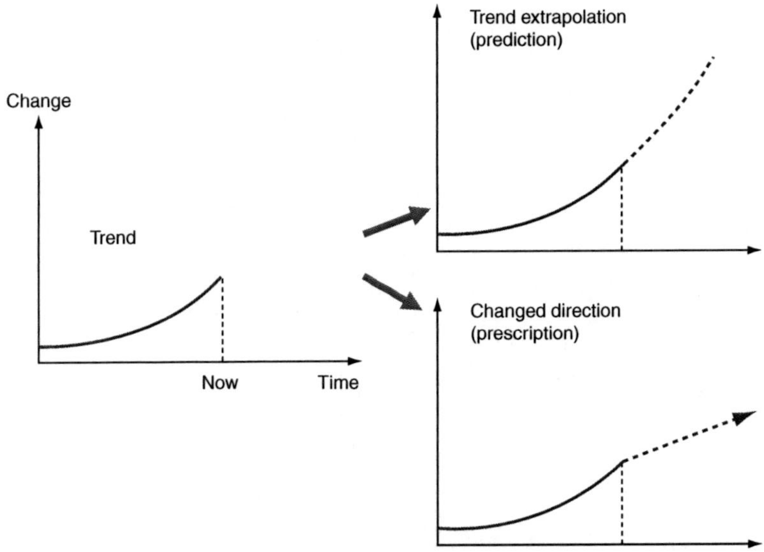


*Figure 6.1* A trend is a change observed over time. In the present, one may either predict that it will continue its course or prescribe that it will alter its course

for public transport, road tolls, peak-hour fees, etc. This is illustrated in Figure 6.1.

Discontinuities are caused by events that result in qualitative leaps or appreciable discontinuous changes in existing trends. This is illustrated in Figure 6.2. The root may, for example, be a natural disaster, a new breakthrough technology or a regime change that has unforeseen consequences and changes action patterns and trends in society. Such discontinuous events are in principle unpredictable and moreover disorder what has been foreseen. The changes can be dramatic, for better or worse. But the degree to which they cannot be foreseen indicates that they can be dealt with only retrospectively. For example, a breakthrough discovery by research scientists that would reduce the effect of gravity would create new technical, economic and market possibilities beyond our current comprehension.

Some discontinuous events can be foreseen to some extent. But their times of occurrence and their consequences most often are difficult to foresee with precision. Obviously, predictable discontinuities can be

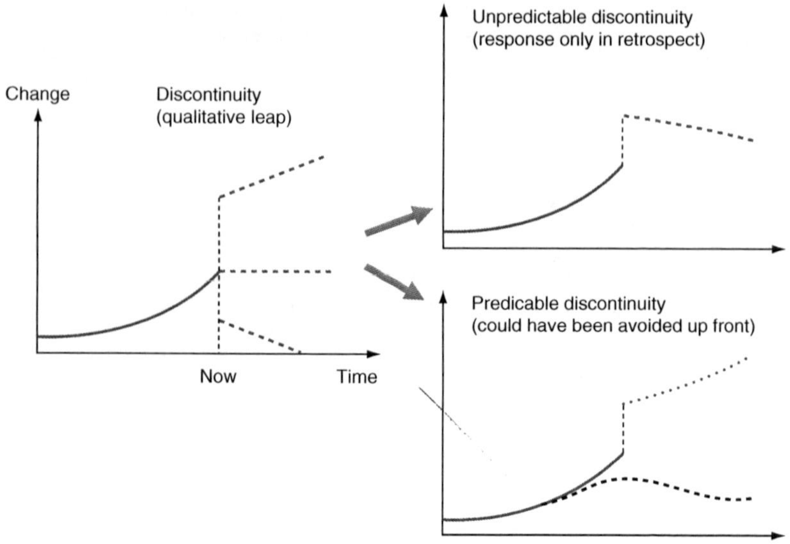


*Figure 6.2* A qualitative leap is a discontinuous change or trend break. It may be unpredictable or partly predictable

prevented in advance. Prevention depends on a controlled change of an existing trend before it is too late, as illustrated in Figure 6.1.

## 6.6 Predictable surprises

Predictable discontinuities either are events deliberately triggered to achieve surprising effects or are events implicit in time. That is, they result from a trend that leads to a discontinuous situation. For example, for several decades after the Second World War, the fear of near total annihilation in a nuclear war led to an arms race that ran wild, both in the East and in the West. Today, we believe that the increasing discharge of greenhouse gases to the atmosphere will lead to unprecedented changes in climate, sea levels, ocean currents etc.

In the case of what is here termed predictable discontinuities, we possess all the information and insight necessary to foresee events. If we take no action, such a discontinuity will occur at some point in time (Bazerman and Watkins 2004). This is illustrated in Figure 6.3. The proposition builds on our deep-rooted conviction that we would rather

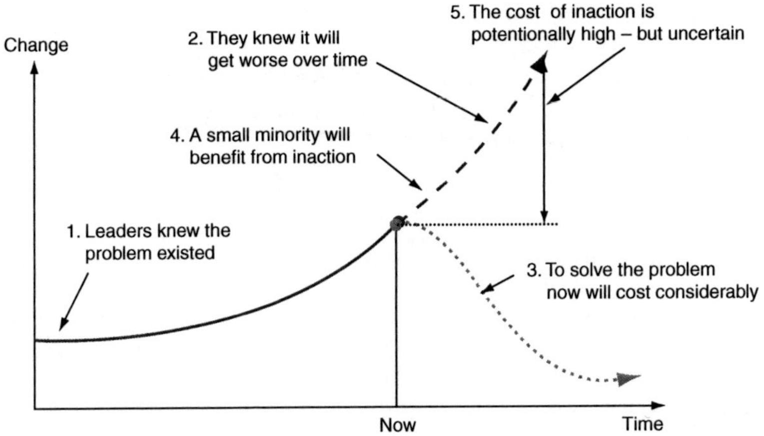


*Figure 6.3* A predictable discontinuity results from an unfavourable trend that has been ignored, despite there having been necessary information and insight to avert the problem

accept a small problem today than pay to avoid an uncertain problem, even though it probably will incur greater costs. We put off problems.

We see problems and their upshots. Often, a small minority is best served by allowing a trend to continue and consequently contrives to slow initiatives for changing it.

In organizing projects, the problems to be addressed are lesser, but often subject to the same mechanisms. For example, a problem that arises might have been anticipated through studying lessons learnt in similar project and thereby might have been avoided. Often, this is not done to a sufficient extent. When a decision has been made and is on the rails, experience shows that it is difficult, if not impossible to stop.

> If you move a frog from a pan of cold water to a pan of much warmer water, it will react immediately and jump out. On the other hand, if you slowly heat the cold water, the frog will stay where it is, until it is boiled to death. This happens because the frog cannot sense gradual changes in its environment. This bit of zoological knowledge is used as an analogy for the paralysis that grips people faced with persistent collective problems.
>
> (New Scientist)

Once one has invested in adequate studies and planning and perhaps started preliminary works, that together have incurred relatively small but real costs, one is more willing to risk considerable future losses in implementing plans than to write off far smaller outlays already made. Pressure groups and individuals often are instrumental in such a scenario.

## 6.7 Predictability and information

The nature of the available information comprises a fundamental question in the front-end phase. To the extent possible, decision makers prefer to base their decisions on facts, but of course they are also willing to make do with assumptions and predictions to a considerable degree. In general, the future is predictable only to a certain extent. Knowledge of previous trends may be used to foresee individual events with high probability. In a situation that is predictable to a certain degree, it is reasonable to assume that uncertainty will merely cause lesser deviations in relation to the observed trend.

How a trend may be interpreted, in addition to information on it, is an interesting question. A good example is that of the behaviour of tanker owners in the oil crisis of 1973–4. Many believe that the oil crisis was caused by the war in the Middle East, but for the tanker owners, it would have arisen regardless, war or no war. Favourable freight rates caused owners to contract for far greater tanker capacity than they needed, and many realized that would influence future rates. This information was widely known in shipping circles and was used in different ways, such as by Næss, Bergersen and Reksten, three major Norwegian tanker owners. Næss believed there would be a serious slump and chose to sell its fleet while prices still were high. He made huge profits. Bergersen chose to switch to long-term contracts (up to 10–15 years at fixed rates) to be less vulnerable to rate fluctuations. His company barely survived. Reksten, the world's largest tanker owner at the time, apparently didn't believe the predictions and chose to pursue the spot market in which rates were highest. He went bankrupt. With hindsight, it subsequently was easy to say which strategy was best, but that hardly was the case at the time the decisions were made. The point is that it is not enough to ensure that information is available. There also must be expertise to interpret what it means and the implications it ought to have in the situation and context in question.

Decision bases are built to a certain extent on assumptions, so the predictability of conditions essential for decisions is a principal question. Several retrospective studies of projects have concluded that most of the conditions that cause appreciable problems in projects were predictable at the time the projects were planned (Morra and Thumm 1997; Pinto and Slevin 1988; Samset 1998). Consequently, early on one should learn from projects conducted under similar conditions. This learning should be recommendatory for the sort of information sought out to support the bases for decision making and for the terms of the project. Such a goal-oriented, steered information search will be instrumental in reducing risk and increasing opportunities.

## 6.8 Scenario planning

A decision on a project rests on a view of the future and therefore involves considerable uncertainty. Analyzing and projecting trends may be useful. However, strategic planning is commonly a one-dimensional projection or prescription of a future situation that fails to consider qualitative aspect of anticipated change and the various factors that might affect the realization of the strategy. Since the late 1960s the concept of using scenarios in forecasting spread from the military to industry. A *scenario* is an account or synopsis of a projected course of action which is used to understand different ways that future events may unfold. Rather than forecast what will happen, scenarios are used to try understand the complexity of the forecast or a strategy.

*Scenario analysis* can be used to illuminate the effect of various alternative strategies or the effect on a strategy of various probable events. Not least, it is used to discuss the effect of disastrous events with low probability of occurrence, for instance the effect of large celestial objects hitting the earth. Such scenarios can be used to design strategies to reduce the effect on society.

*Scenario planning* can be particularly useful in making flexible long-term plans. The chief value of scenario planning might be that it allows decision makers to make tests and learn from mistake without risking failures in real life. Scenario planning starts by dividing knowledge into what would be considered certain developments, and elements that are considered uncertain or unknowledgeable. The first type of information can be used to establish what would seem likely trends, and the other to establish alternative scenarios that can be explored further. Scenario planning is most useful in the early stages of a project when purpose and scope are still under development. The first question to be answered is why the organization decided to consider a project. This question relates to the overarching purpose of the organization wishing to engage in the project and its underlying logic. Project conceptualization is essentially the translation and extension of the organization's business logic into the future (Heijden 2009).

At its best scenario planning exploits the multiple perspectives that people have on a strategic situation. A well-conducted scenario exercise accomplishes many things. It brings about more flexible planning and trends to reduce surprises, particularly because it moves one beyond incremental thinking. Decision makers become more alert to uncertainty and unexpected change. The technique encourages exchange of information and allows speculative thinking and legitimizes imagination.

There are also many pitfalls and difficulties. Clearly a scenario exercise is useless unless if decision makers deal with its analysis. Too many different scenarios on a strategy tend to become overwhelming. Too much detail would make scenarios difficult to communicate, misguided focus would make them useless etc. Scenario planning is a tool for collective learning and not for predicting the future. Clearly, subjectivity and bias will affect reasoning, which might leave many decision makers uncomfortable with the result. Still, while anything but science, scenario analysis has proven a useful tool to help improving our ability to cope with the future.

## 6.9 Costs and benefits of information

The information basis always is incomplete, regardless of the extent of the commitment to charting, analysing and planning a project in the front-end phase. One will have to distinguish between facts and assumptions. Procuring both incurs costs. In principle, in the start-up phase, the benefits of collecting information are great relative to the costs of its acquisition. With time, the cost of collecting additional information increases while the benefit of it becomes more marginal. This is illustrated in Figure 6.4. Consequently, in the front-end phase the challenge is to limit the compilation of information to a level that gives the best possible relationship between benefits and costs. Obviously, it is not the

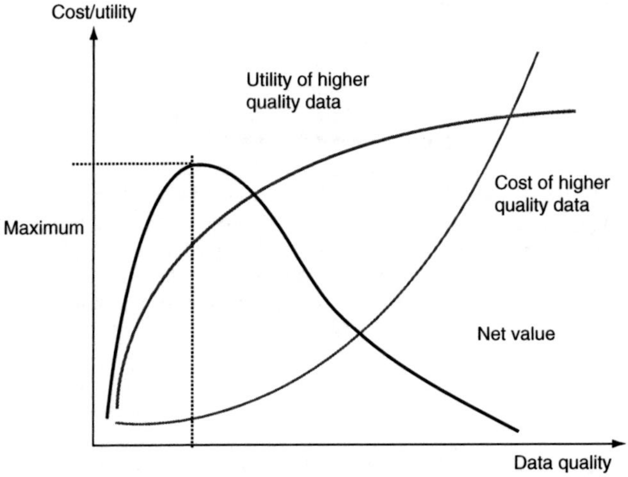


*Figure 6.4* Cost/information ratio and quality of information in a project. It's reasonable to assume that the utility of additional data declines as the cost of acquiring it increases. Hence, the amount of information must be limited to a reasonable level (Jessen 1998)

amount of information that is decisive,[2] but rather the degree to which the information is relevant.

How to determine what is relevant and what is not is itself an interesting question. Some dismiss information as irrelevant if it does not nearly completely suit an initial perception of relevance or correctness. Others maintain that relevant information contributes added value beyond the existing basis of a project or a decision. Still others maintain that relevant information is that which causes one to stop and reflect on one's own assumptions and work thus far. Some emphasize analytical criteria to determine relevance, while others are more concerned with synthesis and reflection. The fact is that interpretations vary on what is relevant and on how this information should be used. For example, consider safety information. We choose to use a recognized solution, but modify it somewhat. On the way, we become aware of several weaknesses in the system, none of which are so serious that they cause accidents. How shall we interpret this information? Should we include correction of weaknesses in our solution? Is the system basically safe because no such event has led to an accident? Or, will our modifications solve the problem? If so, might our modifications create new safety problems, and so on.

> What are facts and what is necessary for information to be seen as fact? What is the connection between facts and validity and credibility? The greater part of traditional decision theory and communication theory assumes that facts exist and are available, but says little on how we may distinguish between facts and non-facts. Recognized studies (Dreyfuss; Mintzberg) have shown fairly clearly that some people to a great degree rely upon their own experience and intuition (silent knowledge), often preferring it to supposed fact. Hence the paradox of the attempts to ascribe the successes of these people to analyses of facts (defined here as information acquired by scientific or controlled methods), while their decisions perhaps build just as much on other types of information and approaches. These people may believe that the information comprises facts, but outsiders will contend that at best it comprises assumptions.

Quality is more important than quantity. In fact, quantity can contribute to uncertainty because it increases the likelihood of having contradictory information that for various reasons cannot be more closely verified. In fact, too much knowledge and information on a matter may make it harder to reach decisions, in part because higher quality is required and in part because admittedly the alternatives are mixed, that is, they contain both positive and negative aspects. In the extreme case this is termed analysis paralysis. One area in which we humans are notoriously poor at decision making is precisely when we are faced with mixed alternatives. How do we weigh advantages against disadvantages and how can we sensibly compare alternatives having dissimilar attributes? It is not without reason that journalists seldom seek out specialists (with some exceptions, of course) when they want clear statements.

Finally, there is also the question of the level of precision to be chosen for information. In general, costs increase with increasing precision. Early on, when the goal is primarily to assess the whole of a project concept than to define the project components, the needs for precision data are limited. Also, precise data tend to be outdated more rapidly than less precise data. The term *half-life of information* is introduced in section 13.3. Consequently, it may be wise to increase the breadth rather than the precision of the compilation of information and to rely more on qualitative data than on quantitative data.

The methods that are available and are used in front-end phase assessments often are simple, rough and holistic, often based on intuitive probability assessments. An example is consensus-based assessment, in which information is generated on the basis of discussions and assessments by a panel of experts with relevant knowledge of the matter in question. However, what all such methods have in common is that they are less costly than advanced, fine-tuned methods that also require information of quality that can be difficult to obtain early on. This makes the methods vulnerable to misuse.

From the viewpoint of cost/benefit, the costs of an initial concept development often are small while the potential reward is large. After the process or project starts, the situation often is the opposite. The reward attained does not always reflect the costs of steering the process. This is particularly the case if the initial concept was wrong. This is discussed further in Chapter 4.

# 7
# Strategic Guidance and Tactical Flexibility

*Concept development is about ensuring a strategically sensible grasp of a project at the earliest possible point in time. However, there are limits to what may be achieved with strategic planning in a changing world. In principle, much is unpredictable. Normally the chances of a precise strategic plan being implemented strictly according to its assumptions are small. When a project starts, the flexibility to make tactical adjustments might be as important as the strategic starting point.*

> *If you don't know where you are going, any road will take you there.*
>
> —*Anon*

## 7.1 Strategic guidance

A long-term, overriding *strategic* perspective for the project is set up in the front-end phase. Strategic planning is advantageous both in projects and in organizations. One of its prime goals is to attain structured and effective continuous management. The strategy shall conduce decision makers at various levels to pull in the same direction by providing a common long-term goal to keep in mind while making decisions. Research has shown that this is essential to attaining good results (Heijden 1996). A World Bank study of more than 1000 projects compared the extent and quality of pre-project studies, appraisals and design prior to project incept with whether or not they were successful. The conclusion was that 80 per cent of the well-prepared projects were successful, compared to just 35 per cent of those that were started without proper preparation (World Bank 1996).

A survey conducted in the US, involving about 600 project managers, contributed to identifying which critical factors influence the level of achievement in projects. The conclusion was that planning the project was by far the most important factor. Problems that could have been avoided with a better project plan arose repeatedly during the entire project cycle (Pinto and Slevin 1988).

An international project that drew on the experience of 60 large infrastructure programmes concluded that projects with great strategic depth, that is an appreciable level and extent of strategic assessments that underlie a project, were more likely to be successful. A clear concurrence showed that the projects that attained the best results had allocated greater portions of their overall costs to their front-end phases. These cost allocations varied from 3 per cent for simple projects and as much as 35 per cent for complex projects. The costs in the front-end phase, before the decision was made to start, varied from 15 to 500 million USD. The conclusion was that such costs often were justified and resulted in considerable cost reductions in the implementation phase, more socially acceptable projects and better risk management (IMEC 1999). The study also found that in particular, three aspects characterized the most successful projects: (1) the front-end phase had been long, that is, several years, (2) the concept had been revised several times, and (3) problem solving was systematic and inclusive. Moreover, it was found that the use of risk analysis was vital and that there was a decided advantage in open debate on project planning.

Typically the less successful projects resulted from authoritative choices made by investors, public agencies or strong interest groups and often were carried out under time pressure. Little time was allocated to pre-project studies or to evaluation or appraisal of concepts. The original concept was maintained to save time, with insufficient emphasis on acquiring relevant information. Consequently, in many cases, projects had conflicting goals and were based on assumptions imposed by interest groups or the authorities.

As discussed in section 5.2, paradoxically, the greater portion of resources expended to ensure project success is used in the implementation phase. Moreover, the greater part of the resources is expended to work out a relatively detailed strategic plan, while only a relatively smaller part of the resources is used in concept development, that is, to identify and test alternatives and delineate a strategic framework for the final project.

This is perhaps one of the principal problems in project activities in general. Early on, before the project or process is initiated, there is often too little attention given to fundamental questions concerning the concept itself.[1] There are fine-tuned, resource-intensive precision instruments for controlling processes, which do not detect whether the concept is sensible or not. In many cases, the methods are used to marginally improve concepts that should have been discarded and thereby contribute to upholding them. Projects with budgets in the billions are precision controlled in issues like time spent, costs incurred and quality delivered, while concepts themselves, such as where an airport is to be located or where a tunnel is to be driven, are insufficiently considered.[2]

The insufficient consideration of the *concept* is due in part to the complexity of assessments, as they depend not only on knowing, but also foreseeing. In the initial phase, uncertainty is greatest and the amount of reliable, factual information smallest. At that stage, method diversity does not sustain because the quantities used have greater tolerances and deviations. Consequently, it makes little sense to use precision instruments.[3]

## 7.2 Tactical flexibility

Research has shown that strategic planning alone cannot ensure success. *Tactical flexibility* is just as important. It must allow for manoeuvring within the strategic framework delineated, as the project is implemented. Additionally, there should be latitude for changing the strategic perspective if that becomes necessary. Strategic planning is built on judgement and assumptions and do not necessarily identify the most suitable choices in situations that may arise. Requiring that a strategic plan be followed strictly can make it a straight jacket. In practice, this means that there is little sense in formulating a detailed strategic plan early on.[4]

This line of thought is underscored by the late US President Eisenhower's remark that planning, rather than the plan itself is most important (Chapter 1). The creative, initial planning process affords the decision makers the opportunities of identifying and assessing the key alternatives and of finding the way to a sensible, realistic concept.[5]

Planning helps decision makers think through alternatives and thereby become better equipped when they later are faced with situations in which they must make tactically vital choices. In some cases, these tactical choices will influence and change the strategy. Normally, the chances are limited that a precise strategy will be implemented strictly according to its assumptions.

A plan presupposes a degree of determinism, a quality of information and a clear cause-effect relationship that at best exists only in the implementation phase. It allows only cursory consideration at an early point in time of the inconceivability of foreseeing the interplay between various involved or affected parties over time, of the incompleteness of information and of the cause-effect relationship being influenced by uncertainty that can change the analytic context that comprises the base of the goals and strategic choices undertaken.[6]

A story often cited in the project literature concerns a Swiss military troop that returned exhausted to base camp after three days in a blizzard high in the Alps. By the troop leader's recount, the men had lost their way and thought that they were doomed until one of them found an old map in his pocket. Courage renewed, the men found shelter, waited until the storm subsided and then used the map to find their way out of the area. Afterwards, they were astonished to find that the map was of the Pyrenees, not the Alps.

The story is used to show that in a situation with high uncertainty, it is not necessarily the quality of the strategic instrument that counts, but rather the tactical response chosen. Yet strategy can be useful even though it is completely wrong. It is principally an aid to point out a main direction. A detailed strategy strictly followed can be worse than any strategy.

Emergence is a concept used in systems theory. It indicates how a project accommodates conditions as they arise and adapts to them as required on the way. This doesn't necessarily mean that it's a magic formula for flexibility and adaptability. But it does indicate that a project can change its structure and focus as it goes from one phase to another, in a manner completely different from that of a conventional organization. This underscores the significance of the process perspective of a project. In it, linked sub-processes give rise to emergence that makes it possible to tackle challenges on the way, but at the same time require an ability to perceive an overriding development pattern, at least to be able to assess some of the future consequences of decisions reached. For one, complexity theory holds that our ability to foresee and influence the future declines rapidly with time. Whenever situations are far in the future, we cannot envision what will happen or find suitable means for exercising influence. Long-term planning can indicate a development direction but cannot dictate the future. Consequently emergence, self-organization and autonomy play key roles in the future development and success of a project.

Research has shown that for the most part projects can organize and manage work so that the degree of success depends less on contextual uncertainty such as social factors, market fluctuations, technical change, etc. A high risk level perceived in the front-end phase is not significantly related to subsequent project output. This suggests that project managers for the most part can manage the risk by applying suitable tactical means to reduce it. For example, factors such as technical complexity, project size and social and environmental change evidently contribute to increasing uncertainty, as shown in Figure 3.1, yet there is no clear connection between these factors and project output or success (IMEC 1999). This is hard to explain in any way other than that in most cases the capacity for tactical problem solving is sufficient to compensate for any strategic weaknesses in the formulation of the project concept. Problematically, this is not done in a systematic way; the principal objection to such an approach is that the cost of a tactical problem solution tends to escalate with elapsed time in a project, as shown in Figure 4.2.

The question is whether the rational choice of project according to some stipulated framework conditions eventually turns out to be the optimal approach. Although projects face major challenges in the form of high risks and definite difficulties, it is often tactical measures that are made to overcome the major difficulties. Successful projects are not chosen by hyperrational actors in structured meetings, but rather evolve over time. They are successfully implemented because they are undertaken by owners, sponsors and other stakeholders who support and contribute project acceptability.

The process of adapting to the surrounding framework conditions is neither systematic nor step-wise, but rather a seemingly chaotic sequence of episodes in which the relevant actors are not always identified at the outset. In it, horse trading is combined with a large measure of entrepreneurial innovation. In this connection, project planning is not so much a rational process as a common, repetitive search for problem solutions (Andersen 1999).

The front-end phase of projects is a process including the formation of coalitions and agreements furthered in the implementation phase. The development process in a project is neither streamlined nor logical, but rather an iterative collection of decisions made by various stakeholders. Planning in such an environment is not as much a rational process as a series of common searches for solutions to problems that finally unites relevant actors.

In the front-end phase, private companies and public agencies exchange ideas, interim agreements and future commitments until the project is strategically shaped at a level where the concept is fixed and the partners enter a binding agreement. At the start of a project, the groups of stakeholders that shape it are not permanently set. Instead, each new hindrance brings in new stakeholders who change the project. All new stakeholders bring in their resources as well as their conditions.

Some projects require less strategic effort, so their front-end phases may be quite short. In contradistinction, complex projects may have long front-end phases and may require enormous investments in strategic development. The relevant decision processes can be prolonged; experience shows that the front-end phase for a nuclear power plant or a hydroelectric plant may last for a decade or more.

## 7.3 Limits to strategic planning and management

Prevailing over uncertainty is not just about the compilation of information in the strategic phase. In recent years there has been burgeoning criticism of strategic planning as an instrument and of its significance in implementing projects (Mintzberg 1994). Several authors argue for more dynamic, strategy-building management models that employ process-oriented steering, network building and creative decision processes to enable project management to devise innovative solutions as new situations arise in the project (de Jouvenel 1982; Forrester 1985; Starbuck 1993).

This book presents some simple aids for concept development in the front-end phase. The quest is for the basic elements of strategy building. But as discussed in section 7.2, it's equally important to ensure a tactical grasp of projects. This is known as project management, which will not be discussed further in this book.

On one hand, a retrospective, overall assessment of a project will illuminate the worth of a project *strategy* relative to what is realistically attainable and what meets user needs. On the other hand, it is necessary to consider the quality of project management and the *tactical* flexibility in the project implementation phase. The distinction between strategic and tactical performance was made in Chapter 2. Taking a closer look at these features, we can use them to characterize projects with varying degree of success. In combination, four possible outcomes of a project are conceivable, as illustrated in Figure 7.1.

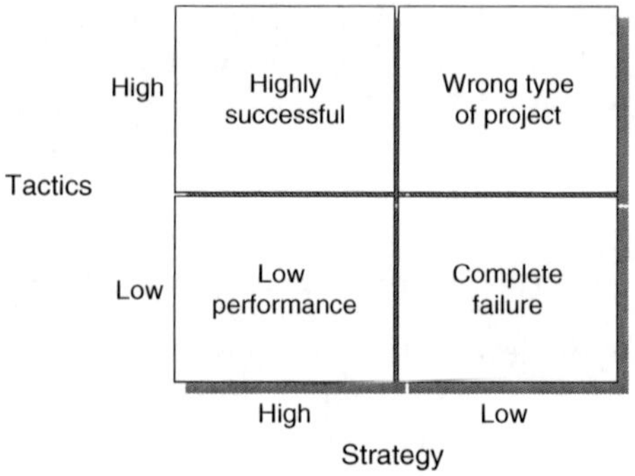


*Figure 7.1* Importance of strategy and tactics for implementing projects. The four project categories are illustrated by examples from Figure 5.2

Good project management strikes a balance between strategic requirements and the tactical scheme. There always are limits to how much should be invested in attempts to develop the best strategy. And it is always essential to ensure that project management adequately affords good chances of realizing the strategy and that the project is sufficiently flexible to tolerate changes necessitated by weaknesses subsequently revealed in the strategy. In real life, the landscape of a project may change so much that the map of it is pointless. For example, the financial assumptions may change, or it may turn out that the project has unacceptable spin-off effects. Four examples of how projects may succeed strategically and tactically to differing degrees are described in the box below and illustrated in Figure 7.1.

**1. Successful strategy and tactics: Earthquake centre in Mexico**

The output of the project was to set up an earthquake emergency centre in Mexico jointly with Japanese counterparts. The strategy reflected an indisputable need, so the project was given high priority. Japan offered superb earthquake expertise. The preparatory work of both parties was extensive and prolonged. The implementation scheme entailed building by local contractors, while equipment and training were supplied by Japanese companies aided by many short-term experts. The local staff was well qualified and motivated, and the centre had capable local leaders and experienced Japanese advisers. The project was implemented according to plan and within four years was completely self-reliant.

**2. Successful strategy, failed tactics: Industrial quality assurance in Eastern Europe**

The outputs of the project were to introduce quality assurance systems in 100 companies in selected countries in Eastern Europe. The strategy reflected an obvious need, and the companies were highly motivated. The potential for improvement was great, even with only small inputs from the project, as quality in industry generally was low. The project was planned and implemented by a leading international agency. The implementation scheme was less successful. The agency chose to serve each company directly. This was extremely expensive and time consuming, and the results attained were meagre compared to the plan. Training consultant consultants and national standardization bodies no doubt would have resulted in better, more lasting effects.

**3. Failed strategy, successful tactics: Small-scale industries for refugees in Lesotho**

The outputs of the project was to enable a group of refugees from South Africa to be self-reliant by helping them start their own businesses in neighbouring Lesotho. The initiative came from a UN agency that hadn't sufficiently consulted local authorities in advance. The implementation scheme itself was successful. The international staff selected and followed up the target group. Training was done by a local organization for industrial development, and subsidized loans channelled through a local bank. Strategically the project was problematic. Few of the many refugees through Lesotho stayed in the country and many were unqualified. A large part of the target group didn't finish training. Some of those who finished training successfully started companies and hired local employees. But a large income gap and poor treatment of employees led to a serious ethnic conflict between the refugees and the locals. In this case, an international organization had favoured a small group of resourceful immigrants in a poor country.

**4. Failed strategy and tactics: Water supply in Zambia**

The output of the project was to improve water supplies in rural villages in Zambia. The project failed strategically, as it became evident that users considered existing water sources to be of acceptable quality. Better water quality wasn't a prioritized need, and the target group had neither the will nor the resources to pay for operation and maintenance of the water supplies. In implementation, the project failed because it relied upon a local government agency to build some 1000 local waterworks. Much of the resources were used to build up the organization with equipment and qualified personnel. After the project, the organization broke up, as there were no public funds for further development. Consequently, considerable investments were lost.

In principle, the result of a project exposed to uncertainty is not just that anticipated, but rather comprises an outcome space, as illustrated in Figure 7.2. One distinguishes between positive and negative outcomes on one side and between expected and unexpected outcomes on the

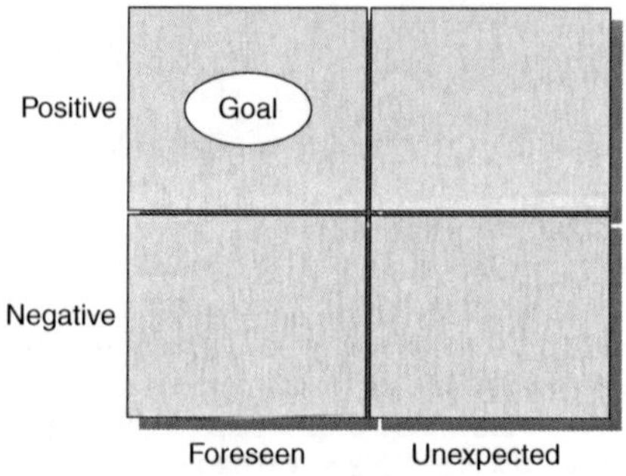


*Figure 7.2* Project strategy and project goals intercept only a few of the possible outcomes of a project within the total outcome space

other side. The goals of a project are concretizations of desired outcomes that are both positive and expected, so they constitute concise limits in the outcome space. But unexpected and negative consequences must also be taken into consideration to assess the relevance and benefit of a project. Moreover, the strategy must be amenable to change should the assumptions and prioritizations of the project surroundings change so much that the project goals no longer are relevant. This means that a project must have a perspective during its implementation beyond the formal, agreed goals – even if this include both the contractor, user and commissioner levels, as discussed in Chapter 3.

In a project exposed to considerable uncertainty, the chances of realizing a predetermined strategy are reduced, and the value of the strategy accordingly limited. Hence, the value of planning is principally associated with two aspects. First, various strategies are identified and assessed, and a choice is made of the one assumed best under the given assumptions. Second, planning affords a possibility of foreseeing various situations that may arise as well as of evaluating how they may be handled early on.

If the contextual uncertainty is less overwhelming and more predictable, the value of strategic planning is more obvious. The chance of realizing a plan then is greater, but only up to a point. Besides, situations that may seem unimportant at the outset may later be decisive in how a project evolves. Moreover, project management often does not sufficiently consider the guidance implicit in the strategy. By and large, success is a question of adapting to external conditions, while failure results from internal conditions in a project (Pinto and Slevin 1988). Consequently, the most significant aspect of planning is that it ensures a realistic correspondence between resources and goals on one side and between project goals and surroundings on the other side. First and foremost, goals must express the priorities and needs of users and society. With a realistic strategy, success is to an extent a question of the flexibility – to make the tactically best choices on the way.

# 8
# The Problem of Cost

*There are two material aspects of project cost estimation. Firstly, the earliest estimates often are far too low, though they frequently are decisive in the acceptance or rejection of a concept. Secondly, minor adjustments usually are made in the last part of the front-end phase to make the budget proposal realistic. The first attracts little attention compared to the second.*

> *A million dollars lost is worth no more than a dollar wasted.*
>
> —*Anon*

## 8.1 Benefit versus cost overrun

Cost is the management parameter that attracts the most attention in the organization and implementation of a project. As discussed in Chapter 2, the focus on costs is considered by some to be excessive relative to other parameters, such as project relevance. In the long-term view, it may turn out that cost overruns are only of minor importance in project profitability and benefit. Yet in other cases, cost overruns may comprise a death blow. Cost is eminently suitable as a management parameter, because it is expressed quantitatively with great precision and is continuously updated as a part of all transactions in a society. Costs are suited to making participants accountable, to gauging progress and result attainment and to comparing expenses with income to assess economic viability over time.

The greatest focus is on cost overruns related to budgets. Major cost overruns can be serious, not least because they may trigger prolonged conflicts between the responsible parties on who shall pay the bills or how costs shall be divided. In some cases, cost overruns may affect long-term economic viability.

But the type of costs involved in budget overruns often is only top of an iceberg. In innumerable cases, the budget increase in the front-end phase, from the first cost estimate to the adopted budget, is much greater. An interesting observation is that the initial cost estimate almost without exception is lower, not higher than what eventually is decided as the final budget. Another observation is that large budget increases in the front-end phase seldom have consequences for the responsible parties. Of course, it's the final cost estimate that's applicable. So, what's the problem?

In principle, there are four causes of cost overruns. They occur successively in the course of the front-phase and the implementation of a project:

1. Initially, planners and decision makers wilfully estimate low costs to increase the chances of a project being considered.
2. The information base and the cost estimation methods are unsatisfactory.
3. Unforeseen situations necessitate changes and governmental directives make the project more expensive.
4. Cost control in the implementation phase is not good enough.

Of the four, the first often has the greatest effect. In many cases, the reason is deliberate underestimation to gain consideration. The principal point is obvious: get on the agenda, because the longer a project has been in the budget process and the further it has been studied, the greater the chances that it will be approved and implemented. Hence, underbidding price in the first round can be decisive. Moreover, underbidding has no experiential repercussions for those involved at this early phase. Evidence pretexts including explanations such as *'we only wanted to start the discussion'* or *'a better estimate wasn't possible because we lacked information'*. Decision makers are surprisingly tolerant of what gets by early on, in spite of it arguably being the most decisive part of the entire project process. The same is true of the cost estimates of projects that have passed the first enquiry and are on the agenda. It has become so commonplace that one no longer speaks of systematic underestimation, but rather of normalization of deviance (Pinto 2006). In other words, a culture with lax views of honesty and compliance has evolved, to the extent that decision makers no longer see reason to trust the figures put forth in the front-end phase. Hence, the possibilities of controlling and influencing cost overruns are going down the drain.

This is serious. It means that poor projects slip through, though they should have been rejected had a realistic estimate put forward up front. Needless to say, it's a far greater problem than marginal budget overruns in the implementation phases of projects.

## 8.2 Systematic underestimation of cost

Cost estimation is burdened with uncertainty. Consequently, cost estimates usually are stated along with their uncertainties. For example, a cost estimate of 100 million currency units will be stated with an uncertainty of ±10 per cent. This means that the cost is estimated at 100 million, but due to uncertainty, it may range from not lower than 90 million to not more than 110 million.[1]

Understandably, the earliest cost estimate is the most uncertain, as only limited information is available and it's long until the final decision will be made. As the process evolves and studies and planning work are in progress, the uncertainty of the cost estimate may be expected to decline. For example, the maximum allowable uncertainty of estimates in Norwegian road projects is ±25 per cent at the pre-project phase. But when the budget is put before Parliament, the estimate uncertainty shall be no more than ±10 per cent.

As mentioned, the expected value also usually increases with time and with the duration of the front-end phase, in part due to general inflation. As illustrated in Figure 8.1, the probability distribution of the cost estimate uncertainty varies with time in the front-end phase.

The picture in many publicly funded projects is far more dramatic, as illustrated in Figure 8.2. Each of the three examples shows how costs rise in percentages above the initial estimates (100%). The time axes are years after initial estimate.

As shown in Figure 8.2, the least dramatic example is the new Oslo Opera House, finished in 2008. Its budget quadrupled over its 11-year construction period.[2] More dramatic is the Stad Shipping Tunnel project, which at the moment (2010) still is in the pre-feasibility stage. For 16 years, local interests at the district and regional levels have put forth proposals for public funding, in spite of the project having been rejected several times after external evaluations found it economically

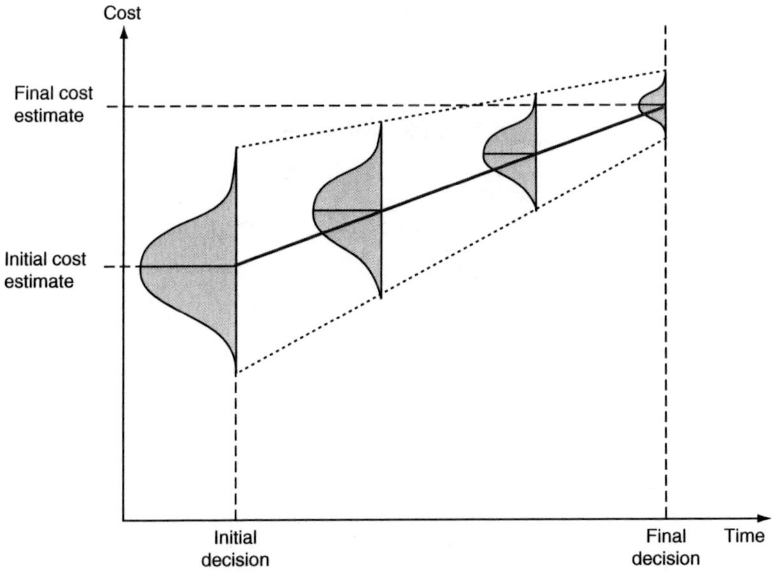


*Figure 8.1* Cost estimates at four times in the front-end phase. A certain increase in expected value over time is tolerable, due to aspects such as lack of information and general inflation. At the same time, the spread of expected value is assumed to diminish with time

unviable. So far, the cost estimate had risen to ten times the initial estimate.

The third example is a Regional University Hospital in the city of Trondheim. At the moment (2010) the project is delayed and in the middle of its implementation phase. In 2008, the project was expected to finish in 2013 at a tentatively estimated cost of ten times the initial estimate.

Systematic underestimation in cases such as these appears to be greatest in public projects, particularly so in local projects put forth for national financing. Hence, the phenomenon has become known as *strategic underestimation*. The principle of it is shown in Figure 8.3. The dots indicate cost estimates in the front-end phase. The plot often ends up in a characteristic S shape. Cost estimates are low in the initial period before the first systematic estimates of costs are undertaken. With time, the information basis improves, and the first surprises come to light. In turn, that triggers greater focus on the effort, demands for greater

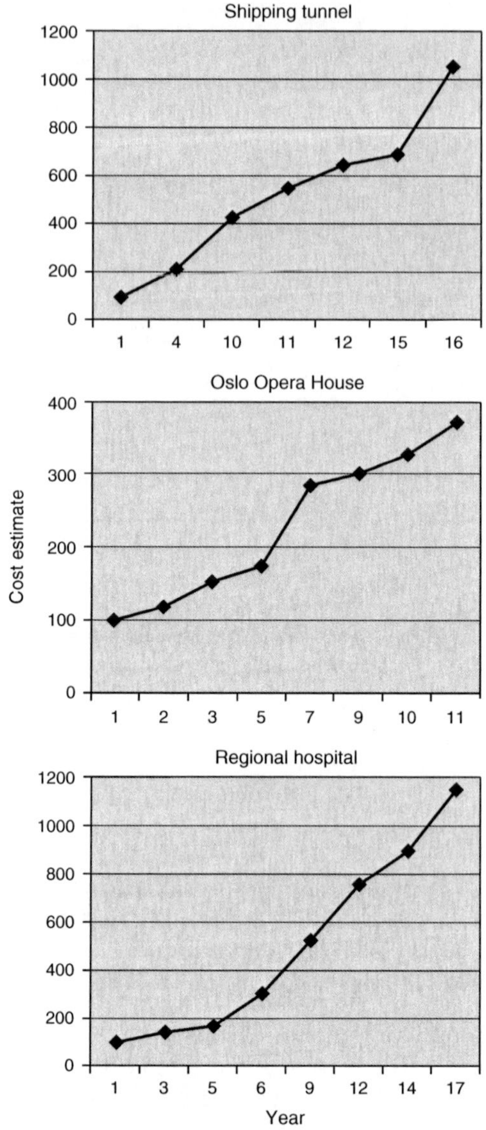


*Figure 8.2* Development of cost estimates in three projects, each of which had an extremely unrealistic estimate at the earliest, decisive point in time. Had the initial estimates been realistic, the initial proposals may not have materialized into projects

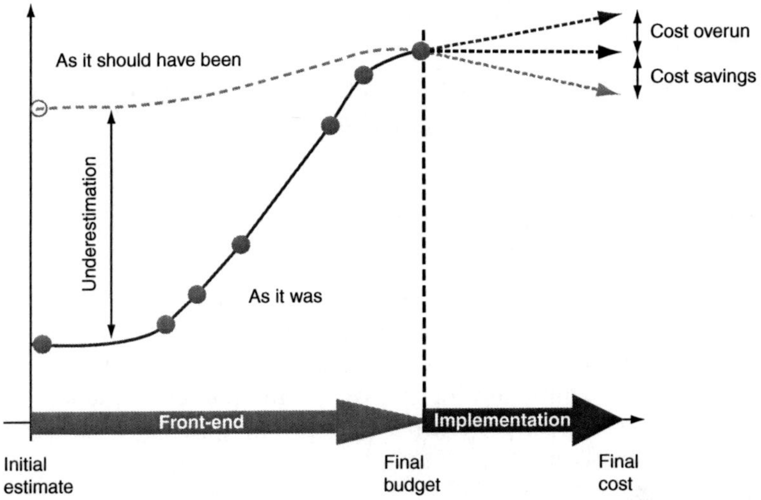


*Figure 8.3* Underestimation relative to the approved budget often is far greater than the cost overrun. Improving cost estimation in the front-end phase conceivably leads to fewer poor projects being chosen and thereby to increasing the overall benefit of investments

openness and realistic estimates, often by independent appraisals, and the cost estimate rises rapidly to the level at which it should have been at the outset. Thereafter, there are minor modifications until the final budget is approved.

The dashed line uppermost illustrates the development of cost in the front-end phase as it should have been had the process started with an estimate at a realistic level, as shown in Figure 8.1. The difference between the dashed and solid lines is called strategic underestimation. That is, a deliberately low budget is often submitted so a project proposal may be considered. In many cases, this is called tactical budgeting, which is a misunderstanding. Here the choice is of the project concept, which is a strategic choice. The early underestimation seldom has a marked effect on cost overruns, which are relative to approved budgets, that is, the final, approved cost estimate.

The development of cost in the implementation phase to the final total at the end of the project is indicated by two dots at the upper right, designating cost overrun or cost savings in the implementation phase.

Strategic underestimation, as it is used here, often is large and in many cases many times the cost overrun.

A disproportionate amount of research has focused on the problem of cost overruns in projects. In light of the discussion above, this might be called tactical cost estimation.[3] The term tactical came from several extensive studies that showed a clear trend toward systematic error, as projects with cost overruns considerably outnumber those that stay within their budgets.

Here we may distinguish between two phenomena. Strategic underestimation in the front-end phase influences the actual choice of project. Improving cost estimation in the front-end phase conceivably is far more important than gaining control of cost overruns in implementation, as it may lead to fewer poor projects being chosen and thereby to increasing the overall benefit of investments.

In this book, we principally regard measures that counter the first two causes of cost overruns in the list of section 8.1, strategic underestimation and poor estimating methods. Strategic underestimation results in systematically unrealistic pictures of economic viability and benefit. Apparently, it principally may be ascribed to preferences, interests, political priorities, etc. Counteracting such penchants will require that decision makers behave differently and that overriding choice and steering principles be improved. A process more concisely set out with clear premises and conclusions as well as greater openness that can identify contributing parties and make them accountable may contribute to a solution. These matters are discussed further in Chapter 14. The second problem, the poor performance of investigators and analysts, most likely results in unsystematic errors. This requires better techniques in probabilistic cost estimation whenever there are shortfalls in the information base. These matters are discussed further in Chapter 22.

# 9
# The Problem of Utility

*Utility describes the character or quality of an output being useful or serviceable. Consequently utility may be estimated. If it is systematically overestimated together with unrealistic estimates of cost, the decision basis gives a distorted picture of whether economic viability can be expected.*

> *Users will tell you what they want – the day you give them what they asked for.*
>
> —*Anon*

The assessment of the utility of an endeavour is about the return we get for the resources we use to implement it. The concept is defined and used in various ways. Some use utility as a collective term for the positive effects of an endeavour. A broader definition might be that utility is the sum of the individual welfare rewards (which in some cases may be negative) generated by the endeavour (Næss 2004). In cost-benefit analyses, the notion of utility designates the financial consequences of an endeavour, both positive and negative. In a broader socio-economic principled approximation, costs and benefits are defined as follows:

> The costs of a project shall principally reflect the value of resources that must be given up to implement the project, while benefit shall reflect how much one is willing to give up. A project in which the benefit is greater than the costs implies that channelling funds to the project contributes to increasing aggregate socio-economic value creation. A positive benefit-cost balance implies that the resources yield greater return than they would have in the best alternative use of resources.
>
> (NOU 1997: 27)

In this book, the notion of utility applies to all positive effects of a planned endeavour. Hence, utility may be classified in various ways, such as direct or indirect, positive or negative, quantitative (expressed in money or other units) or qualitative, etc.

## 9.1 Overestimation of utility

A problem parallel to that described in Chapter 8 often arises in the valuation or estimation of the future utility of a proposed project. Early on, planners and decision makers are inclined to systematically overestimate utility. The widely used benefit-cost ratio is a simple measure of the merit of a project, applicable when utility may be expressed in monetary units. A benefit-cost-ratio less than 1 indicates that a project isn't profitable. Clearly, this indicator exaggerates merit if the benefit in the numerator is overestimated while the cost in the denominator is underestimated. With such an exaggeration, it's easy to 'prove' the worth of a proposed investment. But when the moment of truth arrives, the fall is farther.

For the case of the Oslo airport express rail line mentioned in section 5.3, the estimated utility, based on an assumed annual passenger volume, was 70 per cent higher than that actually attained in the first year of operation. The estimated cost four years before inception was

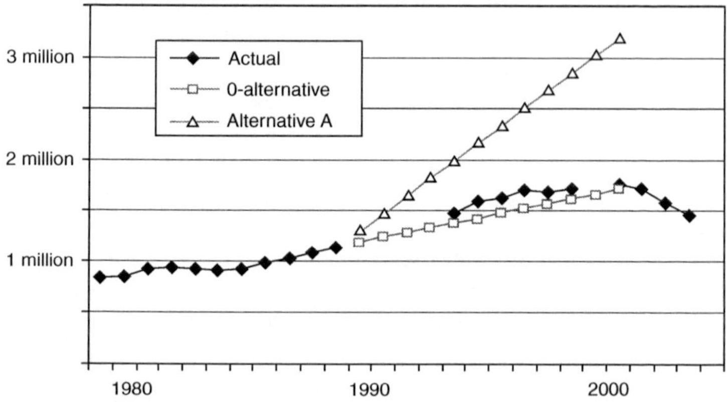


*Figure 9.1* Passenger volume on the western inter-city train, before and after expansion from single to double track. The predicted volume increase was far greater than that actually observed and in fact agreed better with the zero alternative (Olsson 2005)

50 per cent lower than the actual cost at hand-over. Hence, economic viability was merely a third of that anticipated.

In numerous infrastructure projects in the US and Great Britain, the actual benefit-cost-ratio turned out to be 15 per cent to 25 per cent of that assumed at the time funding was approved (Flyvbjerg et al. 2003). This implies that the benefit-cost-ratio was prospectively overestimated by a factor of four to seven. That said, its worthwhile to give heed to the possibility that going backward in time in each of these projects, to the earliest cost estimates and the earliest prognoses on which utility assessments were based, would reveal far greater exaggerations of benefit-cost-ratio or economic viability.

There's cause to believe that this sort of bias, due either to errors or to more or less deliberate manipulation of information, is a prime reason why so many poor projects are chosen. In some cases, a retrospective view has shown the bias to be so large that further consideration of the project would have been unthinkable had more realistic figures been presented in the first round.

It's reasonable to assume that project utility often is more difficult to foresee than cost. The final effect of a project may be assessed only at some time after it has been handed over, and often many aspects difficult to predict affect user and market responses. Experience implies that the same applies to estimates of utility. There's a trend towards systematic skewed estimation. The principle of it is illustrated in Figure 9.2.

In the front-end phase, utility is estimated on the bases of parameters such as traffic volume, turnover, visitor volume and the like. In some cases, the estimates are revised in the front-end phase as more information is acquired. The moment of truth arrives when the project has been implemented and user response is evident. Initial response often is much lower than forecast response. Thereafter, response goes up and perhaps flattens out during the first few years, indicating an S-curve. The gap between the actual response curve and the prognosis amounts to what is here called strategic overestimation of utility. As for cost estimation, the gap may be explained by two situations: systematic skewed estimation, which often is politically motivated, and errors that may be ascribed to flawed information and methods. Likewise, as for cost estimation, it may be assumed that flawed information and methods may result in unsystematic errors, that is, errors in both directions. Whenever the estimates of several projects systematically far exceed what turns out to be reality, there's reason

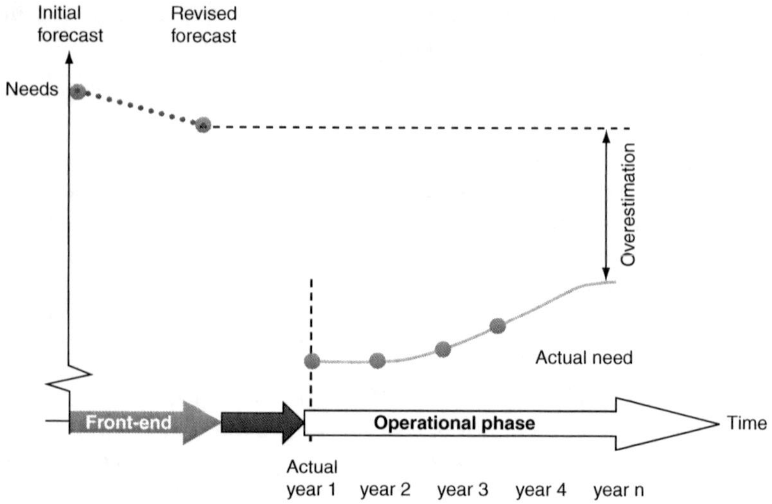


*Figure 9.2* Strategic overestimation of benefit. The precision of the prediction becomes apparent in the operational phase. The actual demand often deviates considerably from that assumed. Such deviations are commonplace, so it's reasonable to assume that they often are due to strategic overestimation

to suspect an imbalance that can be put right only by an overriding requirement making investigators and decision makers more accountable.

## 9.2 Effects and impacts of projects

The expected effect of a project is expressed in terms of its goal and its overall objective. The extent to which an effect is attained is seen in the operational phase. But projects also are often seen to have consequences beyond those expected and sought. Not least the isolated measures of projects that affect environmental cycles and can have unexpected side effects. A bizarre example of unexpected side effects is that of a World Health Organization project of the 1950s to combat a malaria epidemic among the indigenous Dayak people of Borneo. After the area was sprayed liberally with DDT, malaria mosquitoes were almost totally exterminated, and the incidence of malaria fell as anticipated. But after a while, buildings began to collapse, due to an explosive increase in the population of termites, brought about by the disappearance of their natural enemies, the ichneumon flies that had also been exterminated

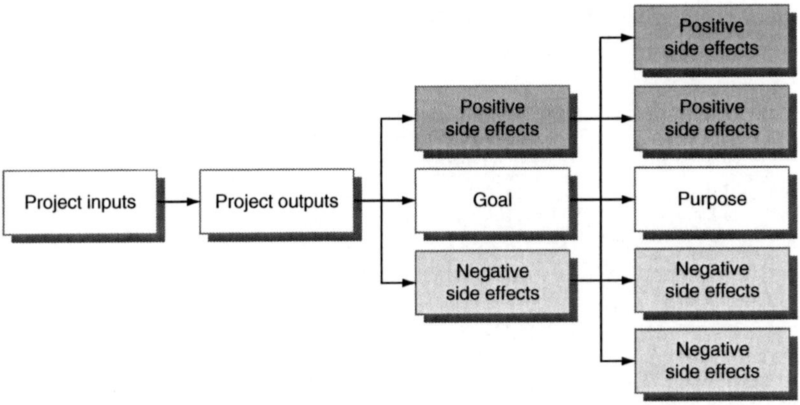


*Figure 9.3* Cause-effect chain including expected effects and side effects

by the spraying. Worse yet, the environmental toxin infused the food chain of insects on which geckos fed. In turn, cats that fed on the geckos died. That triggered an explosive increase in the rat population, with a resulting outbreak of plague and typhus in the area. To arrest the serious problems that had arisen, the World Health Organization released 14,000 live cats in parachutes over the area (Lovins and Lovins 2007).

The outcome space of a project is as depicted in Figure 7.2. In the first place, there is the effect of the project, which is positive and expected. Then come the anticipated negative side effects. Moreover, there are unanticipated positive or negative side effects. Here the consequences of a project may be regarded as a collective concept. Consequently, we distinguish between effects and impacts. They often appear in complete cause-effect chains, as in the example of the WHO project in Borneo. The effects and side effects of a project might be depicted in a cause-effect diagram, as shown in Figure 9.3. The challenge in the front-end phase then is to expand the perspective beyond the range of expected effects and as much as possible try to detect possible side effects and thereby arrange countermeasures that could ward off unfortunate impacts of the project. This perhaps is the most difficult challenge facing planners and decision makers early on, as it requires a multidisciplinary perspective and concerns future conditions that can be foreseen only to a limited extent.

To ensure broad analysis, the Organisation of Economic Cooperation and Development (OECD) recommends that the organization and evaluation of investments and projects should be subjected to intersectorial analysis, that is, be seen from six perspectives:

1. Policy support measures
2. Economic and financial aspects
3. Social aspects
4. Environmental impact
5. Institutional conditions
6. Choice of technology

In terms of *policy support measures*, a project will need to operate within the context of current legislation, and public and institutional policy. If from the very start there are serious discrepancies between the project goal and overriding policy, it is doubtful whether the project should be considered at all. Moreover, the policy climate and priorities may well change over time, so it is important to monitor these. For instance, projects to construct nuclear power plants have been in discredit in Western societies for the past three decades. In countries like Sweden and Austria such projects are banned by national policy. In other countries, the resistance of certain stakeholders such as local communities and environmentalists put an effective end to all such initiatives.

Ensuring compliance with political and legal foundations means that initiatives don't impinge upon top-down priorities or social considerations that are fixed in political decisions or regulated by law. Some measures may overreach in the sense that they are so innovative that they affect the accepted. Yet conflict should be avoided with statutes, such as zoning regulations, which are decisive in most cases.

Appraisal of *economic and financial aspects* has high priority in most projects, but preliminary work isn't always equally good, as discussed in Chapter 8. The problem arguably is greater in cases of public investment than in the private sector. Great importance often is attached to cost efficiency, but not always to a sufficient degree to utility relative to cost. In addition, there's financial sustainability, that is, whether income and expenses will balance through the project operation phase. Appraisal in most projects should at least be of the three aspects of cost efficiency, benefit/cost and financial sustainability.

Appraisal of *social aspects* also is increasingly emphasized, as many projects have consequences at various levels in society, for individuals, groups, local communities or the greater society. The consequences may involve access to or use of resources or means of production, goods and services, or the rights and duties of citizens, the rights of employees, income levels, etc. Early on, dedicated measures, such as user and market analyses, participation analyses, consequence analyses, are essential in many cases, as discussed in Chapter 11.

Awareness of and the willingness to consider the *environment impact* of various enterprises up front has increased since the 1960s when Rachel Carson wrote the book *Silent Spring* on the effects of environmental pesticides. Environmental concern applies upstream, as to the access and use of resources, and downstream, as to waste management, pollution and other environmental impact. Experience dictates that even though the environmental impact of an enterprise may be small when isolated, in the greater perspective, they may be appreciable. These days, political debate on the environment is in focus and various authorities constantly take new political and administrative steps that have consequences for the organization and implementation of projects.

Interaction between *institutions* is one of the more decisive contributory factors to project success. So it's essential to consider projects relative to cooperating and involved institutions and to evaluate the organization of conditions conducive to synergy to avoid working uphill.

The choice of *technology* may be decisive among other factors for productivity, economic viability, safety, environmental impact, etc. In many cases, the choice of technology is itself the starting point for an investment case. This has been proven wrong many times. A principal message of this book concerns avoiding that trap, as the choice of a technology should be the result of a more extensive exercise that from the start focuses on needs, effects and possible side effects.

Not all conditions mentioned above will be prominent in all projects, so the conditions to be emphasized will have to be based on judgement in each case. The point is that you should be open to expanding the perspective, particularly in the front-end phase of a project, even though the problem apparently is simple and the choices obvious.

# 10
# What is a Concept?

*The choice of concept is too often made without systematic identification and assessment of alternatives. Time and again the technical solution governs the choice. Accordingly this chapter focuses on concepts and the requirements that should be placed on them.*

> *There seldom is only one solution to a problem, but always a number of wrong ones.*
>
> —*Anon*

## 10.1 Concepts and strategic choice

In philosophy, the notion of a concept designates an abstract idea or model that corresponds to something concrete in reality or in language. As used in this book in describing the evolution of projects, a concept is a mental construction intended to support the solution of a problem or the satisfaction of a need. The notion of concept is principled in the sense that conceivably several dissimilar concepts may be alternative solutions to the same problem. This means that while the concepts differ, they all share a common property that suits them to solving the same problem. The quality of being principled means that the concepts are not just variations of a particular solution. This is illustrated in Figure 10.1, in which the investment case is distinguished from the project. The investment case is an abstract construction or an instrument used by the financer or the commissioner as a basis for financing measures thereafter implemented in a project.

As discussed in section 4.1, the commissioning party often has a black-box approach to a project. That is, a project is merely a means to attain a goal,

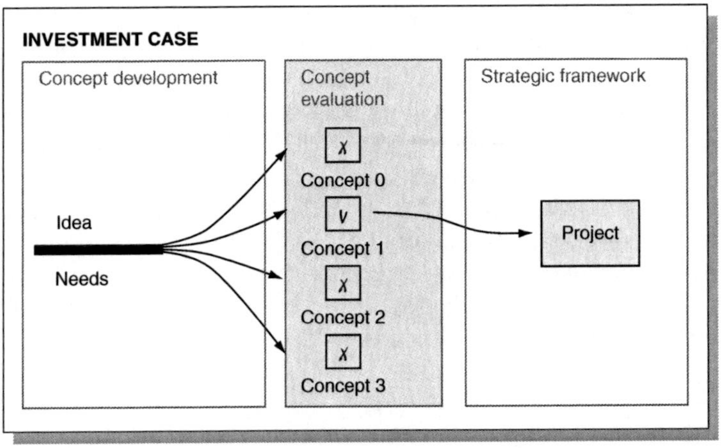


*Figure 10.1* An investment case is implemented as a project after prior assessment of alternative concepts

and that the goal, in the sense of problem solving or satisfaction of needs, economic viability or utility in the long term, is of interest, not the project itself. Consequently, the challenge in formulating the investment case concerns choosing the most suitable concept. When the need or the problem is identified and understood, the task is to identify and test one or more concepts, $C_0$, $C_1$, $C_2$, $C_3$ and so on, see Figure 10.3. The best of these concepts will be chosen as the starting point for designing the project. The implementing party normally organizes and implements the project, while the contractor will be concerned with its being implemented within an agreed strategic framework. Successful implementation of the project results in the desired effect, problem solution, profitability or utility.

This implies that in many ways, the concept is synonymous with the investment case, which is also commonly called the *'business case'*. The concept is concerned with the economic and social aspects of the project, as opposed to the technical aspects. For example, a company may initiate a project to upgrade software to improve the performance of its accounting system. The business case then focuses not on the technical solution but rather on the improvements in system user-friendliness and their effects.

A spectacular example of a choice of concept might be the 1889 World's Fair in Paris. As hosts, the French sought to use the occasion to show France as a modern, forward-looking country, technically lagging no other country. Famously, Gustav Eiffel won the competition for the best concept and implemented a project that even today seems surrealistic. The tower was built in just two years, to a height of 324 metres, just 50 metres lower than the Petronas Twin Towers in Kuala Lumpur that were built more than a 100 years later. The construction entailed an enormous investment with the sole purpose of being a national showpiece. Originally, it was intended to be demounted after the Fair. The project was uniquely successful in its tactical implementation. Moreover, in the long term, it perhaps is one of the most successful and profitable construction projects ever. To date, more than 200 million people have visited the tower, and thoughts of it have prompted many more to choose France as a tourist destination.

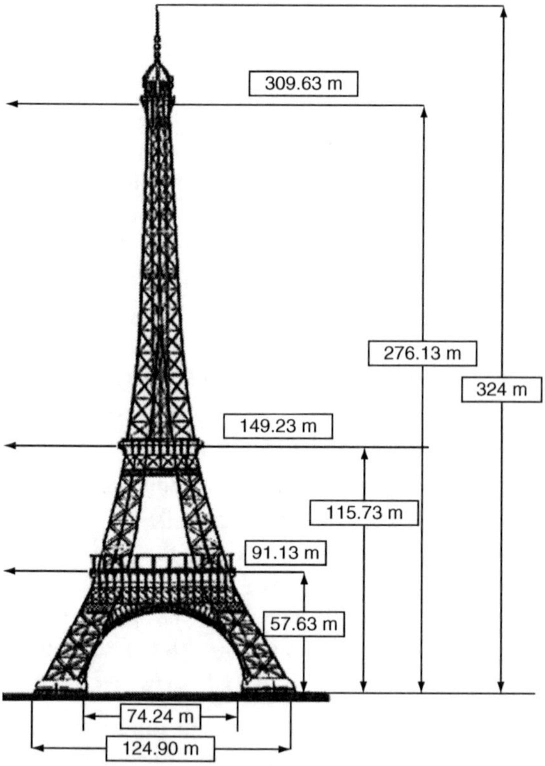


*Figure 10.2* The Eiffel Tower is an example of a concept that against all odds has become one of the most successful construction projects ever

Many projects are troubled by not having had a concept development phase. The concept is decided up front, without studying or assessing alternatives. There may be many reasons why this is so. Often, a key stakeholder puts forth, perseveres with and gains acceptance for a particular idea. Other times, strong political persuasion may exclude other conceivable and perhaps more sensible concepts. An example is road building versus public transport. In many cases, the concept choice is reduced to a banal assessment of technical variants of the same conceptual solution. For example, in planning the new Opera in Oslo, only alternative sites were considered.

Principally different solutions require that the concept is derived from relevant needs or problems so that it is expressed in terms of desired goals or expected effects and not only as possible technical solutions. One of the formal goals of the opera project was that it should result in a diversity of cultural activities across the country. Taken literally, that of course implied that building a new opera house was just one of several possible ways of attaining that goal. An alternative would have been to support a diversity of local cultural institutions, which most certainly would have had a greater impact. In the extreme, the project budget was so large that it could have been used to build splendid small "operas" in all of the country's municipalities.

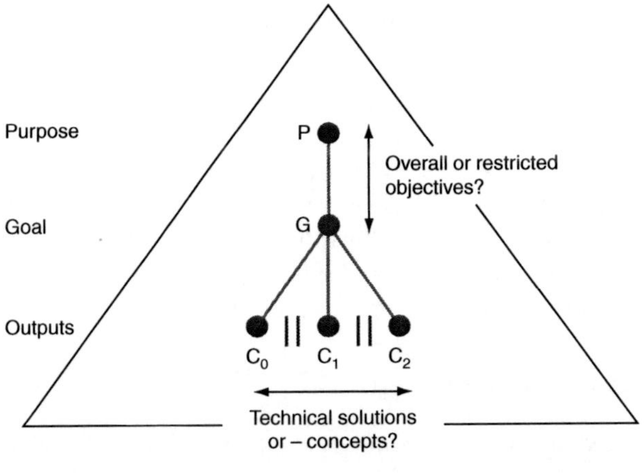


*Figure 10.3* Two persistent problems in projects. (1) Objectives are either too ambitious to provide justification for the project, or (2) too restricted to allow for identification of mutually exclusive concept, so that one ends up considering alternative technical solutions rather that different concepts

Another difficulty in the concept phase is that a zero option is either not considered or is not investigated to the same extent as the other alternatives. The zero option is a concept that entails continuing as before, with no major investment but with adjustments necessary to make it feasible. Neglecting the zero option is often unfortunate. The zero option in the opera project would have been to continue in the old opera building, with some rebuilding, renovation and technical upgrading. Early on, the zero option was rejected without further study. It's quite obvious that in terms of cost and capacity, the zero option would have been far better suited to the opera needs of a relatively small city such as Oslo.

Ergo, the concept concerns finding the best possible solution to a given problem. This requires a high degree of creativity, experience, capability and foresight. Time and again, history has shown that it's possible to devise new and better concepts. Likewise, it's been shown that inadequate resource investment in the front-end phase increases the chance of failure. Often, the simplest has been found best. An example is the first privately funded space project, SpaceShipOne, that in one week in 2004, twice conducted a manned launch to an altitude of 100 kilometres and thereby won the Ansari X prize of 10 million dollars. In the SpaceShipOne project, a small project group used an elegant, simple concept to solve two problems that have been costly for the major space nations. First, conventional vertical launch of a vehicle from ground level involves enormous energy expenditure by huge launch vehicles. Second, the speed of re-entry into the atmosphere is so great as to cause extreme friction heating of the fuselage and thereby high risk of accident.

The group solved the first problem by flying the spaceplane up to an altitude of 14 kilometres before it was let loose and its rocket activated. The second problem was solved using feathering wings in which half of the wing and the tail booms folded upward from the fuselage. The spaceplane then was stable in free fall, with the entire fuselage dragging. Consequently, speed was moderate and upon descending to flying height, the wings were folded out and the spaceplane returned to land as a glider.

## 10.2 Identifying a concept

The black-box approach, also called the system approach, focuses on system characteristics and not on the system itself. It is useful for identifying a concept. This implies that the concept is the system, and we are concerned with its justification and with the impact it will have on its surroundings. For a project, the cause-effect chain illustrated in Figure 10.4

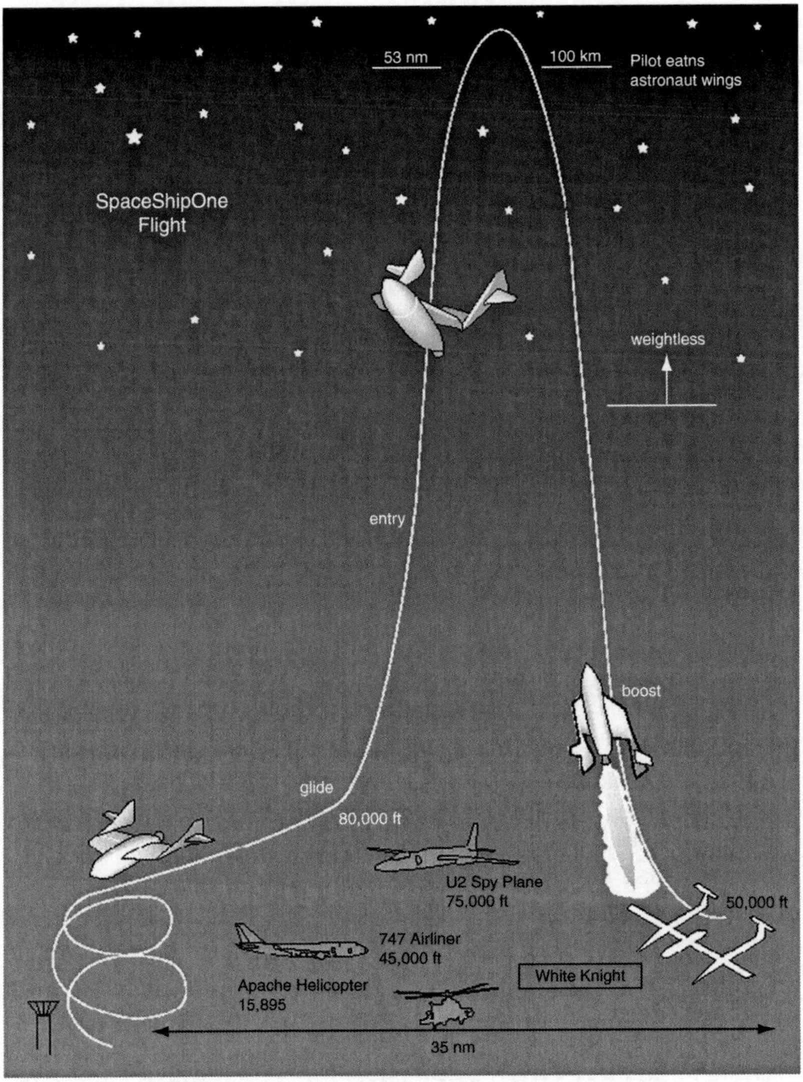


*Figure 10.4* SpaceShipOne is a concept that pioneered the commercial use of space. It employed unconventional technical approaches to avoid the extremely expensive approaches employed in nationally financed space programmes

is pertinent. The starting point is an undesirable condition, here called the problem, which is the cause that gives rise to a need. To satisfy the need, there must be a positive change, here called the goal. If the goal is realized, an effect is achieved so that the undesirable condition ceases. The original problem then is solved.[1] Intervention is necessary to make the cause-effect chain process work. This is called the concept. It comprises the actions that enable realization of the goal. The choice of concept then is guided by the original problem and the expected effect.

Needs, goals and effects may be defined at various levels. The less general the definitions of needs, the more it will provide guidance in the direction of specific types of solutions. That brings in the risk of the project not being suitable to attaining the overriding goals. There are examples in many countries of needs analyses identifying a particular technical solution as a need, and that goals and impact assessments being constrained to concern implementation of a given main concept.

Thus, identification of real alternative concepts must be based on problems and status descriptions at an overriding level. Hence, we speak of a concept level and a strategic level, as opposed to a project level. On one hand, there's a search for alternative solutions to an overriding problem, while on the other hand, the quest is for how each of these alternatives may be realized.

What this means in practice is illustrated by the following example of the planning of a transport project in an urban area suffering congestion of its main streets (Næss 2005). At the concept level, for example, the needs may concern reducing travel time between sectors of the urban area, prompting a more environment-friendly transport mode distribution, and furthering less-travel-generating, car-dependent urban development patterns. The goals at this level must reflect these needs, and the effects of various solution concepts (and their relevant combinations must be assessed).

When a main concept, such as an urban railway, is chosen, demand analyses, goal setting and impact assessment will focus on ensuring that it is designed and implemented in the most socially acceptable manner. Needs and goals at this level may, for example, be concerned with attaining high passenger volumes, financially favourable and environment-friendly routing, and with contributing (through the locations of stations) to urban development in targeted areas.

Whenever demand analyses, goal setting and impact assessment at the strategic level are skipped, and instead the project level is initiated within the framework of a given solution, the initiators' needs can easily be confused with those of the society. Hence, the wishes of special interests for financial gains, prestige or ideologically preferable solutions may take precedence over top-down political goals and the needs of broader social groups. Such constraint of planning at a premature stage is a commonplace weakness in the planning of large, public investment projects.

For example, the analysis that ostensibly spotlighted the need for the airport express rail line serving Oslo focused only on public transport by rail and neglected busses and taxis. The result was a predicted passenger volume that inflated travel by airport express trains by almost 70 per cent and thereby also gave a false indication of the need for this highly expensive rail line.

## 10.3 Requirements and choice of concept

The assumed impact is decisive to the choice of concept. But often the starting point is an undesired condition or a problem that initiates a search for a solution. In such cases, the conditions considered in determining a concept are simple.

First, it's essential to focus on existing problems, not assumed, probable or future problems. Second, problems should not be expressed as absence of particular solutions. For example, the farmers' problem is not that they don't use pesticides, but that their crops are infested by pests. So there are considerable differences in the way the problem can be approached. There are many alternatives in addition to spraying crops.

The problem therefore ought to express an existing undesirable condition, and it needs to be concrete. If the problem concerns traffic congestion, stating it in terms of too few traffic lanes points to just one solution, as illustrated in Figure 10.5.

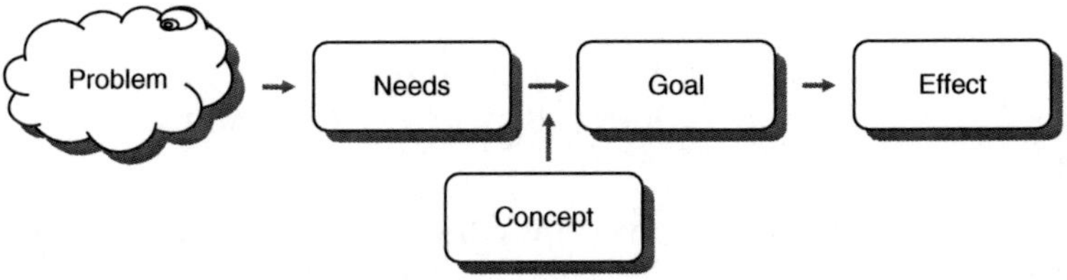


*Figure 10.5* A concept is a contemplated intervention in a cause-effect chain that should result in a particular effect and thereby solve a concrete problem

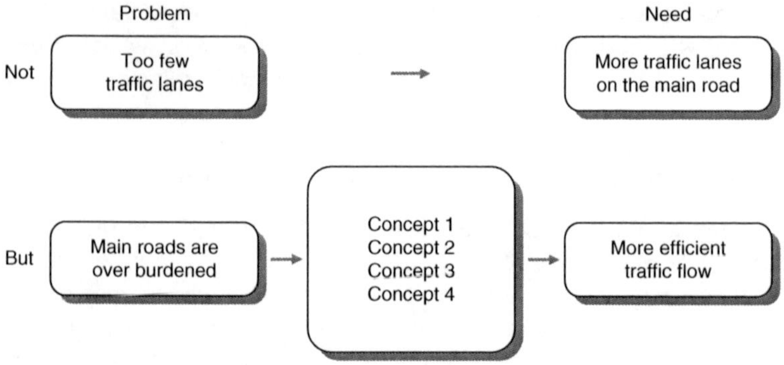


*Figure 10.6* A problem is not the lack of a particular solution but rather an existing or future undesired condition

Expressing the problem in more general terms gives latitude for several alternative solutions. They may not directly deal with the problem of too few traffic lanes, but may seek other indirect solutions, such as by routing some traffic on other streets or by using other means of transport. All are solutions to the overriding problem, which in this case deals with traffic flow, see Figure 10.6.

This example underscores another aspect discussed in section 10.1, namely that the concepts chosen should be dissimilar. Nonetheless, they would have to share common characteristics suited to solving the same problem. If that is not the case, they are merely variants of one set solution. Of course, the final choice of solution also needs to be assessed. But that should happen not at the concept level, but at the project level after the concept has been chosen.

The alternatives also have to be genuine, in the sense that they exclude each other. An oversimplified example is that if you want to start a family and have found two potential spouses, you normally are faced with two mutually exclusive alternatives, unless you wish to be a bigamist. If at the same time, you have three job offers, each in a different city, you have $2 \times 3 = 6$ mutually exclusive alternatives (Løwendahl and Wenstøp 2002).

We have no solid tradition for identifying truly alternative concepts as bases for designing projects. Most often, the choice is made at the starting point, and assessment is mainly at the project level. For example, in a study of a new national museum of art, architecture and design in

Oslo, the choice was between alternatives that all featured collocation of the museums on the same site. The alternatives differed in distribution of space above and below ground, remote or central storage, and the like. So, obviously the concepts merely were variations on the same solution. Genuine alternatives would, for instance, look more closely at which museums should be collocated and where in the city or in the country they should be located. These aspects could then be weighed against the increased benefit envisioned. In this case, the problem, the anticipated effect and the benefit were all vague and gave no clear guide for choice of alternatives. Consequently, there was no substantive discussion of the reality of the proposal put forth.

The reason for the requirement of genuine alternatives is that it would stimulate creative thinking and thereby increase the chances of a good choice. We believe that this is worthwhile, but at the same time know that innovative thinking is no guarantee that it happens. So there's a need to assess several alternatives. Moreover, these alternatives ought to be assessed against the zero option to avoid ending up with something that turns out to be worse than what existed.

- A concept is a mental construction intended to support the solution of a problem or the satisfaction of a need.
- Conceivably there may be several different concepts as alternative solutions to the same problem.
- The concepts should be genuine alternatives in the sense that they are mutually exclusive.
- Nonetheless all the concepts should share common characteristics suited to solving the same problem.

The importance of the choice of concept was probably spearheaded by international development agencies, such as USAID, The World Bank and the UN agencies. The reason may be the seemingly endless series of misguided investments in developing countries where the problems, the needs and the solutions in recipient countries might not have been sufficiently understood by the agencies' international staff and decision makers. At the same time, we have seen that industries have introduced gateway processes to improve the development of their business cases. There is an increased awareness that the project is much more than just a technical solution – it would involve the entire business case, all the various organizations involved, as well as the various mechanisms and arrangements involved in the inter-organizational relationship (Williams et al. 2009).

In the UK public arena the influential "Downey" report laid down the policy that early project definition should take up 15 per cent of the cost and 25 per cent of the time of the project. Later the Office of Government Commerce established gateways reviews as a means to help the departments improve their record in project delivery. Governance frameworks for public projects have been established in several countries. As early as year 2000, the Norwegian Ministry of Finance introduced external quality insurance of the choice of concept in major public projects before they was submitted to Parliament for approval. The requirement includes stipulations for concept studies and alternative analyses of various concepts, including zero options. In the UK, The Office of Government Commerce introduced a Gateway 0 analysis focusing on the choice of concept in 2007.

Hopefully, with time, this will change the attitudes and practices of planners and decision makers and in turn improve the economic viability and benefit of investment cases. Such requirements are discussed further in Chapter 15.

## 10.4 The choice of concept

There are no commonly agreed guidelines for a best practice, here termed concept, for systematic identification and selection of unique and different solution to a problem. Also, there are not a great many studies that offer a systematic inquiry into how this is done in practice, the range of alternative concepts that are identified, and which ones are chosen. One such study, which is not conclusive but that might offer some clues on the state of affairs in the Norwegian setting, is a review of lessons learnt after the quality assurance scheme mentioned above had been in operation for five years (Minken et al 2009). The study concluded that:

- The alternatives being considered were merely different technical solutions to the same problem than mutually exclusive concepts.
- The tendency was that the possible and preferred technical solutions were used to guide the choice of concept rather than vice versa.
- The link between the choice of concept and the underlying societal need or problem was often not made explicit.

- The project-triggering need or problem would frequently be confused with other perceived needs or problems.
- The anticipated, desired effect of the project was often confused with various positive or negative anticipated side effects.
- The Zero-option, or the low-investment alternative solution, was often not identified, formulated or considered in relation to the alternative concepts being analysed.

What this suggests is that in the inception phase, there was no satisfactory inquiry into the project-triggering problems and corresponding needs, possible alternative concepts and their anticipated effects, but more of a narrow technical search for solutions and business as usual. In other words, there seem to be much room for improvement, even though in this case planners had been specifically requested to abide with the requirements of the quality assurance scheme, to do a comprehensive analysis of problems and needs and identify uniquely different concepts. The question why this did not happen needs to be asked. Was it a lack of awareness among planners and decision makers, a lack of competence and imagination, too restricted perspectives and professional focus, or was it a case where vision and advice was overruled by political and economic restrictions. The study further concluded that in the transport sector, the choice of concepts frequently were restricted to alternatives such as the scope and standards of roads, their capacity (2, 4 or 6 lanes), alternative routes (through or around cities, resort areas etc.), technical solutions (ferry, bridge or tunnel), and in more exceptional cases different means of transportation (cars, buses or railroad). Only occasionally the zero-option was considered in detail, such as by applying price regulation, road toll, user restrictions etc. as alternatives to new infrastructure.

The zero option, which is also termed 'the basis alternative' or 'the reference concept', is commonly neglected. In view of the prospects of a new investment project it is frequently neglected or under-communicated as a possibility, even though it in many cases would appear to be the most viable alternative.

The distinction needs to be made between situations where there is a *critical need* in the sense of a problem that has to be solved (for example an unacceptable safety or security problem or an emergency) – and the more *common need* in the sense of an opportunity to increase economic benefits by alternative use of scarce resources (Holst Volden 2009).

Clearly in the first case, proceeding without the investment will not be acceptable and the zero option therefore not viable. The choice of concept will frequently be between different technical solutions to the existing problem or even a replacement of the existing infrastructure: a bridge has collapsed, the air force needs to replace existing helicopters etc.

In the second case, the zero option should typically be considered as an alternative. Building of a new opera house, a merger and relocation of three museums, application to the Olympic Committee for hosting the Winter Olympics – these would be examples of such projects where the zero option would need to be considered.

The zero option is defined as the continuation of the existing situation without the anticipated investment. However, it needs to be defined in such a way that it would not represent further deterioration of an existing situation. Therefore, it should be a viable alternative in the sense that it can be realistically applied, not in conflict with existing decisions, which would typically imply that necessary upgrades and minor investment would have to be allowed to make it a real option.

What this means is that we should introduce a type of mini-concept in terms of investments, to be given a fair trial with the alternatives, and it should be analyzed to the same level of detail. In the assessment all necessary costs and corresponding benefits should be taken into consideration. If this had been done, many white elephants could have been aborted during their inception. Consider the following examples.

In the case of the shipping tunnel described in Chapters 19 and 20 the alternative to a huge and tremendously expensive tunnel, where the socio-economic benefits are uncertain, would be to invest in a system to monitor wave and wind conditions at sea in the area, and provide this type of online information to the public through the meteorological weather services.

Another example could be a project where an island with a small population, now serviced by a ferry, be linked to the mainland by a bridge. Two different zero options could be considered: (1) to maintain the present situation, but with an option to use two ferries should the traffic volume increase above a certain level, and (2) to provide the inhabitants with economic intensives to relocate to the mainland (since this would often be the result anyway: once the bridge is built, residents sell their properties to tourists and move to the mainland).

Hosting the Winter Olympics represents huge investments in infrastructure and usually meagre long-term returns. A reasonable approach would be to apply a time perspective of 10–15 years, and introduce a zero option defined by the economic situation without the Olympic Games in the region, but also to include investment in sport facilities etc. that would otherwise be needed in the period.

A principle consideration in economic analysis is that economic resources are scarce and have alternative uses. When resources are used for one purpose, we implicitly exclude other possible uses of the resources. When economic resources are scarce, the economic viability is determined by the added value generated by applying the resources as compared with the alternative uses of the same resources. In principle, to select the best alternative in economic terms would be to identify the alternative with the highest economic return with that with the next highest return. Then all other alternatives would be inferior (Hagen and Pedersen 2009).

Clearly, the economic aspect is only one of several that need to be considered, as discussed in Chapter 5.1. However, economic considerations are essential, and experience suggests that there is a strong tendency to distort the picture by underestimating costs and overestimating benefits in the initial analysis, as discusses in Chapters 8 and 9. This is commonly done in order to promote one specific concept that for some reason by some is the preferred one. The same goes with the zero option. It is commonly neglected, or not explored and developed into a feasible alternative as compared to the preferred alternative. In times when money is no longer seen as a scarce resource, the crave is for change and the grand choices – not for improvement.

# 11
# Project Alignment: Needs, Objectives and Effects

*Projects are initiated to solve problems or satisfy needs. A problem or a need constitutes a starting point for a strategy that will lead to a goal that expresses what one hopes the project will achieve. After a project concludes, it is expected to have a particular effect on the market or for users.*

*All the facts belong to the problem – none to the solution.*
*—Wittgenstein*

## 11.1 Alignment of needs, objectives and effects

The project strategy and its intended and unintended effects were illustrated in Figure 9.3 . Strategies are designed in response to certain needs. The phenomena of *needs*, *goals* and *effects* are closely related. There must be correspondence between them. For example, a hydroelectric power project is initiated and planned to meet a need for electric power in a market. The project is to build a facility with a stated capacity. The goal is to attain stable delivery to the grid at that level. Need and effect often are expressed indirectly in derived units. For example, the triggering need and effect can both be expressed in economic terms, in this case respectively in well-being and production.

Accordingly, the design of the project shall include the basic requirement of a connection between needs and effect. The goal shall be derived from the needs, and the effect shall at least correspond to the goal set for the enterprise. This is illustrated in Figure 11.1. The needs must be real to attain the anticipated effect. Basic user and market

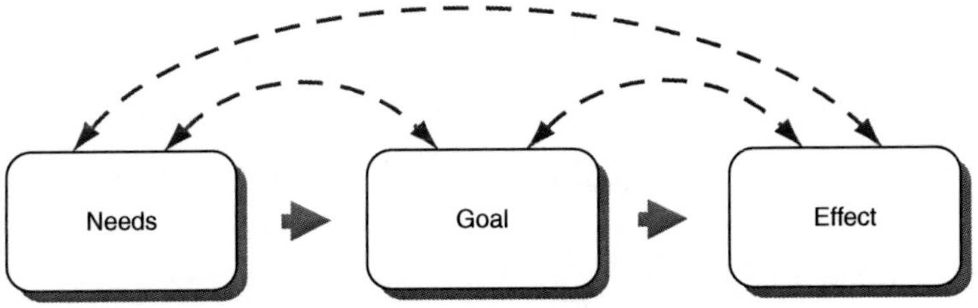


*Figure 11.1* Alignment of objectives presupposes correspondence between needs, goals and effects

research may be used to ascertain whether this is the case. The lack of user or market adaptation lowers the chances of success.

An example of this might be the 1980 decision by the UN General Assembly that the forthcoming decade to 1991 would be the World Drinking Water Supply and Sanitation Decade. The goal was to ensure supplies of pure drinking water to the peoples of all countries. The starting point was that impure drinking water was the cause of many health problems in developing countries. The goal was to build simple, reliable water supplies in villages where the needs were believed to be greatest. The anticipated effect was to reduce the incidence of waterborne diseases. The strategy showed a clear connection between needs, goals and effect, and the programme was initiated with considerable commitment by the UN and donor countries. However, it became apparent that the anticipated goal was not attained. In retrospect, much of the programme was found to be flawed and enormous investments were wasted.

In this case, it was found that the correspondence between needs, goals and effects that seemed good on paper didn't reflect reality. The decision makers had taken for granted that pure drinking water was a basic need of the target group. Water is of course a basic need, as we cannot survive without regular access to it. But in turn this implies that wherever people live, they have access to water. Subsequent studies showed that for the poorest among those the programme intended to help, food production had higher priority than pure drinking water. The poorest viewed impure water that causes disease to be less of a problem than lack of food.

This illustrates the demarcation between needs on one side and wants or prioritizations on the other side. There isn't necessarily a connection

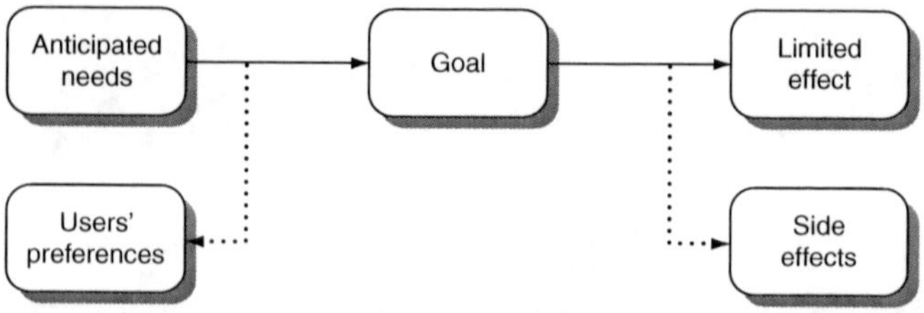


*Figure 11.2* Deficient alignment of needs, goals and effects. Assumed needs are not prioritized by users. The result is inadequate effect and undesired side effects

between the two. In many water supply projects problems arose in the operational phase when users had neither the motivation nor the resources to maintain the installations. In many places, users reverted to the original water supplies rather than obtain parts and fix breakdowns. Therefore, in many cases the investments were wasted. This is illustrated in Figure 11.2.

If the goal had been to build dams for agricultural water, the situation would have differed. There are many examples of projects for the same target groups in which small dams have been built to support local agriculture. This has led to agricultural organization, production and trade. The resultant side effects are precisely those sought for during the Water Decade, that is, improved hygiene and health.

The Water Decade programme was unsuccessful because as seen by the users, the investments weren't relevant. Instead, undesirable side effects arose, including conflicts in the use and maintenance of the water supplies. This example illustrates the importance of project relevance in the sense that it tied to real needs and priorities. The decision process for the World Drinking Water Supply and Sanitation Decade was definitely top-down, and user cooperation didn't come in before the water supplies were built. In many projects, user cooperation in the front-end phase can be decisive for attaining good alignment between needs, goals and effects. In short, success crucially depends on organizing for openness and dialogue between users and affected parties.

## 11.2 Stakeholder analysis

A project involves and affects several parties. One group comprises those involved, that is the project owner and the contractor who

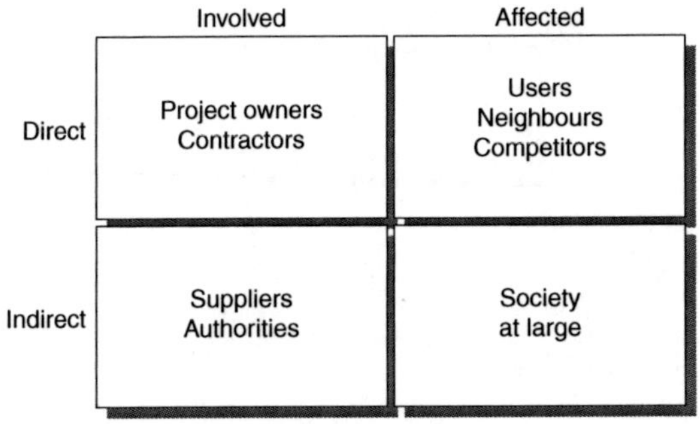


*Figure 11.3* Example of stakeholders in a project

directly impel the project, while the suppliers that provide goods and services and the authorities that approve and organize are indirect participants, see Figure 11.3. Another group comprises the affected parties not directly involved in the project. The users are first and foremost interested in the project being implemented. But often stakeholders such as competitors and neighbours may have other interests in or be opposed to the project. In addition, there are all who are indirectly affected by the project but nonetheless have opinions on it, such as the media and the public.

In open societies, it's generally accepted that for the most part, the various parties and their interests should be taken into consideration to ensure successful organization and implementation. Often, it's easier and cheaper to solve problems upstream. Experience indicates that the converse can cause conflicts downstream, with delays, legal proceedings and sequels that can be far more costly.

Commonly, for example, there's a legal requirement that responsible parties shall conduct extensive consequence studies and open hearings on projects that might have appreciable impact on the environment, natural resources or society and that depend on official approval. The consequence study shall ensure that all consequences are considered in planning the enterprise. The study shall clarify the enterprise, its relevant alternatives, impacts on the environment, natural resources and society, and what can be done to avert damages and disadvantages that might be brought about by it. Approval cannot be issued before the obligatory study is completed.

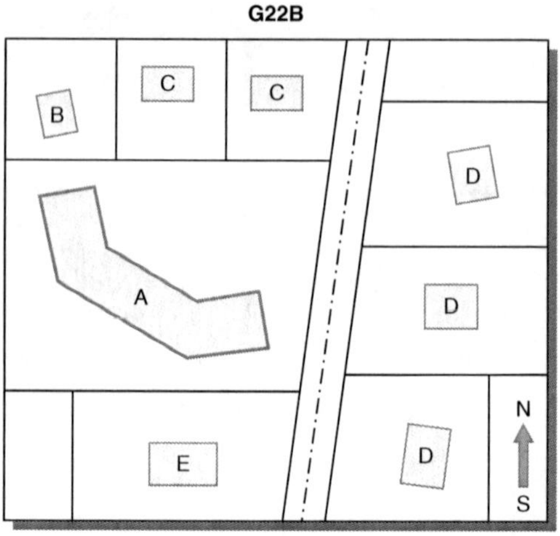


*Figure 11.4* Building project location map. The proposed building is A

Some form of impact assessment or stakeholder analysis is appropriate in most projects, regardless of their size. The following example of a relatively small construction project is illustrative. A simple analysis was used to gain an overview of the stakeholders, the affected parties and potential conflicts of interest.

A contractor has bought a building site in a suburban area. The site slopes to the southwest and is timbered with tall spruce trees. The aim is to build a two-storey building with ten large apartments in the upper segment of the market. The plan requires exemptions from several requirements of the building code, so neighbour objections can overturn the project. A location map with the proposed building is shown in Figure 11.4.

On it, the developer groups the neighbours to provide an overview of the situation:

A. future building residents
B. closest neighbours at same height as proposed building; they are the most noticeably affected
C. neighbours at a higher level to the north, for whom the proposed building is in view
D. three neighbours higher up on the other side of the road; they are less affected by the project
E. a neighbour to the south at a lower elevation, with an unspoilt view

Thereafter, the developer lists the conditions that believably will be essential for the various parties:

1. how the project will affect the future market values of the properties
2. how the individual neighbours may perceive the effects of cutting down the tall spruces
3. effect of widening the road, which is a zoning requirement
4. significance of distance to the building
5. effect of the height of the building

Then the developer ranks the assumed impacts of the project for the individual neighbours, simply as plus or minus or zero if the project may be assumed to be unimportant, and lists the rankings, as illustrated in Table 11.1.

The table shows that distance to the neighbours and building height are the principal problems. The future residents agree with the closest neighbours, B and E, on maximum distance between buildings, while C and D are unaffected. The developer enters an agreement with E to accept the plan if the new building is located 20 metres from the property line. Apparently all parties will benefit from cutting down the trees and widening the road. However, these aspects are weak negotiation counters, as the trees will be cut down and the road widened, regardless of who develops the site. As listed in the table, the project has the greatest effect on B and a lesser effect on C, both of whom are to the north. For both of them, the building height is bothersome.

Of the two, B risks loss of market value due to the project. B, C and D then join forces and threaten to stop the project. The developer then requests a negotiation meeting. All parties know that they have much to lose and most to gain by reaching an agreement. The developer risks

*Table 11.1* Effects of the new building on neighbours

| Effects of the project | A | B | C | D | E |
|---|---|---|---|---|---|
| Tall trees cut down | + | + | + | + | 0 |
| Tall building | 0 | – | – | 0 | 0 |
| Improved road access | + | 0 | 0 | + | 0 |
| Neighbours close by | – | – | 0 | 0 | – |
| Market value change | 0 | – | – | 0 | 0 |

disallowance of the project or perhaps postponement of up to three years. Neighbours B and C risk that the project may be approved as is.

The negotiations result in agreement that the new building will lie lower in the terrain with a lesser roof pitch that will considerably lower its roof crest. Neighbours B and C express wishes to connect to the new sewer for A, which will save them considerable expenses should they be required to remove their septic tanks and install sewage pumps to connect to the municipal sewer. The developer agrees to the connections, as for him the costs are marginal. Moreover, he offers to deliver fill to raise B's garden by two meters and to level and plant it free of charge. The parties agree, and the developer avoids neighbour protests that could have stopped the project.

In this example, the developer employed a simple systematic approach to get an overview of the various parties, their interests and the ways they would be affected by the proposed project. Thereafter, he can propose suitable measures for lessening the disadvantages for those affected and preferably enter contracts with each of them. Moreover, he may be obliged to yield slightly with respect to those most affected. As described here, this often is much less costly than prolonged postponement and legal proceedings.

In new projects, conflicts arise between developers and originators, public concerns and various interest groups. Conflicts arise, because not all interests and needs can be favoured. The example above illustrates a situation subject to ultimate decision by the authorities, in which negotiations between interest groups is a vital supplement to and a bit on the way to making up for public planning. The situation often is not so simple. The arena is dominated by affluent groups who further their interests, while weaker groups are systematically underrepresented in the negotiations and bargaining that take place. This often means that information on the needs and interests of weaker groups isn't disclosed. Consequently, there's a need for governmental requirements of inclusive processes and openness that give rise to solutions that all can accept and thereby prevent major, prolonged conflicts between parties.

The success of a strategy can be assessed partly by the extent to which stakeholders' needs are met and stakeholders are satisfied. Obviously, stakeholders ought to be identified as early as possible. The comprehensive list of stakeholders would include all parties regardless of whether their involvement is strong or weak, positive or negative, direct or indirect. Commonly, a so-called *influence versus interest* grid is used to categorize the

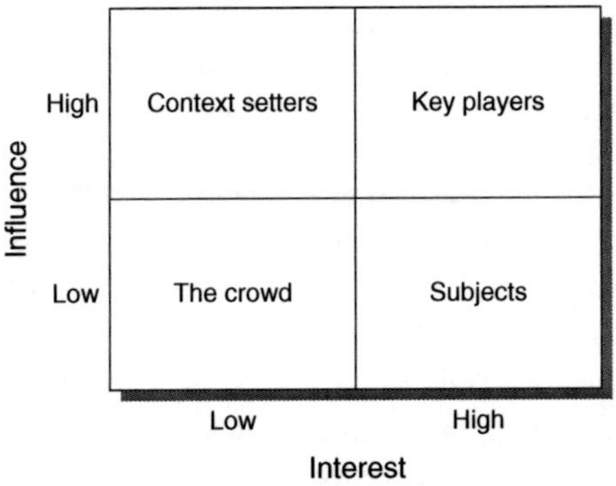


*Figure 11.5* Stakeholder analysis. The Influence versus Interest grid

stakeholders in a way that might help provide greater insight into their role, and how they need to be treated. This is illustrated in Figure 11.5 (Eden and Ackermann 1998). Stakeholders are thus divided into four categories: the Players, Context setters, Subjects and the Crowds.

When deciding on the degree of power that a stakeholder has over a project, the major consideration will be whether the stakeholder has the power to control decisions, facilitate implementation and or affect the project negatively. It may be direct power, for instance of the budget, or indirect, for instance in the ability to persuade or affect others. The power that a stakeholder holds may depend on their formal position, authority of leadership, control of strategic resources, possession of specialist knowledge and or negotiating position in relation to others stakeholders.

- The *Players* are those that are both powerful and highly interested in the strategy. Their consent is essential to the entire undertaking. They have to be fully engaged and there is a need to consult these people, keep them informed and maintain good working relationships. Examples of players are typically owners, shareholders, senior management etc.
- The *Context setters* are powerful, but their level of interest in the strategy is limited. They are generally relatively passive, but may suddenly emerge as result of sudden events to become players on specific issues. The interests on these stakeholders are not high priority for the particular project and they may therefore represent

significant risk to the progress or implementation. It is therefore essential to keep the context setter satisfied. This would typically require engaging and consulting them on their areas of interest, and proactive communication to keep them informed. In many cases, banks may be considered context setters. They provide vital finance for the project, while their interest is often unlikely to extend beyond the financial aspects. However, they can exercise considerable power, in fact, control whether the project goes ahead or not.

- What is termed the *Subjects* in Figure 11.5 would be those with an interest in the project, but with little power. They can be important in that they can influence the more powerful stakeholders and therefore constitute a risk. One strategy would be to keep them informed and consult them in their areas of interest and try to get them involved in low risk areas. This group of stakeholders would typically be the users or the consumers. For instance, a strategy that is not aligned with the needs in the market is almost certainly doomed to fail. Careful analysis of their needs is therefore required, as well as keeping them informed and monitoring their responses.
- The *Crowds* have little power or interest in the project. They are likely to require only minimal effort and monitoring. A feasible strategy will typically be to keep them at arm's length, at minimal resource cost to the project, and inform via general communications as necessary.

Once the stakeholder grid has been established, it can be used to consider the relationship between different stakeholders and how they influence one another. This will help to identify ways and means to satisfy stakeholders. In the example illustrated in Figure 11.4 the player is contractor A. The main context setters would be B, E, as well as the building authorities that will eventually have to endorse the project. It would therefore be essential for A to come to terms with B and E, as was done in this example by entering into agreements both regarding distance between buildings, lowering the roof pitch, the sewer connection and landscaping. Neighbours C would belong to the 'subjects' group of stakeholders. They are concerned parties with little influence, while neighbours D at the other side of the road would only be affected indirectly (and positively) by the project and would be of little concern to the player.

# 12
# Objectives and Their Formulation

*Objectives are used partly to define directions and partly to specify achievement targets at specified points in time. This chapter focuses on how to ensure consistent hierarchy of objectivess and avoid some of the mistakes that are common in identifying and formulating objectives.*

> *Nothing is more dangerous than an idea – when it is the only one you have.*
>
> —*Emilie Cartier*

## 12.1 Using objectives in projects

An objective is a concrete expression of an intention. An intention becomes an objective when and only when something is done to realize it. An objective is a description of a future status sought or to be attained. Hence, an objective is tied to a particular point of time.

Moreover as they are formulated and agreed upon, objectives are a project's prime success criteria. Formally viewed, success is ensured when a project is implemented as efficiently as possible and causes effects that concur with its objectives and correspond to the needs that triggered it. So formulating, furthering and following up objectives is a management function.

Major investment projects are complex and usually have several objectives that are more or less mutually dependent. Customarily a hierarchy of objectives is defined to clarify how the various objectives relate to and support each other. The location of an objective in the hierarchy indicates how general or concrete it may be but doesn't necessarily indicate its importance. The hierarchy displays cause-effect relationships. So, to a degree, it indicates realizability, in other words, the ambitiousness of the individual objectives.

Studies of projects have shown that ambitious objectives motivate better performance, but also that performance drops when objectives are overly ambitious or completely unrealistic. In American literature, this is used to argue that objectives should be formulated so that they are realistic, that is, they can be achieved with the means available. In Scandinavian literature, it's asserted that realistic objectives (that we are certain that we can achieve) are insufficiently challenging in a continually changing world. Visionary objectives are needed to bring out the best performance. This means that overall objectives should be sufficiently ambitious to motivate yet be realistically attainable later on. Of course, impossible objectives are purposeless (Næss et al. 2004).

The formulation of an objective should indicate what's needed to attain it. This is what strategy sets forth. An objective may be expressed at the personal level, such as completing education, building a cottage or having a baby. Or it may be expressed at the project or process level, such as building and furnishing a new opera, or at the organizational level, such as attaining a target market share or membership. Or it may be at the national level, such as in keeping inflation at a specific level.

The purpose of formulating an objective is principally to clarify the direction for that which is sought. The scope of that which is sought also needs to be stated so one may know when an objective is attained. Multiple objectives may confuse that which is sought if they all don't point in the same direction. This is particularly evident if the objectives also conflict with each other. The development of a new oil field hardly can be justified with an environmental objective, as the investment undeniably will result in increased emission of atmospheric pollutants. Here there's a conflict of objectives. Using an environmental objective for a hydroelectric project will not give rise to such conflict, disregarding other environmental aspects, such as those associated with the damming of watercourses.

Objectives should give rise to common understanding among and motivation of all parties involved in or affected by a project. On one hand, this means that objectives should be unambiguous and realistic. On the other hand, to motivate, they also have to be well founded, to the degree that they are accepted. Often, this isn't possible, simply because there are differing prioritizations and needs and because some parties simply may be opponents of the project.

Moreover, the objectives should limit the enterprise or the strategy. This means that the resources allocated and the results anticipated should correspond. Inadequate allocation of resources leads to insufficient conditions for realizing an output. If the objective is overly ambitious, the anticipated effect isn't achieved. Finally objectives should be expressed in ways that permit assessing performance and results. This means that objectives are verifiable and measurable. Such requirements often are expressed in terms of SMART, a mnemonic for Specific, Measurable, Attainable, Realistic and Time-bound.[1]

Practice often differs considerably from this ideal. A study of major Norwegian governmental investment projects conducted by the Ministry of Finance in 1999 found that the formulations of objectives were vague and overly ambitions, unrealistic and little suited to overriding management. The objectives stated mostly were activities or tasks, while there was no hierarchy of objectives between these extremes (Berg et al. 1999). The finding was hardly unique. Rather, it seems to be commonplace practice, as corroborated by several studies, including Samset (1998).

In looking at customary practice in planning projects, the threshold for improvement seemingly is very low and the possibilities of marked improvement accordingly great. This was, for example, the conclusion in a study of major international projects that analysed cause-effect chains that formally comprised the basis for project management, as it was expressed in the steering document (Samset 2006). The study comprised a sample of assumed best-case projects, designed and quality assured to the same norms, as discussed in Chapter 19.

The study showed that all of the projects had substantial flaws. On the whole, the descriptions of the objectives were vague, and objectives

- The objectives are characterised by wishes or expressions of will that cannot be broken down into operative quantities that afford practical bases for management.
- There's no prioritization among the objectives. There are too many of them, and not all can be fulfilled at the same time.
- Closer analyses of the objectives shows that they are tasks, not genuine objectives. Actually, no overall goals have been set.

'Management of Public Investments',
Norwegian Ministry of Finance (Berg et al. 1999)

Why objectives (and what's required of them)?

- Clarify the direction for implementing the project (requires that all objectives point in the same direction).
- Create common understanding and motivation (requires a well-anchored, unambiguous and realistic objective).
- Limit the scope of the project strategy (presupposes alignment of resources, outputs and objectives).
- Allow for monitoring of performance and assessment of results (require that objectives are verifiable and measurable).

at differing levels of ambition were mingled in every project. Some projects lacked descriptions of anticipated effects or had strategic goals that were far more ambitious than realistic. When *'better standard of living'* is listed as an anticipated effect of a small road project, and *'economic growth'* as the anticipated result of a plant nursery project, it's intuitively easy to see that the gap between cause and effect is excessive and that the objectives are overly ambitious for the enterprises. In conclusion, the designs of these projects were so extensively flawed that none of the steering documents were suited to management and overriding decision making. Surprisingly most of the flaws were trivial and should have been avoided, as all the projects had been designed using a proven method that aimed to avoid precisely these sorts of flaws.

## 12.2 Linked and parallel objectives

Objectives are often organized in hierarchies, as discussed in section 12.1. Though useful, the hierarchy is an oversimplification of reality. For example, a hierarchy might be generated with strongly dependent objectives upwards and downwards, but no dependency between objectives at the same level. A more authentic real-world description might locate objectives in a network and define symbiotic relationships between them, as is done in a simulation model. That said, in this context a simplified description is adequate. Hence, we operate with two types of objectives: those linked in a cause-effect relationship and those parallel at the same level.

An example of *linked objectives* is that university studies lead to education which in turn leads to a professional career. These objectives are logically arranged, and the logic is testable. This means that reordering the sequence is a logical error. Education does not lead to studies, and a professional career does not lead to education.[2] A hierarchy may be envisioned in which probability assessment may be used to some extent to chart realism in the cause-effect chain. Assessing probability requires that the objectives are described to some degree of precision. In this case, if a university education is defined as the award of a master's degree, and university studies are set at three years, the probability of attaining the objective is negligible, as the normal period of studies to the master's level is four to five years. The longer the period of study, the greater the probability of attaining the objective. The level of ambition in a hierarchy of objectives can be tested in this manner, by assessing the probability of realisation at each level.

*Parallel objectives* are the ones that we assume will have to be realized collectively to attain an overriding objective. For example, many have found that a formal education is just one of several qualifications that may be required for a particular job. Others that may be decisive in a job application may include social skills, communication abilities, leadership, competitive instinct, etc. Consequently, an ambitious student probably will see work and organization experience as an objective parallel to education, hence, the motivation to become involved in extra-curricular activities such as sports, organizational involvement, vacation jobs, etc.

The hierarchy of objectives may be used to analyze the formulation of objectives. A commonplace problem is that objectives often are presented in complex, compound sentences that contain several objectives, both linked and parallel. The compounding of several meaningful elements renders a statement unsuitable for formulating an objective. This problem often is glaringly obvious in opinion surveys. Consider the question:

> Have you had or been treated for influenza or colds in the last 12 months?

In the formulation, there are two maladies and two degrees of treatment in the same statement. The opinion survey allows just two alternative answers, yes or no, so it is impossible to answer the question. The answer may be elicited only by four separate questions. An answer to a compound question is possible only by separately answering its parts.

Consider the following statement:

> Our wilinlgenss to comrephend meinanlgess stematents ouplatys comomn sesne.

Though the statement is meaningless, most readers will perceive sense in it. Moreover, most will interpret it in the same way. The intent of the statement comes through and proves that it is true: our willingness (and perhaps also ability) to understand meaningless statements goes beyond common sense. Regrettably this also applies to interpretations of the statements of project goals. Experience indicates that we have a unique, remarkable will to accept goal statements without critically considering their meaning, even when the statements are meaningless. Or, in any event, if they are insufficient or illogical, as often is the case. Four examples to illustrate this phenomenon follow in section 12.3.

The underlying cause may be an inability to analyze and interpret complex statements. Or it may be that the project culture allows that formally accepted goals are neglected when projects are implemented. Or both. It's possible that we are so accustomed to tactical operation that formulation of objectives has only ritual meaning.

In section 12.3 below, the formulations of objectives in four major public investment projects are examined to illustrate some of the more common flaws. That said, the assessments are of the objectives as they are stated in official documents and not of what may be the realities of the projects. Hopefully the relevant project documents contain

Specification of objectives:

- The Purpose shall specify what specifically is sought and be the point of departure for choosing the concept.
- There shall be one unifying objective at each objective level, if needed with underlying, parallel sub-objectives specified.
- For all parallel sub-objectives, the mutual allocation of resources on different sub-objectives should be clarified.
- The Purpose shall be sufficiently ambitious so that it provides justification for the project and latitude considering alternative concepts.
- The overall objective shall not be higher than its realization to a reasonable degree can be attributed to the project.
- The Goal shall be realistically attainable within a stated time frame, provided that the outputs are realized.

supplementary information that clarifies project strategy. Here we look only at the statements of objectives to illustrate the prevalent penchant for accepting vague, complex statements.

## 12.3 Identifying objectives: Four cases

### A top-heavy subproject

The first example is the 'Campus in Trondheim (CiT)' building project contemplated to collocate the university and the college in the city of Trondheim. The formulation of objectives was:

> The project shall contribute to the university and the college being enabled to operationalize and realize the Parliamentary goals for the institutions within the sectors: education, research, dissemination, innovation, external relations and resource management. The project shall contribute to the further development of Trondheim as a leading centre of knowledge, nationally and internationally.

The first noticeable failing is 'contribute to' that appears twice in the statement. A formulation of objectives should describe a desired final state. Saying that something should 'contribute to' weakens the statement. The project is said to contribute to realization, but there's no clear statement of the extent. Hence responsibility is disclaimed for whatever happens. This is commonplace. And here, in the same sentence, 'being enabled to' further weakens the statement, almost ludicrously, as it's not binding for anyone.

The second failing is the complexity of the statement. Each of the goals set forth in a meaningful formulation of objectives should be stated in terms of one and only one future condition to be realized, stated in a complete, meaningful sentence. Conjunctions and commas show that is not the case here. On one hand, it deals with operationalizing Parliamentary goals, on the other hand, with realizing them. Realization obviously is far more ambitions than operationalization. Moreover 'education, research, dissemination, innovation, external relations and resource management' are mentioned in one go. They are however different phenomena and should be seen as different goals. The city as a knowledge community is said to aim for prominence, both nationally and internationally. Clearly international recognition is far more ambitious than national renown, so these two aims should be different goals.

In this case, ten different goals have been packed together in a single formulation of objectives. It's illuminating to see how these goals might be related in a goal hierarchy, as shown in Figure 12.1. The overall goal obviously is that the city of Trondheim shall become a leading international centre of knowledge. That can come about only if it happens first at the national level. This entails a direct cause-effect relationship. At the lowest level of the hierarchy, the project is concerned with building facilities. This is a link in a plan for collocation of two institutions. The next link in the causal chain concerns operationalizing the Parliamentary goal of merging two institutions. The remaining six goals of the formulation are specified thematically and stated in a comma sequence in one sentence. Hence, together they may be seen to comprise parallel objectives. They are concerned with education, research, dissemination, etc. They must be realized if the overall vision of Trondheim becoming a leading centre of knowledge is to be fulfilled. So they're located high up in the hierarchy.

The layout of Figure 12.1 connotes correspondence between the goals in the upper part of the strategy, that is, the parallel goals and the overall goals. The collocation and strategic planning in the lower part of the hierarchy also appear connected. But in between there is empty space. Realization of the parallel goals obviously presupposes the inclusion of other elements in the hierarchy. Conceivably they may include better organizing and improvements in internal resource allocation to improve the efficiency and effectiveness of the institutions, better arrangements for reach, more funds for research, higher salaries to attract more capable professionals, etc. A gap can clearly be seen in the goal hierarchy as described in Figure 12.1. So ambitious an overall goal as in this case can only be achieved by the realization of underlying goals. Obviously the construction project should be seen as a limited sub-project. If the overall goal is fixed, as shown here, consideration must be given to what will contribute most to it. New buildings arguably would become merely marginal measures in an overall assessment, so the building project itself is of little relevance. To put it differently, the way the objectives are formulated in this case, the project lacks justification.

### A project with fleeting justification

The second example also involves a compound statement used as the starting point for a qualitative analysis or decision, as illustrated by the following example of the Norwegian '*combat aircraft project*'.

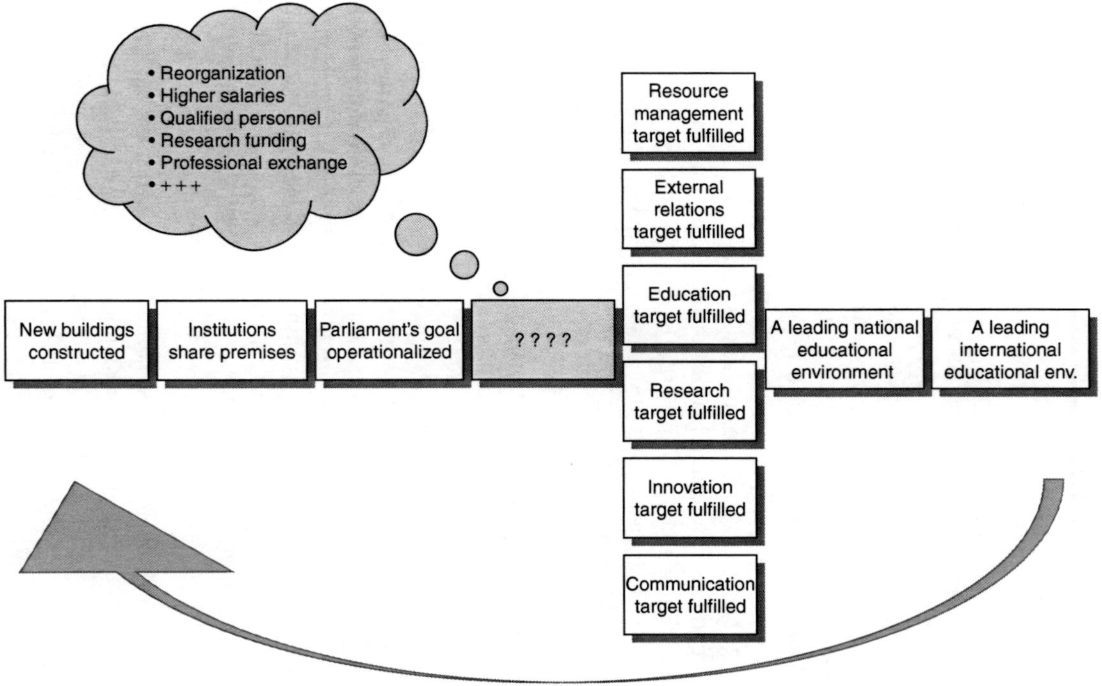


*Figure 12.1* Campus project. Hierarchy of objectives

The strategic objective underlying the acquisition of a new combat aircraft for Norway was formulated in the following way:

> Air strike capability that shall contribute to national security, sovereignty and freedom of action.

The formulation contains not less than four objectives, that together perhaps have meaning, but separately constitute four completely different objectives at differing levels of ambition respective to the endeavour, that is, the acquisition of a number of combat aircraft. The project strategy can be properly analyzed only by considering each of its individual elements. In fact, strategy with such a compound statement cannot be analyzed without splitting it up into separate meaningful elements. This applies not only to strategic analyses, but also to other endeavours, such as describing and testing differing scenarios, assessing risks, etc. Highly compounded formulations of objectives are due in part to there being no clear unifying reason for the project and in part to the penchant for taking in all good intentions without understanding their implications. In such cases, causality, that is, the connections between objectives, should be studied.

As mentioned above, the formulation of objectives contains four objectives. The connection between them arguably is incidental. However, the expression *'contribute to'* denotes causality. That is, the *'air strike capability'* is the cause and the remainder of the statement comprises the anticipated effect. But as Norway already has national security, sovereignty and freedom of action, *'contribute to'* is illogical; it should be *'maintain'*. The formulation then is: *'Air strike capability to maintain national security, sovereignty and freedom of action'*. The goal of *air strike capability* tells us only the project output, that is, that a number of combat aircraft are delivered and are operative. This objective will be realized upon delivery and consequently isn't a strategic objective. It should be deleted in the formulation of objectives.

The remaining three objectives are separated in a comma sequence that doesn't indicate causality. The question then is if they shall be considered parallel objectives. The answer lies in whether there are cause-effect connections between them. Understandably, sovereignty, which Norway already has, is the attribute that first and foremost ensures national security as well as freedom of action. The connections might be pictured in a cause-effect chain as shown in Figure 12.2. Other views of the connections are of course possible.

The choice of strategic objective then is between the three remaining objectives. To a degree, the question reduces to a probability assessment: will the combat aircraft aid the realization of national freedom of action, national sovereignty or national security? Or in other words: given adequate air strike capacity, what are the probabilities that each of the three objectives will be realized? *National security*, whatever that means, arguably is the objective closest to realization. That said, national security presumably is more extensive than security from attack by outside military forces and also includes questions concerning the economy, the environment, food supply, self-sufficiency, etc. It may be that *national security*, or perhaps *credible defence capability* in the sense of deterring military intervention by other countries, is a central objective as it is at a lower, more realistic level of ambition in relation to the endeavour. If so, it may plausibly be a strategic objective that replaces the others, that are no more than buzzwords that have crept into the parliamentary proposal in an effort to substantiate a public investment, which is not unusual. The cause-effect chain then is as shown in Figure 12.3.

Air strike capability is one of several elements that comprise the credible defence capability that also includes Norway's participation in greater alliances. The overriding reason is expressed in the strategic objective, namely maintaining the country's national security.

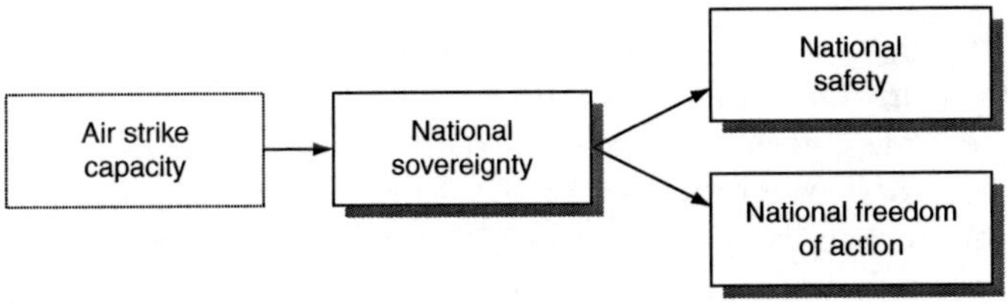


*Figure 12.2* Cause-effect chain for a combat aircraft

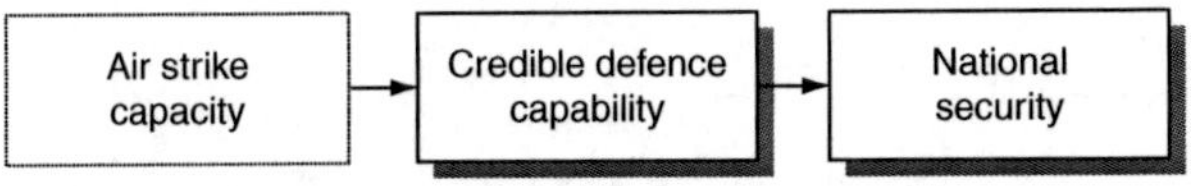


*Figure 12.3* Final cause-effect chain

## A project with no obvious justification

Another project with a yet more compounded formulation of its objective is the *Stad shipping tunnel* that calls for building a tunnel for smaller vessels between two fjord arms on the route between two minor ports on the Norwegian coast. The strategic objective of the project is said to be to:

> Enhance the operating conditions for maritime transport along the coast by increasing accessibility and safety for sea transport in the region, as well as support local employment and population.

The formulation contains five meaningful elements: (1) operating conditions for maritime transport, (2) increased sea transport, (3) increased safety at sea, (4) higher employment and (5) increase in local population. The word '*by*' refers back to the first objective, in contradistinction to the first example in which '*shall*' points forward. As it stands, the 'operating conditions for maritime transport' is the effect, while the other aspects are causes. This is an obvious error. The '*operating conditions for maritime transport*', whatever that means, should lead to increased sea transport, increased safety at sea, higher employment and a population increase, not the other way round.

In this case, a down-to-earth interpretation of the concept of '*operating conditions*' must mean the shipping tunnel itself. Employing the old adage that one should call a spade a spade, the cause-effect chain is as shown in Figure 12.4.

As in the previous example, the shipping tunnel (or the 'operating conditions for maritime transport') may be enhanced as it is no more than the project output. *Increased safety at sea* and *increased sea transport* along the coast believably are the first-order effects of the project. All that's left of the strategic objective is the support of *employment*, which is a precondition for increasing a *population*.

This is the logical structure that leaves a question that must be clarified more by politics than by logic. What is the underlying reason for

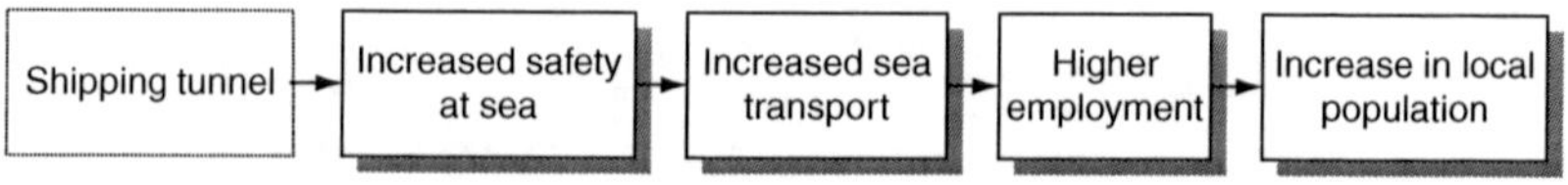


*Figure 12.4* Shipping tunnel cause-effect chain

the project? Is it the population issue? If so, is the shipping tunnel an enterprise that with sufficient probability will attract new residents? Or is employment the principal aspect? If so, can the project be justified from a greater socio-economic assessment of the impact of the anticipated increase in small-ship traffic? The statement of the overall objective in the bill put before Parliament gave no concise answer to such questions and consequently no credible grounds for the project.

**A purposeless project**

The fourth project regards *a road connection* from a small town at the end of the Lofoten archipelago to another town on the Norwegian mainland, originally planned for completion by the end of 2007. The bill before Parliament correctly defines the output as *'about 30 kilometres of new roads, including four tunnels, two longer and nine shorter bridges'*. However, the bill contains hardly any mention of a goal or a strategic objective for the project. The closest statement to a justification is:

> The project will give a region with a population of 25,000 a permanent road link to the mainland and thereby provide a ferryless mainland connection for the Lofoten archipelago.

This statement contains three meaningful elements: (1) road to be built, (2) permanent road link to the mainland and (3) ferryless connection to the mainland. The linking words *'give'* and *'thereby provide'* comprise a cause-effect connection, as shown in Figure 12.5.

Of course, the new road is just an output, not a strategic objective. The two other outputs mentioned are merely different ways of saying the same thing, so causality is meaningless. Both will be realized the moment the road is completed. This means that the project has no overriding objective. The 25,000 residents that will benefit from the new road most likely will get it. But the parliamentary bill has no description of the intended effect that can justify that funds are appropriated to the project. This also is not unusual in public decision documents.

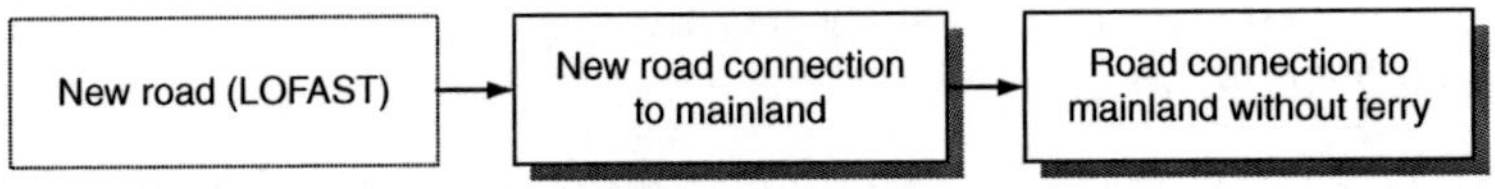


*Figure 12.5* Formally agreed LOFAST cause-effect chain

## 12.4 Causality and probability assessment

As discussed in the examples of section 12.3, assessments of causality and probability are aids. Both are based on judgement. A cause-effect chain is a logical construction based on experience and common sense. Consequently probability assessment is required to test the sense or strength of the links in the chain.

The starting points of all three examples are the project outputs. They are easily identified, as they are what the project delivers upon completion. The probability test of the merit of the output simply is that the probability of realization is 1, assuming that the resources are available for implementation. The respective outputs of the examples are acquisition of aircraft, a shipping tunnel and a road connection with bridges and tunnels.

The probabilities of realizing all the other objectives are less than 1. This is because the realization of an effect-oriented goal and an overall objective depend not just on the project, but also on other aspects that are external to the project and with which uncertainty is associated. A realistic objective is one for which the project helps realization, that is, the probability of realization is relatively high. A low probability of realization implies that the objective is overly ambitious for the project, so another objective at a lower level of ambition should be chosen. This is discussed in more detail in Chapter 19 and illustrated in Figure 12.6.

All of the above goal descriptions are qualitative only, without specific statement of the scope of achievement. Needless to say, this is unacceptable. However, it is often difficult to specify anticipated achievements without using separate indicators. Consequently, as implied here, early discussions of principles at an overriding level may do with qualitative expressions, provided, of course, that they are followed up more precisely using quantified indicators for intended achievements.

The assessment in the case of the combat aircraft was that the project contribution was marginal in relation to the overriding goal of national sovereignty. Consequently, a probability assessment resulted in the recommendation that the objectives be replaced by a goal and a strategic objective that were more realistic, in this case credible *defence capability* and *national security*.

In the example of the Stad shipping tunnel, it's reasonable to assume that it most likely will increase safety for users who bypass the

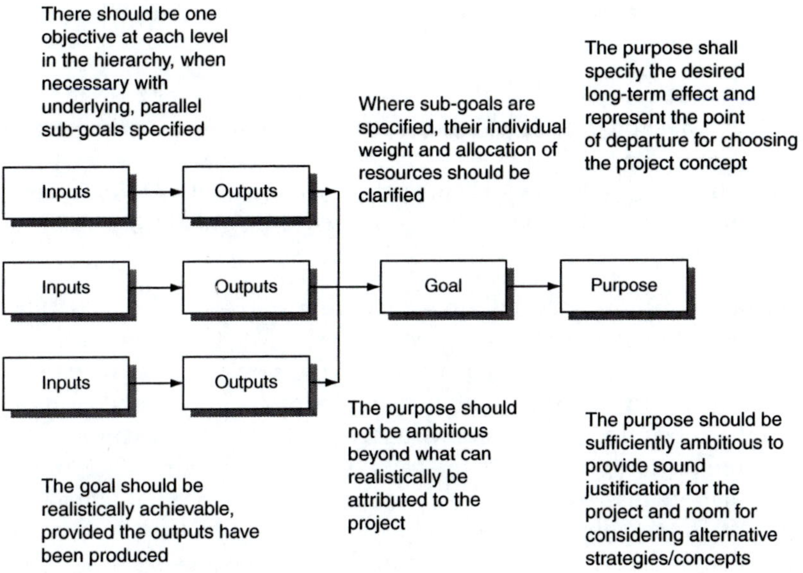


*Figure 12.6* Requirements when designing a hierarchy of objectives

> Requirements: Formulation of objectives
>
> - Singular expressions – no linked statements
> - Specify end situation – not a process or 'contribute to'
> - Specific – not general statement or reference to some overall strategy or policy
> - Unambiguous – so that it can be understood in the same way by all involved
> - Verifiable, if possible measurable

treacherous waters around Stad. This means that 'increased safety at sea' is insufficiently ambitious as a goal. The increase in sea transport is probably more uncertain, as it depends among other things on needs and fees charged. This would be a suitable goal, assuming that the probability of realizing the objective is sufficiently high, and assuming that the tunnel is built. How well the project will contribute to increased employment and population is even more uncertain. If the probabilities of realizing these objectives are low and assuming that the tunnel is built, there's cause to search for other objectives that can give better justification for the project. If this is not the case, the project should be abandoned.

For the road project, a probability assessment was also the basis for curtailment. The probability of a new road is 1, assuming that the project is realized. The same is true of the connecting road being ferryless. There are two implications: there's no cause-effect relationship between the outcomes, and hence there's no overriding justification for the investment.

Qualitative information is not something chosen for a particular situation, but rather something we all use in daily communication. To a great extent, we rely on qualitative expression that itself may inadequately describe what we wish to communicate, but nonetheless most likely will be understood as we wish. The credibility of the content of a communication depends on the basis of its information. Much of the information that we use is based on underlying systematic analyses of facts, often comprising qualitative information. Other portions of information are based on assumptions and judgement. An initial assessment of aspects such as needs and assumed effects of possible project alternatives will to a great degree refer to qualitative information based on assumptions and judgement. This isn't just a disadvantage. Operating for the most part with concepts and not with figures may simplify the visualization and discussion of complex situations. Accordingly the level of precision in such cases is low. Consequently one must be particularly vigilant in securing validity of definitions for the concepts used to ensure that the information used as the starting point for further concept and project development is as unambiguous and consistent as possible. Much qualitative information comes to light in complex, compound statements. Analysis of such information presupposes that a relevant text is broken down into its constituent meaningful elements. Much of the analysis comprises *categorization* (as by SWOT analysis, see Chapter 18), identifying or building *structures* (log frame analysis, see Chapter 19) or assessing *characteristics* (such as risk assessment, see Chapter 24). In such cases, the assessment of causality and probability are useful aids, as discussed in this chapter.

There's little doubt that the formulations of goals of the above examples are problematic. Worse yet, they're not unique, but comprise the rule rather than the exception. In fact, goal hierarchies and formulations of objectives in accordance with the principles outlined in this chapter seldom are so.

This raises at least four questions that should be answered:

- Are we at all aware of the intent of our project when we have not formulated its goal?
- Can we choose the most suitable concept when the goal has not been clarified?
- Is the goal something that we won't deal with in practice?
- If so, what should be changed, the formulation of objectives or the entire project culture?

The big question then perhaps concerns our attitude to management by objective as a principle and the extent to which flexibility and tactical manoeuvring should be allowed. They are not mutually exclusive, and in most cases, both are prerequisites for success. Regardless, practice indicates a need for more concise formulation of objectives in the front-end phases of projects, at any rate to establish common understanding of where a project is going and how it will get there.

# 13
# Methods and Analyses in the Front-End Phase

*Research has shown that many of the problems that have arisen in projects could have been avoided early on by considering experience from similar projects. Early analyses are to a large extent based on assumptions and judgement since they concern a future situation. Key issues involve the probability for realizing and the consequences of various choices. Consequently precision quantitative methods often are unsuitable. Simple, consensus-based processes, calling upon key decision makers and professionals with relevant expertise and experience relevant to the project to be analysed, often are more useful.*

> *We have excellent methods for calculating answers – but poor methods to ask the right question.*
>
> —*Albert Einstein*

## 13.1 Simple methods, facts and judgemental data

In the front phase, the need for information is most urgent and the uncertainty greatest. At the same time, the possibilities for improvements through acquiring better information are greatest, as discussed in Chapter 5. But one also faces the fundamental problem that the basic data are inadequate and uncertain, with large margins and deviations and is supplemented with judgemental data. Hence, precision instruments are little suited to analyzing data. This is why the choice of methods available for use in the initial concept appraisal is more restricted than in the planning and management phases.[1]

Such methods are simple, rough and holistic. Experience implies that even though the information base is derived from more or less intuitive estimates and assessments, qualitatively excellent results can often be attained by using such tools systematically in assessments performed by groups of people with relevant insight and experience. Also, such methods typically are inexpensive in use. Consequently, from the viewpoint of cost/benefit, the costs of initial concept development often are small while the potential reward is large. After the project starts, the situation often is the opposite: the reward attained doesn't always equally well reflect the costs of steering the process.

In terms of the basic data, the distinction is between *facts* and *assumptions*. Both types of data may be presented quantitatively in numbers or qualitatively in descriptions. That said, qualitative information needs to be quantified as much as possible, such as by using scales, rankings or various forms of weighting. To the degree possible, qualitative information suited to statistical presentation is sought. One must ensure that essential information is not lost because it is difficult to quantify. Whether or not an information element may be represented by a number has no bearing on its worth. Both numerical and descriptive information are necessary. Qualitative information is necessary to build understanding and depth. Quantitative information can impart precision and undergird analyses.

## 13.2 Four types of analyses

Whenever statistical data doesn't exist or is unavailable, the so-called experts may be engaged to generate information. The relevant collective term is expert judgement, which connotes a structured way of handling subjective analyses. For example, experts used in stochastic analyses customarily generate triple estimates of the most likely, assumed highest and assumed lowest value of a variable. These values are used as the principal parameters of an assumed probability distribution. The resulting expert analysis data comprises estimates of unknown values in the system to be analyzed, stated by experts possessing know-how relevant to the system. This type of analysis is illustrated in Chapters 22 and 25. Experts are people with relevant knowledge of and experience with the system.[2]

In general, there are four alternative approaches to building an information basis for decision. They are illustrated in Figure 13.1 and discussed below. Their approaches range from the use of purely statistical data to the use of informal, individual judgement (Øien et al. 1996).

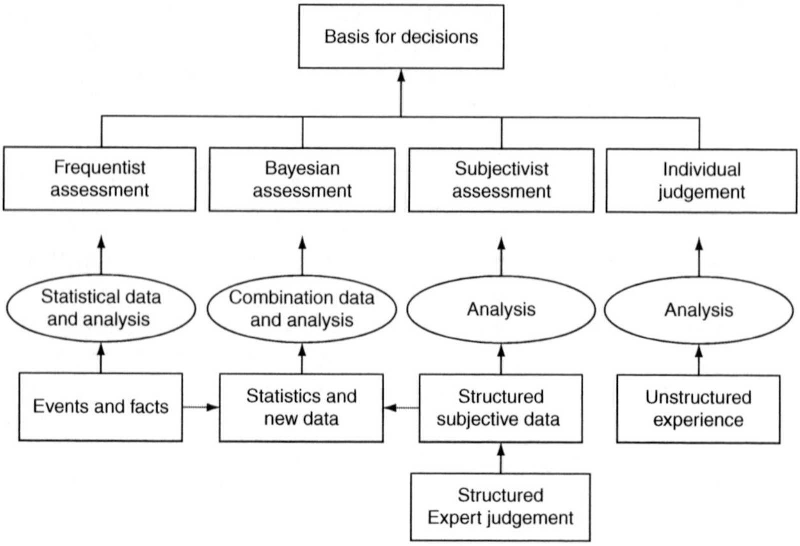


*Figure 13.1* Four types of assessments that may be used as decision bases, from statistical analyses of facts to subjective judgement

## Frequentist assessment

A frequentist assessment presupposes sufficient statistical data for use in the model, so the analysis can be carried through and gives a result. 'Sufficient' means that the number of observations registered or data is large enough to provide a basis for reaching reliable conclusion on what may be anticipated. They may, for example, be cost figures used to compile a budget proposal or estimates used to assess future economic viability.

Such assessments based on facts may be regarded to be the ideal alternative. Reliable qualitative data may be used analytically in various ways. First, it may be used to *precisely describe events* or courses of events. Second, it may be used to test *correlation between variables*. Third, it may be used to establish a basis for drawing conclusions that can be *generalized* to a larger sample or another situation. These uses may require advanced statistical analyses, and today there are innumerable such tools built into various common computer programs. Using computerized statistical analysis, of course, risks that the analysis is more advanced than the basic data, which often is the case. In front-end phase analysis, the aim is to describe future situations for which the outcomes are by and large influenced by uncertainty. Consequently, in principle, the result of a precise analysis doesn't necessarily yield a better approximation of the outcome of a future situation than does a more primitive analysis. This means that even though historical data and facts are 100 per cent reliable, there's always some uncertainty associated with how these data can be used to predict what will happen in the future. This is discussed in Chapter 6. In turn, perhaps a less advanced analysis serves the purpose better if it is cheaper and its results are easier to understand and communicate.

### Bayesian assessment

Bayesian assessment may be applied whenever there's some statistical data, though insufficient for a reliable statistical analysis. It can for instance be applied to update forecasts as data is supplied with time, or to update projections based on historical evidence by supplying subjective data based on expert judgement as time passes. In this type of analysis, probability estimates may be gradually refined as more data is acquired. The analysis presupposes that there is an *a priori* assumption of probability for a given outcome. Moreover, statistical information is available, such as error percentages or measurement inaccuracies. Bayes Theorem may be used to calculate the most likely *a posteriori* outcome or the probability of a given outcome. The precision depends on the original probability estimate and the quality of the supplementary information. When new information becomes available, the most recent *a posteriori* estimate may be used as a new *a priori* estimate that then is revised using the new information. Such chains of computations have the weakness that the effects of errors escalate and that the directions of estimates may be rapidly lost.

Following is one example to illustrate the above mentioned. In 1968 the US nuclear submarine Scorpion failed to arrive as expected at her home port. An extensive search failed to discover the wreck. A Bayesian search methodology was then adopted. Experienced submarine commanders were interviewed to construct hypotheses about what could have caused the loss of the Scorpion. The sea area was divided up into grid squares and a probability assigned to each square stipulating the probability that the wreck was in that square, considering various hypotheses. A second grid was constructed that represented the probability of successfully finding the wreck if that square were to be searched and the wreck were to be actually there. This was a known function of water depth. The result of combining these grids gave a grid that stipulated the probability of finding the wreck in each grid square of the sea if it were to be searched.

This sea grid was then systematically searched in a manner which started with the high probability regions first and worked down to the low probability regions last. Each time a grid square was searched and found to be empty its probability was reassessed using Bayes Theorem. This then forced the probabilities of all the other grid squares to be reassessed (upwards), also by Bayes Theorem. Thus systematically guiding the search, the Scorpion was found about 740 kilometres southwest of the Azores later the same year (Wikipedia).

**Methods and decision bases**

| Traditional | Front-end phase |
|---|---|
| • Facts | • Subjective/collective judgement |
| • Deterministic analysis | • Stochastic analyses |
| • Quantitative data | • Qualitative assessment |
| • Disciplinary approach | • Interdisciplinary approach |
| • Focus | • Perspective |
| • Mathematical models | • Global outcome charts |

### Subjectivist assessment

Subjectivist assessment builds on expert judgement, in a systematic, structured manner. The worth of subjectivist assessment lies in the expertise of the experts on which it depends. Credibility is enhanced by correcting for bias and systematic errors in assessment. Consequently, the expert judgement procedure can be intricate. Hence it's usually divided into preparatory, exploratory and computational phases.

In the *preparatory phase*, the problem and existing data are analyzed to chart how the expert judgement shall be used. The various methods usually prescribe how individuals are to be chosen and how their expertise is to be evaluated. Then the computational method is chosen, by deciding whether individuals or groups will estimate, by setting the rules for group consensus and by specifying the uses of qualitative or quantitative data. Individual estimation usually is used for analyses of events, while group estimation is used for cost analyses. Finally guidelines are compiled for how interviews shall be structured to acquire information. In them, the information should not be broken down into so many details that the overview is fogged and trivial discussions of details take over. At the same time, the perspective should not be overly top-down, so as to maintain adequate linkage to the problems at hand.

The goal of the *explanatory phase* is to elicit as much relevant and reliable expertise as possible from the experts. The experts need to be well informed on the problem and the intent as well as on possible sources of systematic errors in judgement that can influence results. The most commonplace of such cognitive biases, also called heuristics, include:

1. *Anchoring and adjusting,* which imply that judgement is influenced too much by the initial value that comprises the starting point of the assessment.
2. *Representativeness,* which implies that the estimate is influenced by perceiving the entity to be assessed as representing or resembling another phenomenon of known probability.
3. *Control,* that implies the estimate is affected by a wish to influence the situation.
4. *Overconfidence,* which for instance might imply an overly narrow interval between the highest and lowest estimates around the chosen anticipated value.

The *computational phase* uses the estimates of individual experts or groups of experts to generate the results and estimates put forth to the decision makers. In it, the expert results are calibrated and weighted, such as by using control queries. The method provides guidelines for the computation of a common estimate based on processing individual or group consensus expert judgements. See Merkhofer (1987). Typical applications of expert judgement include the bases for stochastic cost and progress analyses, discussed respectively in Chapters 22 and 25.

**Individual judgement**

Individual judgement may be used whenever there are neither acquirable data nor concrete events that can be analyzed. As its name implies, individual judgement relies on subjective assessments gathered in an unstructured, often arbitrary manner. Rules of thumb that draw upon experiential data from similar situations are often used. In these cases, the decision basis usually is weak. That said, individual judgement often is used as the first approximation to a problem that later is analyzed in a more systematic way. Individual judgement also is used in simple assessments of the results from compound analyses and consequently may be of value in eliminating unreasonable outcomes.

That said, problems arise when vital decisions are by and large based on individual judgement, as is the case in many projects. Typically, an idea is hatched by someone having the power, position or experience to be heard and takes hold early on as the accepted concept. It becomes the basis for subsequent assessment and planning and is likely to become the final choice. In many cases, the greater problems that arise in a project may be written back to decisions of this sort. See Goodwin and Wright (1996).

The methods described in this book are chiefly based on frequentist assessment and subjectivist assessment. That is, actual information and quantitative information are used as much as possible, supplemented with expert judgement as necessary. Systematic expert judgement is used increasingly. This trend is not necessarily due to a lack of actual information. Expert judgement can be far more cost effective than detailed analyses of data, such as in the initial cost estimates for large project concepts. Experts also can contribute copious information not expressible in statistics. Not least, a dialogue among experts can conduce to bringing experience and silent knowledge (intuition) to the surface, so it may be communicated to others. Moreover, expert judgement often enhances communication among those involved, which is advantageous.

Expert judgement has been more thoroughly examined in a study of decisions made on weak information bases (Williams et al. 2009).

## 13.3 The half-life of information

The validity of information throughout the front-end phase is a major concern. It's rather obvious as well as commonly accepted that the more precise the information, the more rapidly it's outdated. It's tempting to speak of the half-life of information. For example, the planning value of information on demand in a rapidly developing market can diminish within months, even weeks. However, there are many examples that qualitative assessment tends to remain valid for much longer. Consider the assessment of users' fundamental preferences within a market segment. While it might not be possible to make a valid prediction of the actual demand three years into the future, it may be assumed that demand will continue for a long time and can therefore be relied upon in strategic planning.

The principle is illustrated in Figure 13.2, which shows the decline of the validity of information with time. Conceivably, a situation might arise in

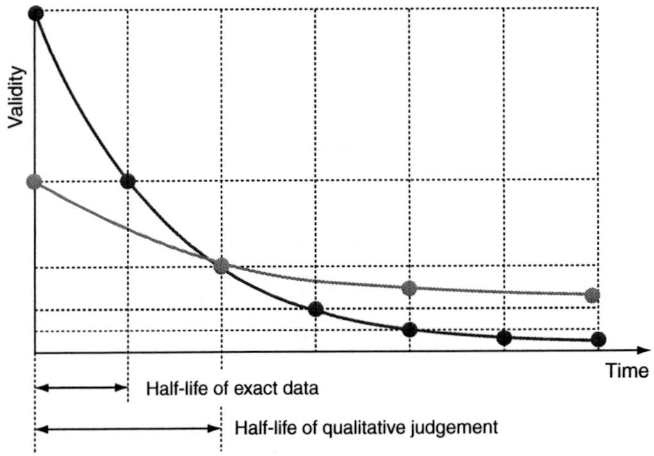


*Figure 13.2* Half-life of information. Validity tends to decrease over time during the front-end phase. More rapidly for accurate estimates than for less accurate ones

which an exact statement of a quantity at the ratio level has a relatively short half-life, so validity sinks rapidly and the number is soon nearly worthless. The same type of information stated at the ordinal level, such as ranked in larger groups, may have a half-life that is twice as long. Its validity is lesser at the starting point, but at once more durable, so its validity over time is better than that of exact information.

Matters such as these don't necessarily give rise to problems in the front-end phase. The need for precision and detailed information increases gradually as the process progresses towards the time for detail planning and project inception. This agrees with customary practice. Problems arise when the decision process drowns in a wealth of detail at a premature point of time. This is colloquially called *analysis paralysis*. Conversely, one might remark that the older the exact information, the less its utility.[3] This is yet another argument for avoiding a flood of details and quantitative information in the initial process.

# 14
# Quality of Information

*The need for information changes throughout the front-end phase. At first, there's little information, and one relies by and large on assumptions and qualitative assessments. With time, the scope expands rapidly to include facts and numerical information of increasing precision. In this chapter we discuss how to ensure firmness of the basis for acquiring and processing information. In this discussion, quality means valid and reliable information.*

> *If you don't provide people with information, they will come up with something to fill the gap.*
>
> —*Clara O'Dell*

## 14.1 Qualitative versus quantitative information

The IT revolution and the persisting steep upswing in available computing power of the recent decades has made reality ever more fine-grained. It has enabled previously unthinkable degrees of detail and precision. For example, a GPS-enhanced mobile phone can indicate where you are at any time with an accuracy of a few metres. The volume of information underlying this capability is enormous. Multiplied by the number of mobile phone users, it's incomprehensibly large. This is just one of the myriad services that are available to everyone. This makes us volume consumers of information. Not everyone is so aware, but nonetheless we take accessibility and high precision for granted.

The developments in IT have led to generally high expectations of precision and testability. Consequently much of the education that shapes the intellect increasingly is based on information in numerical form. Not least, this is the case in technical and economic fields. Needles to say,

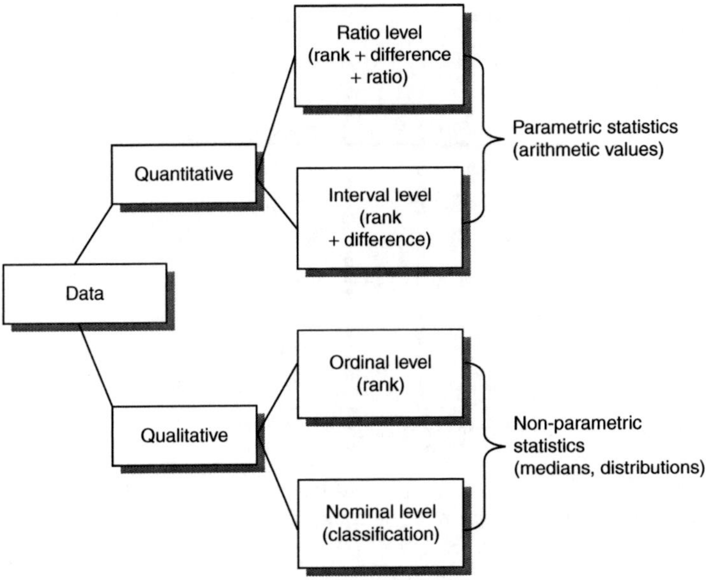


*Figure 14.1* Qualitative and quantitative information by level of scale (Olsson and Sörensen 2003)

numerical information is more suited than textual information to the systematic analyses that may undergird generalizations or substantiate highly probable connections. The relevant statistical processing presupposes that the information used is qualitative, at the interval level or preferably at the ratio level (with an interval scale and a zero point), see Figure 14.1.

The increasing requirements of detailed documentation as a basis for decision making lead to occasional failure to see the potential of systematic use of textual information. The principal hindrance is that its precision is low and its testability limited. Moreover, qualitative information often reflects or depends on individual interpretation. This may give rise to credibility problems and misunderstandings. The statistical processing and presentation of such information is mostly limited for instance to medians, quartiles and distributions (non-parametric statistics). That said, in a given case it may be possible to classify textual information with relatively high resolution, as shown in Figure 14.2, even though so doing often dilutes credibility, because subjective assessments are involved, which attractsquestions of interpretation and categorization.

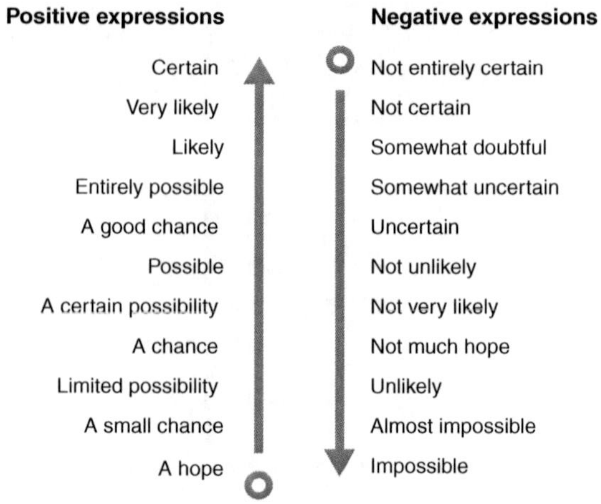


*Figure 14.2* Qualitative expressions of subjective probability. The starting point for classification of information at the nominal level (Teigen 2006)

The frequently excessive urge to emphasize the worth of numerical information leads to easily overlooking the principal advantages of using textual information, namely that it can be generated quickly and that it is the prime basis of human communication, and also that it is necessary to give the whole picture of complex situations involving numerous cross-cutting issues.

Moreover, much information simply cannot be quantified. Also, whenever numerical information is not reliable, it may be more appropriate to use qualitative expressions until more reliable information can be acquired. Finally there's the recognized phenomenon that a large assemblage of numerical data or highly aggregated data often can contribute to blurring rather than clarifying a situation.

Of course, in practice it's not a question of either-or, but of having it both ways. Qualitative assessment helps describe the whole, while quantitative information imparts precision to a description. This is why we mainly use qualitative information for communication. The messages of our communications may be regarded as parts of an information hierarchy in which the underlying, implicit information often is quantitative. The credibility of communications rests principally on the assurance that underlying information exists and can be accessed if need be.

## 14.2 Information and validity

In research, the term *validity* is used to characterize the degree to which information reflects the phenomenon being studied. Validity denotes a correspondence between reality and interpretation. A general model illustrating this is shown in Figure 14.3. Information is valid provided two criteria are fulfilled. Firstly, construct validity must be substantiated, that is, the interpretation must correlate with the phenomenon described, such as a body temperature over normal being a sign of illness. Secondly, there must be *reliability* to ensure that the expression is dependable, such as the degrees indicated on a thermometer matching body temperature.

The example illustrates the worth of quantitative information. In this case, body temperature is one of many signs of illness. Alone, an indication of fever is inconclusive information on what ails the patient. Increasing the precision of the measurement, as to several decimal places, which would improve reliability of measurement, obviously is futile. The doctor needs additional information to credibly assess the patients' condition. Some of the additional information is qualitative, not possible or practical to measure quantitatively, such as malaise, swollen glands, rash, headache, cough, etc. In other words, one must seek out high validity indicators that would in combination provide sufficient basis for a correct diagnosis. The qualitative information often is decisive in a diagnosis. The quantitative information is important in judging the condition.

The possibilities for ensuring reliability in qualitative assessments are limited. In some cases, such as in analyses mostly based on assumptions,

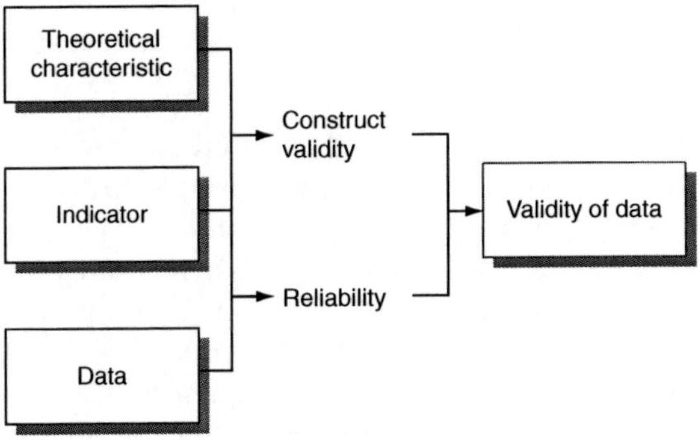


*Figure 14.3* Validity as an expression of the quality of information (Hellevik 1991)

the construct validity decides the worth of the assessments. The challenge then is to ensure that the concept or information element used is a good expression of what we wish to describe. In that case, we can at any rate be relatively certain that the information is relevant to the situation to be analyzed, even though is may be short of reliability in terms of precision.

A validity problem arises whenever the connection between the phenomenon to be described and the expression or statement chosen is weak. In a transport project with the goal of *'improving traffic safety'*, a validity problem arises if *'local employment'* is chosen as an indication of attaining that goal. It may be assumed that there's no clear connection between traffic safety and employment. More direct indicators of high validity will, for example, be *'the incidence of various types of accidents'* or *'the numbers of people injured or killed'*.

A reliability problem arises when the level of precision in a statement or expression used is poor. In the above example, a reliability problem arises principally because the statement of it includes the adjective *'improves'*, which gives considerable leeway for interpretation, and the noun *'safety'*, with no indication of its meaning. The level of precision might be increased by being more explicit as to for *whom* are they applicable, in this case the composition of the target group, the *degree,* here of anticipated change, and the *timing,* here how long it will take for the change to come about, etc.

As discussed in section 6.2, in the initial idea phase of a project, assessments and conclusions are by and large based on qualitative information. This is because quantitative information either is unavailable, because the resources for acquiring it are inadequate or because it's impractical, such as in cases where the realization is several years ahead and it's obvious that the applicable values will change appreciably and unpredictably with time.

Moreover, in the front-end phase it is often most *desirable* to waive the precision afforded by quantitative information and instead do with adjectives such as *'good'*, *'to a great degree'*, *'important'* or *'considerable'* to describe extents, amounts or levels. This may afford considerable freedom in assessing various models or concepts, facilitate their being placed in the greater context and permit assessing the principal consequences of changes in them. Consequently, the requirement of precision undoubtedly can be temporarily lowered, but in no case is it acceptable to modify the requirement of construct validity. In other words, we can accept some uncertainty and spreading in our attempt

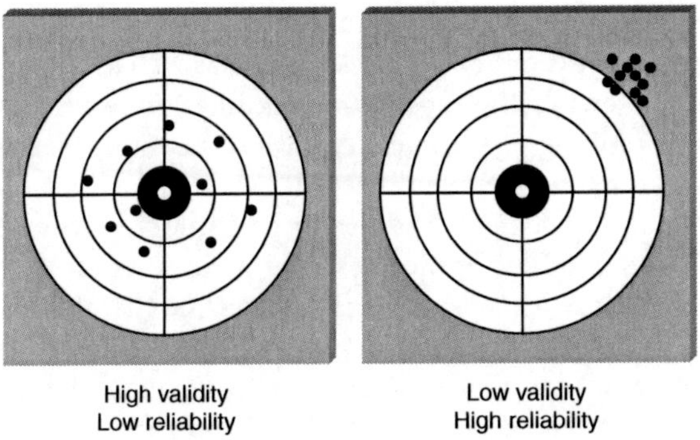


*Figure 14.4* Validity and reliability, focus versus precision

to hit the target, but a complete miss is unacceptable, even though reliability may be high, as illustrated in Figure 14.4.

## 14.3 Judgemental, probabilistic assessment of utility

*Reliability*, or whether information is dependable, can in principle be tested or re-examined. It is ensured whenever indications are unambiguous or measurements have no systematic errors. It can be proven if several people independently use the same indicator for the same problem and obtain the same result. Sources and methods of acquiring information are decisive in order to ensure reliable information. For example, in generating qualitative information using survey responses, the informants, who are the sources, may have poor information or may more or less deliberately give erroneous information. Moreover, answers depend of course on how questions are stated, on how the survey is conducted and on any misinterpretations or misunderstandings that may arise in communication between the two parties.

The *validity* of information cannot be re-examined but in principle may be based upon judgement. Hence the choice of indicator is decisive. Two principles for indicators should be considered to ensure that the information is valid for the phenomenon described: (1) choose indicators that provide the most *direct* measure, and (2) use *several indicators* that together comprise a good indication of the phenomenon described.

For example, *'number of graduates'* is a direct indicator of the phenomenon *'university education'*. But that number alone gives an incomplete picture of what is attained. So it naturally should be supplemented with information on marks or *'level of achievement'* as well as the relevant *'type of education'*. Likewise, the *'quality of education'* may be characterized, such as by the ranking of a university with respect to other universities. Other aspects may be included, such as *'duration of studies'* compared to an average and *'drop outs'*, the number of students who leave before finishing. Together, these indicators give a more complete picture of university education. This example illustrates the hierarchical character of information. Education is the overriding phenomenon studied. It is described using subordinate indicators or information elements that together afford an acceptable, valid description of the phenomenon. Some elements are vital for a valid description and therefore have high validity, while other elements are unnecessary or directly flawed and have low validity.

Precision may be low when working principally with qualitative information, so ensuring information validity then is no less important. As discussed in section 6.3, probabilistic assessment then may be used. Consider an example of the evaluation of a project to build an office building some time after its completion: the aim is to find *'how well users are satisfied with the building'*. Some indicators that might be used to acquire information are listed in Table 14.1.

Information validity may be tested indirectly by estimating how well each of the indicators distinguishes information that helps describe the phenomenon. For example, opinion on *'building functionality'* is a direct indicator and consequently a good term for testing. On the other hand, *'job satisfaction'* is influenced by many factors other than perception of the building and hence is less valid. The extent of *'evening overtime*

*Table 14.1* Selected indicators of user satisfaction in assessing an office building project

| **Validity** | **Indicator** |
|---|---|
| High | User opinion of building functionality |
| High | Tenant turnover |
| High | Office market demand |
| Medium | Building maintenance |
| Medium | Price level of the offices |
| Low | Extent of evening overtime work |
| Low | Tennant company profitability |
| Low | Users' perception of job satisfaction |

*work'* presumably is little influenced by the building itself and hence has low validity. The indicators are ranked in the table, so it's easy to spot those that are useful and those that should be taken out. Clearly, valid information is useful while information of low validity is not only unnecessary but may blur and perhaps skew the conclusion. So there's good reason to strictly adhere to the requirement of validity, to focus and enhance the worth of assessments and save resources.

## 14.4 Precision – clarity and unambiguity

As discussed in section 14.3, unambiguity is a precondition for dependability of information. This applies to the indicators that designate the information sought as well as to the acquired information on which assessments are based. Word usages can lead to ambiguity in statements. Hence, as in many other fields, semantics are crucial, as terms used should be well defined. Two sorts of definitions are relevant: lexical definition and précising (stipulative) definition.

The lexical definition of a word is the one usually found in dictionaries. So it's often called the dictionary definition. It is the meaning of the word in common usage, usually presented with descriptions of nearly similar meanings without use of the word. A lexical definition often is too broad to be used for specific purposes.

Hence, a lexical definition can be amended or narrowed down to a précising definition. For example, the principal lexical definitions of the word 'resistance' are 'the action of resisting' and 'armed or violent opposition' (Concise Oxford Dictionary). However, 'resistance' has other meanings in physics, medicine, finance and politics. A précising definition used in physics and electrical engineering is a statement of Ohm's Law: resistance is the ratio of voltage to current in a conducting medium. Ambiguity of understanding may be prevented by amending the term slightly to indicate the sense of the précising definition, as by writing 'electrical resistance'. Professional people use terms in these ways, to ease communication within their fields. Even so, definition problems often arise in communications between disciplines and between professionals and the general public, who rely mostly on dictionary definitions.

That said, more precise definitions cannot solve all problems of linguistic precision. This is particularly true when vagueness enters in the use of adjectives to indicate quality, quantity or size. Words such as 'good', 'high' and 'substantial' are categories in classification at the nominal level, as illustrated in Figure 14.2, and consequently may be misinterpreted. Moreover, many words may be understood with differing meanings, depending on one's point of view. For example, the word 'normal' used to describe a transport project may be understood by one party as (1) within the usual limits, and by another party as (2) within limits of what is acceptable, or perhaps considerably lower. Many words have several meanings. For example, what exactly is the meaning of 'the mercury content of drinking water is normal'? Does 'normal' mean 'in comparison to other lakes', 'in comparison to lakes in virgin wilderness' or 'with respect to the legal health hazard exposure limit'? (Hansson 2003).

Choices of words and concepts as well as precise words designating worth are significant in obtaining and disseminating information. Not unusually, different stakeholders may have sundry interpretations of the same phenomenon or may define it in various ways, such as in relation to the planning of a controversial project. Not least, various parties often disagree on the interpretation and information content of concepts such as 'needs' and 'benefits'.

## 14.5 Rational choice, causality and probability

In its broadest sense, logic is taken to mean correspondence with reason or with generally accepted principles of rational thought and action. That which does not correspond is illogical. Fallacy is a collective term for arguments that have logical form but are invalid. As a branch of knowledge, logic deals with the principles and applications of the rational. This is not least the case in linguistics, as in how we use, combine and give meanings to words. We usually rely on rational bases in planning actions or projects. *Causality* and *probability* are two essential principals that underlie the analyses and assessments of rationality.

*Causality*, or cause-effect correlation, helps us decide which action should be initiated to attain a desired effect. Conceivably, different alternative actions may have the same effect. By definition, the rational choice is any one of them, as all achieve the effect. But, if alternative strategies differ, such as in time taken or resources required, the strategy requiring the least resources will be the rational choice. Equally conceivably, a specific action may result in various effects in addition to the desired effect, as discussed in Chapter 9. This complicates assessment, as other cause-effect relationships must now be taken into consideration. Some side effects may be undesirable and in some cases unacceptable. A rational choice must then weigh up the impact of possible undesirable effects and maybe eliminate strategies that could result in unacceptable side effects.

This sort of rational thought is easily applied to physical systems but is far less tractable for social systems. This is because events in physical systems follow natural laws and thus in principle are predictable. In contradistinction, events in social systems, that is in society, are in principle unpredictable. This is because the units in the system can make their own decisions. Consequently, attempts at large-scale rational planning are more or less doomed to fail. The cause-effect relationship also is more problematic than it is for physical systems. Happenings in society do not necessarily follow a one-dimensional cause-effect chain or a two-dimensional activity tree. They are described better by dynamic systems with mutual influences between their elements. Such systems may be described mathematically and to some extent be simulated, but experience augurs unpromising results, as such systems are in principle unpredictable.

A simple approach to this problem, which obviously may be used early on in the planning process, is to maintain efforts to chart simple cause-effect relationships, but also bring in probability assessment to consider the uncertainty that may affect the relationships. If so, the strategy will be rational if the *probability* of success is at least as great as the probability of success for some of the alternative, equivalent strategies.

## 14.6 Constructing valid information hierarchies

The examples of sections 14.4 and 14.5 are of interest not for their conclusions, but because the models used represent schemes for assessment on a qualitative basis when only qualitative information is used. Of course, this is only at the upper level of the information hierarchy. If the conclusions are to be valid and credible, they need to be supported by more information at underlying levels. In practice, this means that several underlying parameters or indicators must be identified and accordingly documented. More indicators at underlying levels contribute to bettering validity at an aggregated level, provided each of them is valid with respect to what they aim to measure. In an assessment of the realization of the goals of the project to build the new University Hospital in Oslo, discussed in section 2.2, it's natural to consider indicators that reflect the provision of healthcare, such as the hospital's capacity, capacity utilization, range of services, quality of healthcare, etc. Farther down in the information hierarchy, these indicators may be split into more detailed indicators that together provide a more precise picture of the situation. For example, capacity utilization may be expressed in terms of total number of beds, polyclinic capacity, use of various types of equipment, medical staff, etc.

Such an information hierarchy contains a mix of qualitative and quantitative information. Information tends to be more qualitative upward in the hierarchy and more quantitative downward. A third dimension of time might be added, so the information hierarchy is depicted at various points of time in a project's front-end phase. Early on, the initial information hierarchy may be shallow, simply because in-depth information is unavailable. It will build extensively on assumptions and therefore be of limited utility. As the process progresses, the information hierarchy will grow naturally with the acquisition of more detailed information, that increasingly is quantitative and increasingly builds on facts, not just on assumptions.

Purposeful construction of information hierarchies emphasizing systematic assessment of validity and reliability are valuable in analyses, decision making, monitoring of progress and project management. The aim is to capture the most important aspects of the idea to be assessed, that is, the project concept in context. This may be done numerically, such as with data on costs, scope, progress, etc. However, in the initial phase, much of the information will be qualitative and purely textual. Superfluous detail may be avoided by building small information hierarchies that clarify what is to be included and which indicators are needed and are useful to support the flexibility needed to assess the various alternatives within unalike scenarios. Provided that the information hierarchies are valid, they will be durable in time, to the degree that they comprise textual information. As the analytical process, the decision processes and the implementation of the project progress, these information hierarchies will expand and be based on qualitative information of increasing precision.

The uses of qualitative information in the front-end phase are described further, discussed and illustrated in Part II, specifically in Chapters 17–22.

# 15
# Front-End Assessment and the Decision to Finance a Project

*The question of which concept is the best concerns more than the systematic, rational identification and assessment of various alternatives. In the front-end phase, the interests and prioritizations of various parties become evident, intervene and lead to decisions that often are far from that which appeared logical and rational at the outset. Hence, understanding this process is as vital as questions regarding the information base and the rational analysis choice of method.*

> *Logic is a means to arrive at the wrong conclusion with complete certainty.*
>
> *—Gudmund Hernes*

## 15.1 Reason and experience

Reason and experiences are illustrated by the following small experiment. A bottle lies on a window sill, its bottom against the window and sunshine outside. A bee and a fly are inside the bottle, trying to escape. What happens? The intelligent bee flies towards the light. It buzzes constantly against the bottom of the bottle, until it drops dead of dehydration and exhaustion. The fly, with its lower intelligence, flies randomly, in all directions, until it by chance flies out through the narrow bottleneck and escapes. Chance triumphs over reason.

In the front-end phase of a project, we often see much the same thing. The forward march towards a final decision to finance is characterized by mixes of reason and chance. Sometimes one starts with a well thought out strategy. In other cases, strategy is based on happenstance. However, a rational, well-founded starting point is no guarantee of a fitting decision. The process is influenced by the decisions of stakeholders and politicians. The end result may be something different from the beginning. Correspondingly in other cases, a poor starting point can be improved in a process that more or less depends on chance.

From the bee in the bottle we might learn that it's futile to rely on reason only, even though most of us are more comfortable with it. If the bottle had been turned around, its mouth towards the window, the bee would have escaped first. Nonetheless, with no latitude for flexibility and chance, we fall out of step with reality and probably reduce our chances of success.

In Chapter 12, realism as a basis for rational choice was discussed, with the conclusion that much of the work of the preparatory phase is equally justified as it helps us get ready for any tactical adaptations in a future uncertain situation, such as making the optimum strategic choice. At the same time, experience shows that strategy work is essential in identifying worthy concepts.

Much of the discussion on front-end phase assessment has focused on the information base used, on the choice of method and on the quality of the decision basis. The IT revolution that started in the late 1960s brought about dramatic change that extended beyond technology. As a consequence, the social sciences have also become increasingly sophisticated. For example, dynamic simulation models have come into use to describe complex social systems.

Since then, many questionable analyses have been presented as credible and have met harsh professional criticism.[1] Consequently, mathematical simulation has increasingly been acknowledged as unsuitable to the analysis of self-adjusting, societal processes. The root problem is that the output of an analysis is no better than the quality of its input data, as reflected in the neologism of quantitative analysis, GIGO, the abbreviation for 'Garbage In, Garbage Out'. Worse yet, applying simulation models in the social sciences risks 'Quality In, Garbage Out'; even with good input data, the results may be useless.

In recent years, there's been a trend of using simpler methods. The methods are simpler in the sense that they go to the opposite extreme in using analytic processes mostly based on qualitative assessment. The methods may be extremely simple and, for example, conflict with basic mathematical principles of stochastic analyses. On the other hand, there's been greater emphasis on better information bases in such analyses. Systematic expert assessment is increasingly used to generate estimates, as a counterbalance to excessive reliance on individual judgement and experience. Consensus-based processes in which experts jointly select input data have often proven useful, but the quality that comes out of such exercises is controversial. Accordingly, the question of the quality of the decision basis after methodical processing of these data is equally inconclusive.[2]

Regardless of one's standpoint in this discussion of methods and information quality, it's obvious that it focuses only on a narrow part of the challenge faced in seeking the most suitable choice of concept early on. A conceivable expansion of perspective is illustrated in Figure 15.1, which diagrams the front-end phase from the time the information base is available until the decision is made on what is to be the result of the project over time.

The process follows the information flow and is depicted as a chain with subsequent events. Needless to say, it's a simplification. In reality, much of what happens involves iterative processes with replays and new rounds on the way. The Figure 15.1 also shows learning loops to illustrate the stages of the process that have advanced sufficiently to permit learning about what has happened at earlier stages. For example, how well a message has been understood is essential to evaluating the quality of communication (boxes 4 and 5). Only when the project is realized can one can speak with certainty on the choice of concept and on the information that comprises the starting point for it (boxes 1 and 7). The purpose of the figure is to probe which and in what way links in the chain may be improved.

## 15.2 Information processes up front

### Information base

As indicated in Figure 15.1, information that provides the base for analysis is the starting point. The idea that initiates the process is of course an important part of the information. In some cases, it may outlive the process and become the final choice, as discussed in Chapter 14. In other cases, the idea triggers involvement and real analytic and democratic processes.

Obviously it's essential to more closely examine what available information may be used as a base for choosing input data. One distinguishes facts from judgement (box 1). On one hand, there are questions of the relevance and availability of *information sources*, of how available

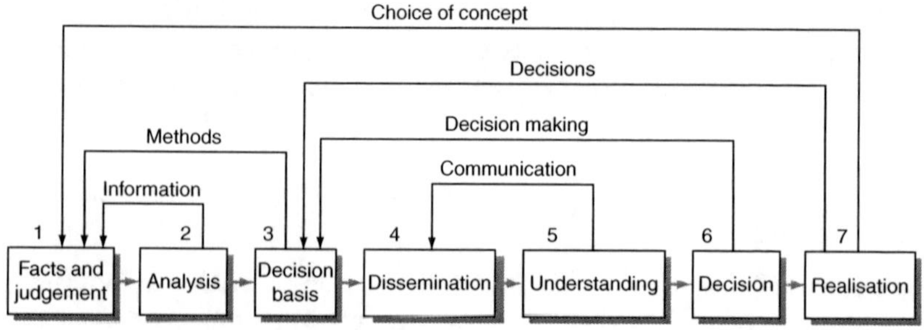


*Figure 15.1* Front-end phase process from the information basis to what actually will result from the concept chosen

information may be organized and used, of the aggregation level at which information is useful, of empirical data from other projects, etc. There's a wealth of information on projects that may be valuable, but little has been done to systematize it and make it available. This brings in the issue of benchmarking and not least questions of the costs and benefits of information, which are bound up with other matters, such as the extent to which information is relevant.

On the other hand, there are questions of the relevant types of *experience* and of how systematic error and error sources may be avoided in individual assessments and group processes, etc. It may be beneficial to see if expert assessment may be developed further through tighter coupling between systematic use of facts and for instance Delphi techniques in front-end phase assessments.

Moreover, there's the question of data choice. It's not just a technical issue, but also one concerning processes and their results, interactions between individuals and institutions, the extent to which data reflects reality and the interests and prioritizations that may exist. Most will agree that it's sensible to emphasize the process and choices of information to ensure that less garbage and more substance underlie analyses. This probably cannot be attained by focusing only on available knowledge and experience. In complex cases it presupposes the arrangement of time-consuming processes that support dialogue and clarification between the parties involved.

## Methods and analyses

The question of methods (box 2) is central in viewing the worth of the front-end phase process. Chapter 16 comprises an overview of selected methods and connections between them, which are more explicitly described in Part II of this book. The question of methods concerns the empirical results of various methods in analyses, not least the comparisons of complexity and applicability. Presumably it's useful to weigh the needs for processing data and for precision on one side against the value of easy-to-understand analytic processes that enable critical reflection upon results on the other side. In some cases, dissimilar methods are used for the same type of analysis. In such cases, the merit of the various methods should be tested, such as by using the so-called Successive Calculation Method and Monte Carlo simulation in stochastic cost estimation. These matters are discussed in Chapters 22 and 25.

### Decision basis

As illustrated in Figure 15.1, it is a long way from analytic results to decisions and actual realization. The merit of the decision basis is central (box 3). Of course, its quality cannot be assessed solely on the grounds of the method used or the quality of the input data, but must be viewed in connection with what happens later in the process. All too often a decision basis is linked to a detailed assessment of just one alternative. An example is a probabilistic analysis that results in expected values of costs and time expenditure that are considered favourable. Such a decision basis is too narrow for most projects. The assessments must first embrace more than the narrow contractor perspective, as discussed in Chapter 3. They should also consider the long-term consequences of the project. Moreover, they need to build on real assessments of various concepts. An analysis of the decision bases of projects in general shows that this often is not the case. Additionally, of course there's also the question of the quality of the decision basis. This is discussed further in section 15.3.

### Communication and decision

The part of the front-end phase from analysis to decision often is the least predictable and most time consuming. The questions concern openness, the dissemination of the decision basis, the degree of understanding in communication, and the resultant decisions made (boxes 4–6). In large projects, this may be a prolonged, iterative process from when the decision basis is available in the first round until the final decision is made on financing and initiation of the project.

Much implies that there's considerable room for improvement in communications and decision making. Not least, there's arguably a need for a new perspective on what's needed to arrive at a good project concept as well as for how long a choice of concept should remain open before being narrowed to one alternative. Such narrowing often happens too early, so perhaps contemporary practice in the public and private sectors should be re-evaluated. Matters to be considered include communication of the decision basis, the involution of the process, the openness of the dialogue between the parties, the parties' uses and accessibility of resources, how conflicts and disagreements are resolved, etc. Communication principally is about dissemination, availability and understanding, while the decision-making process is concerned with how the deciding bodies formally handle the processes that lead to the final decision.

### Reality check of the front-end phase

However, the big question concerns the merit of the front-end phase in relation to what actually happens, that is the choice of concept, the realization of the project over time and that which realization helps (box 7). The answer entails useful learning and understanding of the whole chain described. It also indicates the potential of systematic front-end phase assessment. Moreover, it provides a basis not just for testing the correspondence between decisions and events, but also for testing the information basis, the choices of information, the worth of methods, etc.

## 15.3 Quality assurance of the bases for decisions

The private and public sectors use different approaches to and measures for quality assurance of matters in the front-end phase that lead to major decisions. There's much focus on costs as management parameters. For example, usually a set of formal decision points are established in the front-end phase. At each point, there's a statement of a maximum allowable uncertainty margin in the cost estimate. The requirement is that the uncertainty be reduced with time, which leads to the extent and depth of detail of studies and planning with time. The principle is illustrated in Figure 8.1.

Such schemes are useful for gaining control of the costs of a new enterprise, but raise no questions about the founding choices. They contribute probably more to cementing the initial choice at an early point of time as planning becomes more extensive and detailed.

In Figure 15.1, the project processes are depicted as a sequence of events. In Figure 15.2, they are depicted as iterative; there are repetitions on the

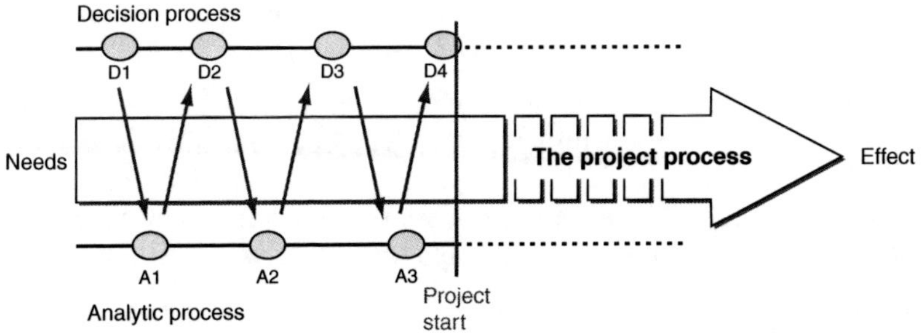


*Figure 15.2* A technocratic decision model with perfect interaction between decision makers and experts

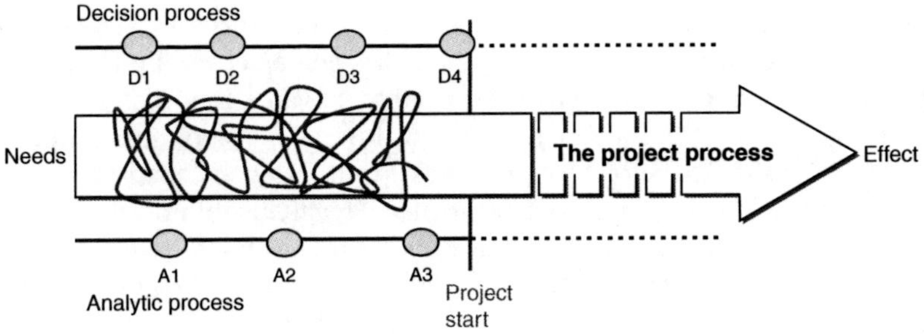


*Figure 15.3* An anarchistic type decision model, open and unpredictable

way. A decision process and an analytic process run parallel throughout. The figure depicts an ideal situation in the which the triggering initiative results in decision D1, which in turn initiates analysis A1. Its results lead to a new decision D2, which clarifies some overriding questions and recommends additional analysis A2. The process continues forward until it ends with the final decision to start is made.

This is known as the technocratic decision model. It assumes perfect interaction between experts and decision makers in an ideal and relatively predictable world. It results in the best choice being made on a 100 per cent rational basis. It's a captivating model that has been tested over the past hundred years with varying success across the world, perhaps particularly by the former Eastern European regimes. Empirically the model doesn't imply a preference for more open and inclusive processes. Quite the contrary; many believe that it's incompatible with basic democratic principles and practices.

The other extreme, illustrated in Figure 15.3, is anarchy, in which there is no concise, prearranged action pattern. It's an open, inclusive process. It's less predictable and perhaps takes longer, but it finally also will end up with a decision. The chances of ending up with the best choice may be less, but the process probably is more compatible with democratic principles.

Perhaps reality may be described as something between the extremes of Figures 15.2 and 15.3, and most of us probably agree that we can live with it. But the big problem remains: how does one ensure the choice of concept?

Many have attempted to answer that question. Major investment projects, such as the building of roads, airports and hospitals, the procurement of defence materiel, etc. have a front-end phase that lasts several years, or in some cases several decades. This period is characterized by its lack of predictability and by its stepwise evolution towards the final decision. It is urged on by the influence of various interests, by political compromise, by media exposure, by public debate, etc. Such an open process is in accordance with democratic principles. Prevalent opinion disfavours a stricter, more technocratic, expert-driven process based exclusively on rational planning. Admittedly the complexity and unpredictability of the process limit the long-term value of rational planning at an early point in time. At the same time there apparently is a need for an idea phase, as mentioned in section 14.2. In it, intuition and experience are to a great

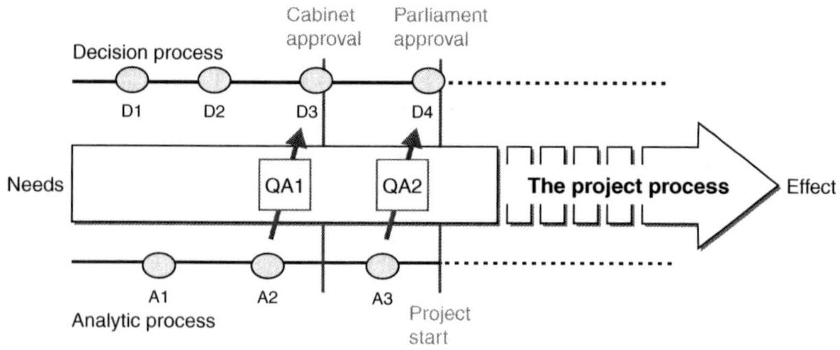


*Figure 15.4* External quality assurance for major public investment projects. The first concerns choice of concept (QA1), the second formulation of the concept (QA2)

extent supplemented with rational analysis and assessment. Moreover, there's an obvious need for the best possible decision basis at the decisive stages of the process in which the principal decisions are made.

A requirement introduced for major public investment projects in Norway addresses these questions, as indicated in Figure 15.4.[3] Quality assurance measures are designated QA1 and QA2. The front-end phase accordingly is divided into a concept phase and a pre-project phase. The concept phase leads to the choice of the main concept. The choice shall be made at a point of time sufficiently early that the choices between the real concept alternatives remain open. Needless to say, this point of time cannot be exactly specified in general terms.

In Norwegian projects covered by the quality assurance requirements, the responsible Ministry is obliged to come up with at least two conceptual solutions of a problem in addition to the zero option (doing nothing). The Cabinet formally approves the choice of concept. That triggers a pre-project phase in which the preferred concept alternative is studied further and planned, before Parliament reaches its final decision on financing.

Hence, the principle is to require qualitative assessments of a concept as well as to require equivalent assessment of real alternatives at an early point of time. The relevant quality assurance is performed by external consultants, from consultancies or from research institutes. These consultants shall not consider the alternatives but only assess the merit of the decision basis. Thereafter, it's up to the Cabinet and the Parliament to reach a decision.

The upshot is that the arrangement doesn't intervene technically in the democratic process, but permits actors to operate without requiring changes in formal practice and procedures. At the same time, the threshold is elevated for the quality of documentation that administration must provide, which hopefully will grad\ually improve administrative conduct and practice.

# 16

# Three Steps in Front-End Assessment: Definition, Development and Appraisal of Concept

*The focus in this book is exclusively on the concept phase. This chapter comprises an overview of the simple methods used in appraising concepts. They are associated with each other and represent a uniform, systematic set of analytical steps, in which the choices of parameters and processing of information form a whole. Concept appraisal is divided here into three separate sub-phases to illustrate uses of the methods. Further descriptions of the methods and examples of their uses are given in Part II.*

> *No one listens to what you say, until it resembles something they have thought themselves.*
>
> *—Nils Fredrik Nilsen*

Decisions may be made on very simple bases. One might toss heads or tails, or, if reliable information is available, undertake a simple assessment of foreseen reward relative to costs.[1] But the decision bases also may be comprehensive. Projects of some extent usually have a thorough, detailed pre-project study. In some cases, a pre-project study may take years and include complex analyses, simulations, pilot studies, etc.

However, in such cases, the type and extent of studies in the *initial phase* often are severely limited. This may be unfortunate. The terms of the final project often are shaped more by the events of the initial phase than by the pre-project study. At that point of time, the terms of the pre-project study are determined. With a prior, top-down assessment of the concept itself, strategic guidance could be included in an initial phase that also puts the pre-project study on a sensible track.[2] This may be extremely profitable, both in the short term and the long term, not least because the costs of top-down concept studies are relatively small.

The extent of effort in the initial phase of a project apparently is either pretty limited or relatively comprehensive. This may be ascribed to formal requirements, such as for impact assessments and quality assurance, first being imposed when the project exceeds a certain size. Hence, there is no accepted tradition for systematic front-end phase appraisal of smaller projects. The same is true of systematic use of risk analyses in project activities. Today, the consultant sector has no relevant satisfactorily developed and proven offering, compared to what's available for project management in the implementation phase. There are no widely used method tools or standards for such analyses. Here it may be argued that some fields, such as the offshore sector, obviously have come farther than others. In the public sector, particularly defence, transport and construction are so engaged.

## 16.1 Tools in front-end assessment

In 1999, the Norwegian Ministry of Finance took up the problem of front-end phase assessment of large projects. As discussed in section 15.3, the result in 2000 was a requirement that all publicly financed investment projects budgeted at more than NOK 500 million (about 75 million Euro) be subjected to external quality assurance in the front-end phase. In turn, this heightened public and private sector awareness of front-end phase issues. This book was compiled in the wake of that initiative.

**An example of inadequate concept assessment: A Regional University Hospital in Norway**

On the way from the initial idea to the project, the concept phase was skipped. The project aimed to improve hospital offerings in mid-Norway by upgrading and expanding the Regional University Hospital. The first step should have been an assessment of how that might best be done in relation to the existing needs and to the physical, economic and institutional conditions, and based on the background of experience with similar projects in Norway and other countries. Instead of a top-down assessment of the concept, an architectural competition was initiated for the physical design of the hospital. The proposals that came in were consistent with the terms chosen, namely the development of a large, central, public hospital with existing buildings in the city centre as the starting point.

At that, the physical frame was established that curtailed the chances of finding the most effective solution of the problem, namely enabling efficient hospital operations, research activities, medical teaching, etc. The question remains open as to whether a top-down concept appraisal at an earlier point of time would have resulted in another, more suitable strategic choice. Perhaps locating the hospital in the outskirts of the city would have been profitable in the form of gains from building site sales and would have afforded space for expansion. Perhaps dividing the hospital in several independent units, in which privatization of some functions could have contributed to overall efficiency at critical links in the treatment chain and would have reduced administration problems. Perhaps reorganization of operations with more treatment being offered by polyclinics as an alternative to hospitalization would have contributed to lower costs, etc.

The architectural proposals were compiled on the assumption that a central, public hospital wasn't adaptable to such possibilities. Initially skipping the concept phase before the physical framework was set brought in disadvantageous physical constraints for developing the project. Should future political hearings require changes of the concept itself, the possibilities of realizing them would be severely limited.

This book is based partly on the author's experience in concept development and assessment in international development projects. Such projects are characterized, perhaps most conspicuously, by the donor organizations' greater willingness and abilities to finance than their practicality in choosing concepts. This has led to an increasing awareness of the need for overriding studies that can draw up terms for donors and recipients at an early point of time. The quest has been for more sensible strategic guidance to avoid the most scandalous projects that now and then are exposed in the media. This background has spawned an international consultant sector with considerable experience in systematic concept appraisal. This experience may benefit many countries round the world.

The chapters thus far in this book have detailed a methodical scheme for systematic front-end phase appraisal, as illustrated in Figure 16.1. In line with the discussion of Chapter 4, the concept phase up to the principal decision to finance and plan is distinguished from the project phase which usually starts with a detailed pre-project study and planning after the decision has been made. This distinction can be hazy, in part because not all principle decisions lead to concepts being realized, and in part because analyses in the project phase may oblige a reversion to new appraisals of concepts.

The focus in this book is exclusively on the concept phase, which in the figure is divided into three sub-phases, *concept definition*, *concept elaboration* and *concept assessment*. This drawing shows how the methods

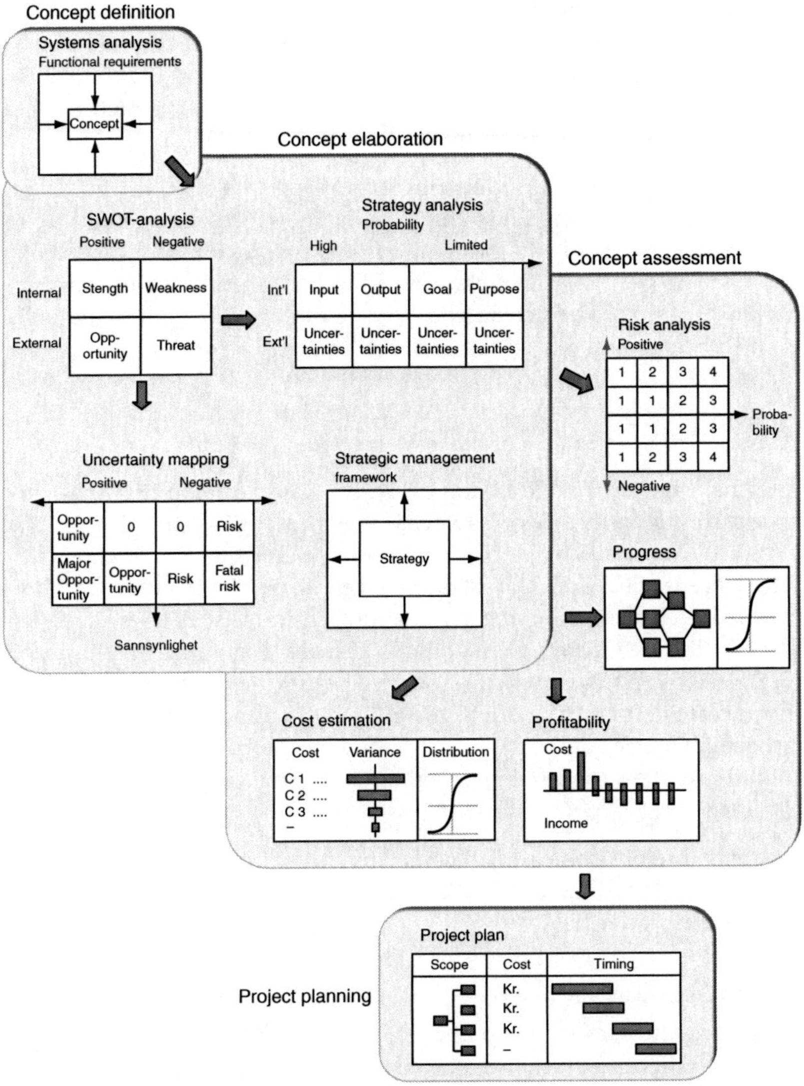


*Figure 16.1* Overview of the method tools for systematic front-end phase appraisal

described are associated with each other and represent a uniform, systematic set of analytical steps, in which the choices of parameters and processing of information form a whole. The phases and methods illustrated in Figure 16.1 are summarized below. In Part II, the methods are described in greater detail along with examples of their applications.

This approach is of course just one of many possible. Still it builds on known, much-used methods and thereby shows how they build upon each other by gradually bringing in new parameters. Conceptually appraisals may to considerable degree build on qualitative information handled within predefined outcome spaces that are divided into mutually exclusive categories and thereby are methodologically consistent.

## 16.2 Identifying the concept

The challenge is to avoid taking off with a particular solution that later may turn out to be a poor choice. The goal is a principal solution that affords the most suitable response to one or several more or less concretely stated needs. The principal solution gives us the flexibility to think of alternatives later. A comprehensive approach implies that we must first identify the needs and the system – societal, economic, institutional, technological, environmental or political – in which the concept will be incorporated. Then, it's natural to seek out the functional requirements that ought to be fulfilled so as to attend to the needs. Thereafter, one should take steps toward defining alternative concepts.

The process that leads to identification of a project concept should first and foremost be open. This means that it is not bound to predetermined choice but rather allows for unbiased identification of the various alternatives.

### Systems analysis

Systems analysis, as its name implies, involves systematization and procedures to this end. Its hallmark is that it starts with an open perspective and no predetermined notion of the optimum concept, as that might block creative contemplation of alternatives. Accordingly the emphasis is on clarifying needs and functional requirements systematically in a 'without-to-within' process that leads to identification of potential concrete concepts. Thereafter these concepts ought to be tested against the functional requirements and the framework conditions within which the project will operate to identify those most suitable. The base method used can be anything from simple conceptual models to dynamic simulation. However, as discussed in Chapter 13, bringing in relevant experience from similar situations or projects is indispensable. Time and the system life cycle are principal parameters in systems analysis. The method is more explicitly described in Chapter 17.

## 16.3 Developing the concept

Once one or more promising concepts have been identified, they should be made more specific and developed from ideas to candidates for strategic choice. This can be done through more explicit concretization of what should be achieved, what the project shall produce, which resources are available, and what possibilities exist and what limitations may be imposed in implementing the project. A further appraisal of the concept and the environment in which it will operate also may be appropriate.

### SWOT analysis

The first step may be to conduct a Strength, Weaknesses, Opportunities and Threats (SWOT) analysis. SWOT delineates an outcome space to describe the characteristics of the contemplated project. As can be seen in Figure 16.1, a distinction is made between the project itself (internal conditions) and its surroundings (external conditions). Likewise, there is a distinction between that assumed to be positive and that assumed to be negative. Hence the outcome space is divided into four parts that describe the *strength*, *weaknesses*, *opportunities* and *threats*. Of interest is that the method is *consistent* in the sense that the outcome space can accommodate all possible events and that events are grouped in mutually exclusive categories. SWOT analysis presupposes a closer examination of a project to perceive it in an institutional, technological, environmental, social or some other context. The method is more explicitly described in Chapter 18.

### Strategy analysis

The next logical step comprises a strategy analysis. It builds on the SWOT analysis and again describes a methodically consistent outcome space in which *internal* and *external* conditions are distinguished along one axis, and the probability of realization is introduced as a parameter along the other axis. This is shown in Figure 16.1. A principal point here is the demarcation between what is *factual* (that is, realizable) and that which is *hypothetical* (that is, desirable). An outcome space divided in eight parts, as shown in the figure, is called a logical framework. It's used to describe project strategy uppermost and uncertainty factors affecting strategy lowermost. The method is also known as the 'logical project analysis'. The framework is used to discuss and analyze the probability of realization with the aim of finding the most possible realistically feasible concept at an early point of time. The method is more explicitly described in Chapter 19.

### Uncertainty mapping

Once a strategy has been defined, the next obvious step is to appraise the uncertainty associated with realization of the strategy. The figure includes a framework for rough analysis of uncertainty factors. In it, the distinction between the assumed positive and assumed negative of the SWOT analysis is extended to distinguish between opportunities and risks. Again, probability is introduced as a new parameter. Dividing this outcome space in subcategories identifies low risk and low opportunity events for which both impact and probability are low. These are events that may be disregarded. On the negative side, events may be identified that will have major impact and high probability of occurrence and consequently require redefinition of the concept. This is known as the fatal risk. This type of rough analysis provides an overview of the remaining uncertain factors that must be taken into consideration in further appraisal of the strategy. The method is more explicitly described in Chapter 20.

### Strategy and strategic frame requirements

These analyses may now be used as a base to delineate strategic frame requirements for the contemplated project. The frame requirements indicate the principal control parameters that the project owner or commissioner consider as guiding for the enterprise. The strategy provides the principal control parameters for those who execute the project. The drawing in Figure 16.1 illustrates how frame requirements are defined to the extent that they provide the necessary tactical flexibility for those who implement the project, that is, they afford leeway for handling uncertainty and unforeseen events in implementation. The strategy and the frame requirements comprise a complete description of the contemplated investment case at the concept stage. The method is more explicitly described in Chapter 21.

## 16.4 Appraisal of the concept

Once the concept has been elaborated, the next logical step is to appraise the proposed project with regard to some of the most important decision criteria, which are costs, profitability, timing and risk. The extent and quality of available information will vary. In the course of the front-end phase, more and better information gradually becomes available. Still, for the most part factual information must be supplemented by empirical data, subjective assessments, expert assessments, etc. Hence, it may be suitable to use stochastic analysis in which probability distributions of estimates are included in assessments.

### Cost estimation

Cost estimation traditionally is based on a collocation of a large quantity of cost data. These cost data at the detail level are aggregated to a collective cost estimate. Such analyses from the ground up are time consuming and expensive. In concept assessment, it's preferable to use top-down analyses based on expert assessment. Starting with a rough estimate, assessments are made of the uncertainties of the individual parts of the estimate, and thereafter winnow out the estimates that have the greatest uncertainty of attaining good estimates. The detailing continues until it seems that one has attained sufficiently good estimates that may be aggregated to a total. This approach has proven to provide a sufficiently good cost estimate relative to needs at an early point of time, more rapidly and with lesser use of resources. The method is more explicitly described in Chapter 22.

### Profitability appraisal

With a reasonable estimate of a project's anticipated costs and duration, profitability may be appraised, provided that one also has realistic estimates of income expected. The major costs normally are concentrated over a relatively short period, while income usually extends over several years. Cash flow analyses consequently consider the dimension of time by discounting investments, future income and operating costs. Profitability is expressed in terms of net present value or internal rate of return. The method is more explicitly described in Chapter 23.

### Risk analysis

The uncertainty factors identified in concept development may be classified in greater detail and analyzed to provide a base for closer assessment of ways of reducing risk and realising opportunities. The method is more explicitly described in Chapter 24.

### Progress analysis

Network analyses are customarily used to analyze progress of a project. In principle, a project is broken down into activities that are sufficiently limited so their durations may be stated precisely. Elements in series and/or parallel are coupled in sequences with the intent that organizationally the project may be implemented as efficiently as possible. The network structure enables calculation of a project's duration as a whole and identifies critical activities or bottlenecks. However, in the concept phase there's no detailed knowledge of the contemplated project, so one will have to make do with a rough division of principal components. As for cost estimating, a stochastic analysis may be used to estimate the durations of the individual project components. Whenever the uncertainty of an estimate is large, it may be broken down into smaller parts to reduce uncertainty and increase the dependability of the estimate. The method is more explicitly described in Chapter 25.

### Project planning

Once the concept has been chosen and the principal decisions made on financing and implementation, the time has come for more detailed pre-project studies, for planning, etc. The goal is to ensure a good grasp of the project's principal parameters in the implementation phase. The traditional focus has been on scope, cost and timing, as shown in Figure 16.1, which are brought out by the methods and techniques of project management and risk management. Such matters will not be discussed further in this book. The interested reader is referred to the literature of project management.

# Part II Tools and Techniques

This Part II comprises ten chapters, each describing a method or tool, customarily used in sequence from an initial idea to a project concept, as illustrated in the block diagram of chapters below.

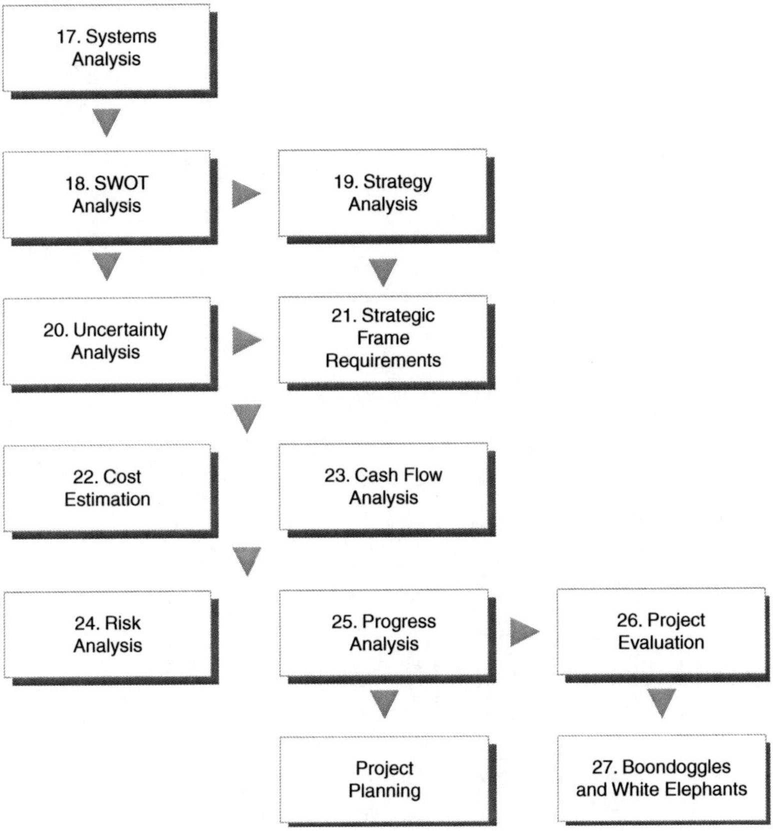

# 17
# Systems Analysis

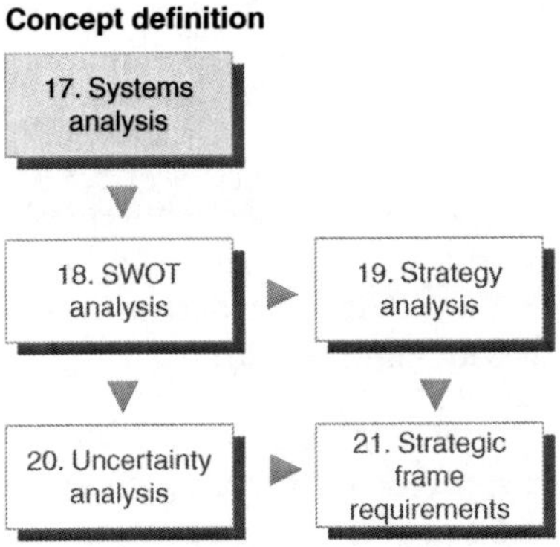


*Systems analysis is a collective term for various methodological approaches to find an optimum solution to a problem. Instead of springing from an assumed best solution, systems analysis considers the problem to be solved in its context, described as a system, and asks which conditions must be fulfilled for the system to function. The solution is that which best satisfies the conditions. Such an open approach makes systems analysis a useful tool as an initial approximation on the road from a problem to a successful project.*

## 17.1 An open-ended systematic process

In principle, a concept is the best response to one or more tangible needs. A comprehensive approach implies that one must first identify the relevant needs as well as the corresponding functional requirements

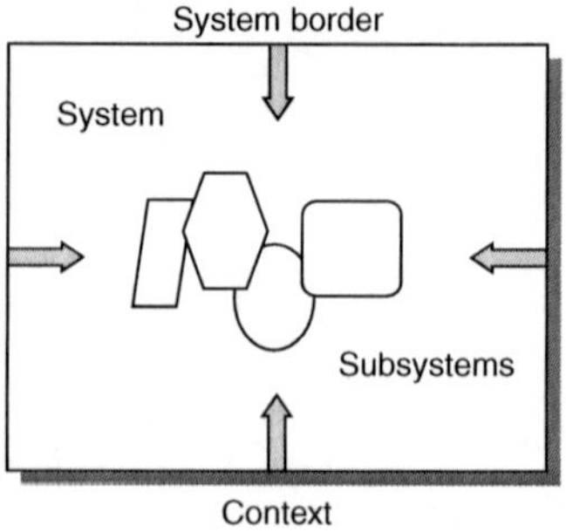


*Figure 17.1* General view of a system. The choices of components or subsystems are decisive for how the system functions. In systems analysis, these components are chosen after having assessed the whole

to be met by the concept in the context in which it will fit.[1] The process that leads to identification of a project concept should be as open as possible, in the sense that it's not excessively constrained to specific operational solutions or tied to a predetermined choice. The process should facilitate unbiased identification of various alternatives.

Traditional problem-solving often derives from a central actor's perspective and is characterized by the basic choices having been made before systematic analysis begins. Thereafter, the analysis will be associated with and restricted to the choice already made. Systems analysis is a stepwise approach to problem solving. The problem to be addressed is first described as a system along with its concomitant external conditions for success. Then, concrete solutions are identified and tested against these external conditions. This affords a basis for making a choice. Systems analysis accordingly is an outside-in approach, as indicated in Figure 17.1.

Processes that involve people over time are intractable to modelling, regardless of whether they are simple or complex. Nonetheless models are useful aids to understanding reality. Systems analysis builds a model comprising subsystems or components, system borders, the context, resources and results (input-output). The subsystems may be regarded individually or as parts of a larger system. All of the subsystems as well as the main system are limited in time and space, have goals, are dynamic elements and may change their properties over time. The system is assumed stable when inputs balance outputs. The capacity

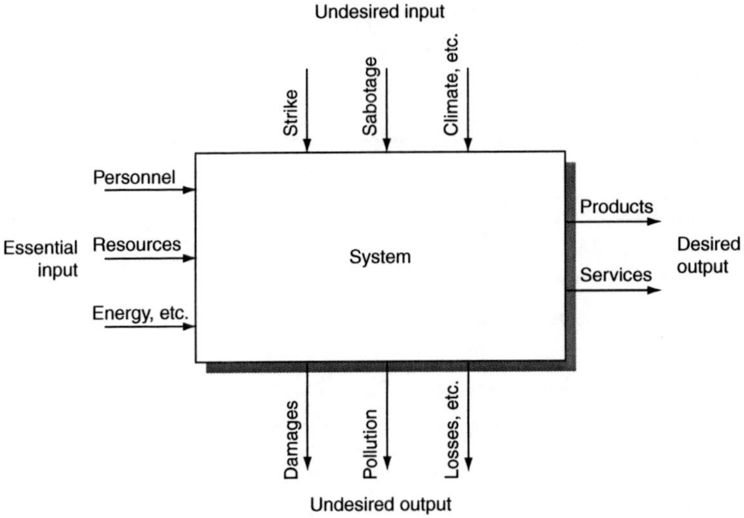


*Figure 17.2* Production system described as an input-output-model

of the system is determined by the scope and number of subsystems incorporated within its limits.

Most circumstances may be regarded as systems, including natural phenomena, production processes, societies, technical and physical undertakings, etc. Popularly put, a system may be assumed to consist of a combination of processes, people, technologies, material components, etc. that together unify to be able to satisfy certain defined needs.

In systems analysis, the concern is with the components of the system, their properties and the relationships between the components, as they impart the combined properties of the whole system. Popularly put, systems analysis is an indisciplinary approach used to ensure success in systems. Systems analysis often focuses on a system in its entirety, that is, its capacity (such as in products or services) and its vulnerability (such as in damages, pollution or losses), as illustrated in Figure 17.2. Or, as in the following example, the focus may be on those subsystems that enable the whole system to function as well as possible.

The level of methodological sophistication applied may be anything from a simple conceptual model to dynamic simulation. However, as discussed in Chapter 13, bringing in relevant experience from similar situations or projects is indispensable. Time, that is the system life cycle, is a principal parameter in systems analysis. A general procedure might progress in the following nine steps:

1. **System definition:** Focus on the complexity of the issue and delimit the system.
2. **Identification of needs:** Identify involved or affected stakeholders, along with their needs, prioritizations and any changes with time over the life cycle.
3. **Requirement specification:** From the needs under consideration, identify the demands placed on the system, including:
   a. functional – how the system should work
   b. physical – how the system should be built and what it must sustain
   c. operational – how the system should run
   d. economic – the costs of system development and operation.
4. **Alternative subsystems:** Identify technologies or concepts that may help meet system requirements.
5. **Performance appraisal:** Test the subsystems against the requirement specification.
6. **Concept choice:** Evaluate alternatives to find the most suitable concept.
7. **Control of choice:** Test the concept over the life cycle and more closely examine the financial conditions, the environmental conditions, logistics, impacts of technological change, operation and maintenance, etc.
8. **Vulnerability testing:** Simulate the system in various scenarios with changes, errors and disturbances, such as by using models.
9. **Describe** the system.

Various tools and techniques may be used in carrying through such a procedure. They may be databases and networks for securing relevant information on experience in similar projects, Delphi techniques or Monte Carlo simulations to forecast or estimate, scenario tools and mind-mapping techniques to describe and visualize, multi-attribute evaluation to rank alternatives, and dynamic simulation models for evaluating effects and conducting sensitivity testing. The example in section 17.2 below illustrates the use of the procedure described above in a simple conceptual evaluation of ensuring energy supply, a principal issue in many countries.

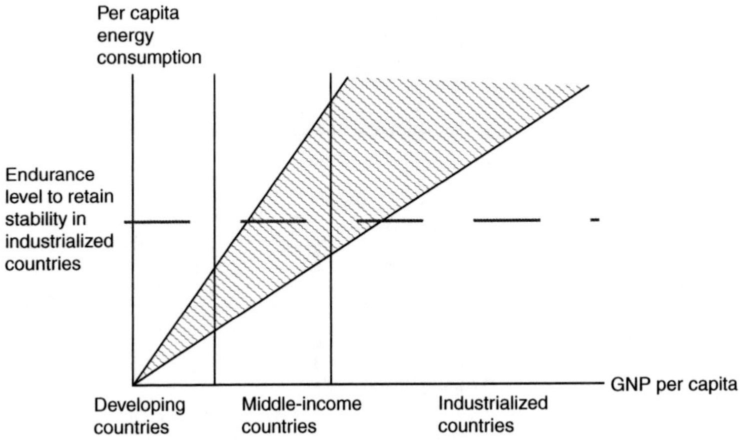


*Figure 17.3* Energy consumption in countries at different stages of development. Most countries in the world locate in the hatched area, developing countries clustered at the lower left and industrialized countries dispersed at the upper right

## 17.2 Example: Choice of energy system

A small country on the Arabian Peninsula has undergone rapid economic development and consequently needs to expand its energy system. The country has neither hydropower nor its own oil resources, so at the outset, its choice of an energy carrier is completely open. The country aims to develop tourism and appreciates the potential of being forward-looking. Its vision is to be an international showcase for clean energy and environmental sustainability. It wants to conduct a broad analysis of how various alternatives will affect future needs and hence which of them should be more closely evaluated.

The big picture of the problem, which is the principal trigger of the initiative, is illustrated in Figure 17.3, which shows that

1. Increased energy consumption is a prerequisite for economic growth, even though per capita energy consumption varies considerably across countries with the same GNP per capita.
2. The economic, political and social stability of industrialized countries depends on maintaining energy consumption above a certain level.

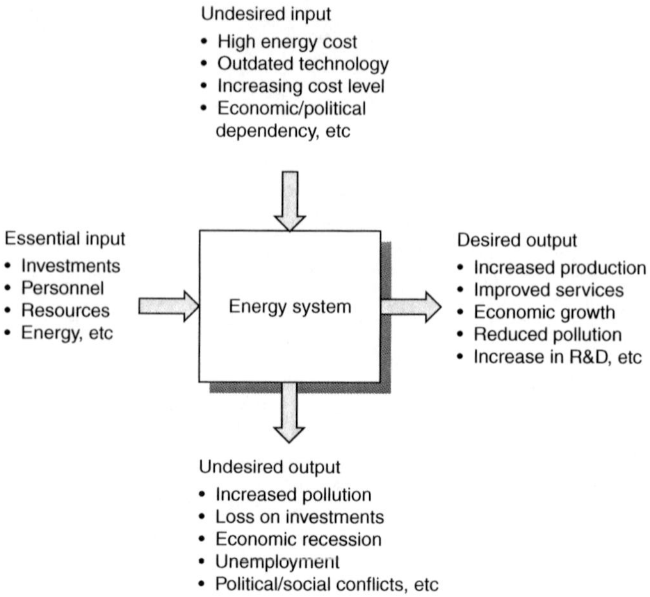


*Figure 17.4* Conceivable comparative framework for an energy system showing the input-output parameters

## System definition

Here, the system is the country. So the system border is delineated by the country's attributes, including its economy, geography, resources, environment, etc. The time horizon of the analysis is well in the future, and the life cycle is limited to the lifetimes of the individual energy systems incorporated as constituent subsystems. A conceivable comparative framework for such a system is shown in Figure 17.4.

A systems analysis must have a perspective that includes all affected parties at all levels. In this case, where one aim is to be innovative in environmental aspects and resource exploitation, the perspective should transcend the nation, as the system will work with the environmental, political and economic aspects of the global whole. The evolution of the greater whole will be decisive to what happens at the national level. The perspectives from four different vantage points, from the global to the individual, are listed in the first column of Table 17.1. These considerations may be used to gain a general picture of the overriding requirements of the system.

*Table 17.1* Identification of needs

| Perspective | Needs | Justification | Demands |
|---|---|---|---|
| Global level | • Predictable basis for sustainable development | • The survival of mankind | • Thermal stability<br>• Ecological pluralism |
| National level | • Permanent solution to meet energy needs | • Large energy consumption<br>• Politically and economically vulnerable system | • Control over energy resources<br>• Improved efficiency in energy consumption |
| Energy producers | • Profitable production of energy | • Large investments that need to be discounted<br>• High profit margins | • Stabile access to resources<br>• High market share |
| Consumers | • User-friendly energy | • Largely dependent on energy in daily life | • Inexpensive<br>• Accessible<br>• Safe |

## Identification of needs

The second, third and fourth columns in Table 17.1 list the overriding needs, what justifies the needs, and the demands they trigger.

As evident in Table 17.1, there are no obvious basic conflicts between the needs and the demands at the four levels. The contrasts seen in contemporary practice, such as between the demand for atmospheric thermal stability at the global level and energy consumption at the national level, are primarily associated with choices of subsystems, such as the type of energy carrier used and the efficiency of energy use at the consumer level. For example, burning fossil fuels results in copious discharge of greenhouse gases, and energy inefficiency worsens the problem.

## Requirement specification

Considering the needs of the various actors entails imposing different demands on the energy system. The relevant demands are summarized in Table 17.2. The focus in the columns of the table is on the four types of demands listed in section 17.1 above: functional, operational, physical and economic.

This concretization leads to general demands on the system. No one system can be expected to meet all demands, but the one that meets

*Table 17.2* Requirement specification

| Functional demands | Operational demands | Physical demands | Economic demands |
|---|---|---|---|
| 1. Based on renewable energy | 1. No pollution of environment | 1. Unlimited supply of energy | 1. Unaffected by political changes |
| 2. Short life cycle (regeneration time) | 2. Easy to transport | 2. Less vulnerable to acts of war | 2. Accessible to industrial and developing countries |
| 3. Non-toxic | 3. Easily convertible to electric energy | 3. Production safety | 3. Low costs of resources |
| 4. No change in the global thermal balance | 4. Could be used in existing applications | 4. Storage safety | 4. Low development costs |
| 5. Short development perspective (10–20 years) | 5. Short implementation perspective (20–50 years) | 5. Transport safety | 5. Small investments |
| 6. High energy density | 6. Utilise existing infrastructure | | 6. Low transport costs |
| | 7. Reduced need for storage capacity | | 7. Diminishing cost trend |
| | 8. Decentralized production | | 8. Profitable |

*Note*: Grey backgrounds indicate demands not fulfilled by non-renewable energy sources.

demands to the greatest extent should be selected in the next round. The demands that will not be fulfilled by non-renewable energy sources, such as oil and natural gas, are shown against a grey background in the table.

## Alternative subsystems

A control of the attributes of the various energy carriers listed in Table 17.3 shows that commonplace non-renewable energy sources can be excluded on the bases of their regeneration cycles and pollutant productions alone. That leaves the alternatives of nuclear fusion, geothermal energy, solar energy, kinetic energy and potential energy.

Adding other demands, such as on unlimited capacity in relation to needs, rules out some of these alternatives. That leaves fusion energy, geothermal energy and solar energy in the form of heat, photoelectric energy or hydrogen production.

*Table 17.3* Characteristics of energy systems

| Energy source | Energy carrier | Regeneration cycle (years) | Capacity in relation to needs | Pollutants |
|---|---|---|---|---|
| 1. Nuclear energy | • Fissile material | – | Unlimited | Fissile pollutants |
| | • Fusion of isotopes | continuous | Unlimited | – |
| 2. Fossil fuel | • Oil | millions | Limited | COx, SOx, NOx |
| | • Natural gas | millions | Limited | COx, SOx, NOx |
| | • Coal | millions | Limited | COx, SOx, NOx |
| 3. Geothermal energy | • Water/steam | continuous | Unlimited | – |
| 4. Solar energy | • Heat | continuous | Unlimited | – |
| | • Electricity | continuous | Unlimited | – |
| | • Hydrogen | continuous | Unlimited | Water, (NOx) |
| | • Plants/trees | 1–50 | Limited | COx, SOx, NOx |
| | • Micro-organisms | continuous | Limited | COx, SOx, NOx |
| 5. Kinetic energy | • Wind | continuous | Limited | – |
| | • Waves | continuous | Limited | – |
| 6. Potential energy | • Hydro-power | continuous | Limited | – |
| | • Tidal power | continuous | Limited | – |

*Note*: Grey backgrounds indicate attributes not fulfilling the requirement specification.

The attributes not fulfilling the requirement specifications are shown against a grey background in the table.

## Performance appraisal

Performance may be appraised in part through comparison, as in Table 17.4, in which fusion, bio-energy and hydrogen are compared to fossil fuel, the principal base of present-day energy systems. The table lists the results of a multi-attribute evaluation with a very simple three-tier ranking of meeting the functional demands: incompatibility with requirements as –1, acceptable as 0 and highly suitable as +1. The functional demands themselves are not weighted. This is a degree of simplification that would probably not be applied in practice, the scale would allow more detailed scores and the different attributes would be weighted.

By sums of rankings in this case, the hydrogen alternative is best. Though the fusion alternative ranks high, it is considered unrealistic, as it still is

*Table 17.4* Evaluation of energy systems

| | Fossil fuel | Bio-energy | Fusion | Hydrogen |
|---|---|---|---|---|
| **Functional demands** | | | | |
| 1. Renewable energy | –1 | 1 | 1 | 1 |
| 2. Short life-cycle | –1 | 0 | 1 | 1 |
| 3. Global thermal balance | –1 | 1 | 1 | 1 |
| 4. Non-toxic | –1 | 1 | 1 | 1 |
| 5. Short development perspective | 0 | 0 | –1 | 0 |
| 6. High energy density | 0 | 0 | 1 | 1 |
| **Operational demands** | | | | |
| 1. No environmental pollution | –1 | 0 | 1 | 1 |
| 2. Easy to transport | 0 | –1 | 1 | 0 |
| 3. Easily convertible to electric power | 0 | –1 | 1 | 1 |
| 4. Short implementation perspective | 0 | 0 | –1 | 0 |
| 5. Uses existing infrastructure | 0 | 0 | –1 | 0 |
| 6. Reduced need for storage capacity | 0 | 0 | 1 | 1 |
| 7. Decentralised production | 0 | 1 | –1 | 1 |
| **Physical demands** | | | | |
| 1. Unlimited supply of energy | –1 | –1 | 1 | 1 |
| 2. Less vulnerable to acts of war | –1 | 1 | 0 | 1 |
| 3. Production safety | 0 | 1 | 1 | 1 |
| 4. Storage safety | 0 | 1 | 1 | 0 |
| 5. Transport safety | 0 | 1 | 1 | 0 |
| **Economic demands** | | | | |
| 1. Unaffected by political changes | –1 | 1 | 1 | 1 |
| 2. Accessible to industrial and developing countries | –1 | 1 | –1 | 1 |
| 3. Low raw material costs | 0 | 0 | 0 | 1 |
| 4. Low development costs | 0 | 0 | –1 | –1 |
| 5. Small investments | 0 | 0 | –1 | 0 |
| 6. Low transport costs | 0 | –1 | –1 | 0 |
| 7. Declining costs | –1 | –1 | 1 | 1 |
| 8. Profitable | 0 | –1 | 1 | 1 |
| **Total** | 10 | 4 | 8 | 16 |

at the basic research level, and continuous fusion processes probably still are a long way off. The time frame and the development costs of ongoing international research in fusion energy prohibit its consideration as a real alternative. The hydrogen alternative also has the drawback of the costs of development of operational systems and the time it will take before they are available for everyday use.

### Choice of concept and closer evaluation of choice

Nonetheless hydrogen as an energy carrier gets the highest score by far, and should be examined further. This requires a new review of the extent to which the energy carrier satisfies the specified demands, based on more extensive and updated information. Such a comprehensive review is beyond the scope of this book. That said, information available today implies that hydrogen may in the near future meet most of the requirement specifications. This applies also to the development perspective and costs, as it may be assumed that hydrogen-based energy systems need no fundamentally new technical solutions and can to considerable extent exploit the existing infrastructure for distribution to consumers. The analysis also indicates that significant problems remain to be solved. The key problem, of course, is that hydrogen is only an energy carrier. It must be produced in a process that requires more energy than what the resulting hydrogen as a fuel yields. Consequently the greatest challenges are the choices of an energy source and a process for producing hydrogen. Moreover, other problems remain to be solved, such as those of safety at high temperatures and in storage and transport, among them embrittlement in certain metals when exposed to hydrogen.

The relevant processes for hydrogen production and consumption, respectively, are illustrated in Figures 17.5 and 17.6. The salient trait of the hydrogen-based energy cycle is that it is closed, in the sense that water is the medium, so energy can be stored and extracted without involving other substances. This makes hydrogen unique as an environment-friendly energy carrier, provided a clean energy source can be found as a basis for the process.

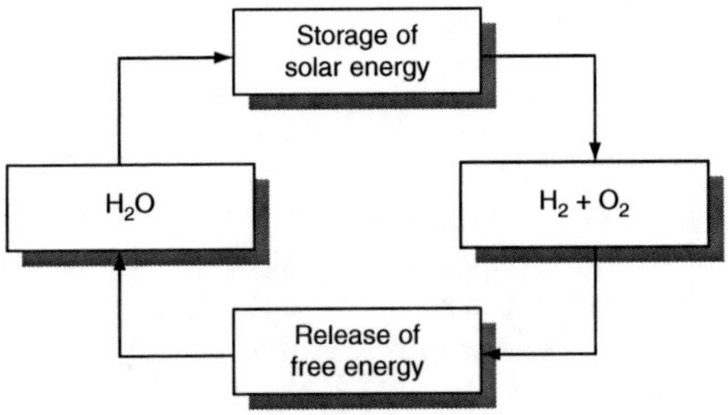


*Figure 17.5* Hydrogen as an energy carrier. The energy process is closed in the sense that it only stores and liberates energy without use or production of physical resources or waste

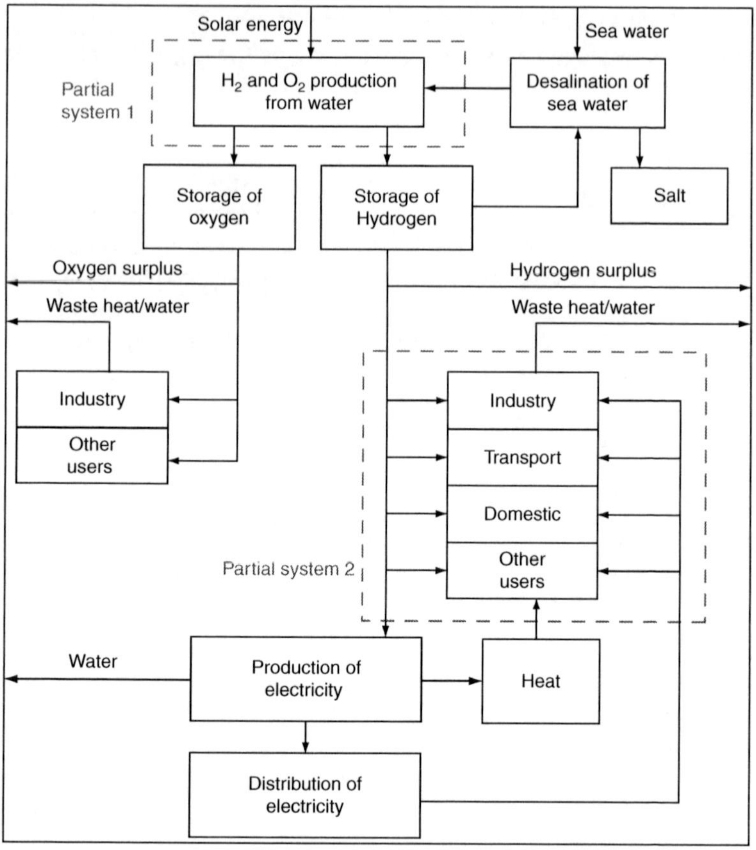


*Figure 17.6* Hydrogen-based energy system showing intervention across system borders

## 7. Description of the system

From the ecological viewpoint, the total energy system comprises a series of closed processes that include the production and uses of energy. So everything is absorbed by the environment with no changes other than the transfer of energy and matter in time and space. Solar energy is converted to various forms of usable energy, that is, fuels, heat and electricity. The by-products are elements and compounds that may be used directly, such as oxygen, water and salts.

Moreover, hydrogen can be used to supply the energy required in several sectors, such as in the processing industries, construction and transport, using known processes based on mechanical power, electrical energy, light and heat. Consequently the chances that commercial processes will be developed in the near future seem sound.

Overall the analysis shows that hydrogen as an energy carrier is interesting, from the environmental, economic and technical viewpoints. Provided that a clean production process is found, most environmental problems associated with the reliance on fossil or nuclear energy will be avoided. The reservation is that thus far, as an energy carrier, hydrogen is not commercially competitive with oil and gas, due to the high cost of producing hydrogen using current processes. Therefore, the realization of large-scale, hydrogen-based energy systems presupposes extensive research and development of commercial production processes, information and opinion campaigns directed to national and international opinion leaders and decision makers, international agreements and regulations for the uses of non-renewable resources, etc.

# 18
# SWOT Analysis

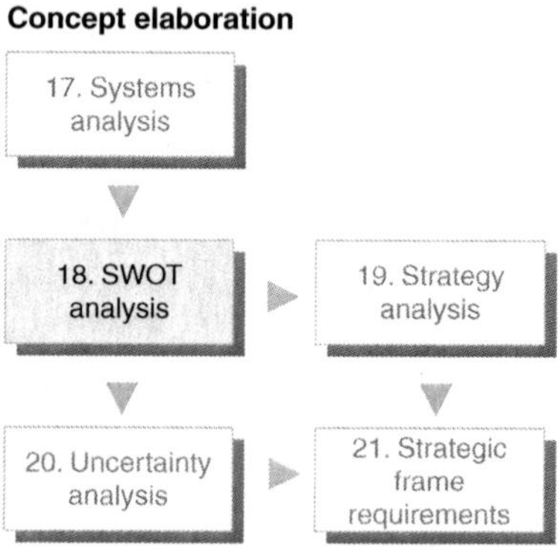


*Systems analysis yields an overview of the functional requirements and external assumptions relevant to a successful project concept. SWOT analysis uses this and other information to produce an overview of the strengths and weaknesses of the concept viewed in the broad perspective. In turn, this affords a better basis for strategic choice.*

## 18.1 A review of pros and cons

In the 1950s, SWOT, the abbreviation for Strength, Weaknesses, Opportunities and Threats, emerged as an aid to strategic planning and market analyses. It's a simple, qualitative, generally applicable method. The essence is a description of reality within an outcome space divided into four categories, as illustrated in the matrix of Figure 18.1. Internal and external attributes are listed in its rows, positive and negative aspects in its columns.

| **Strengths** | **Weaknesses** |
|---|---|
| • Unambiguous goals<br>• Professional expertise<br>• Motivation<br>• Experience, etc. | • Cost<br>• Internal conflicts<br>• Choice of technology<br>• Progress, etc. |
| **Opportunities** | **Threats** |
| • Needs<br>• Market potential<br>• Demand<br>• Political priorities, etc. | • Competition<br>• Environmental effects<br>• Unforeseen effects<br>• Public response, etc. |

*Figure 18.1* Concretization of aspects that may be important in strategic planning of projects

The SWOT method is used principally for acquiring information as a basis for creating strategy. The strategy emerges at the interface between charting and evaluating the opportunities and threats confronting the project or organization within the context of its operation, also taking into account its strengths and weaknesses.

The goal of the strategy is to exploit the opportunities available on the bases of the project's strengths, while at the same time avoiding external threats and taking account of internal weaknesses. However, the objective of the method is limited. Principally it is used prospectively as an aid to charting essential conditions relevant to strategic planning in the front-end phase. In many cases, it also is used retrospectively as an aid to charting positive and negative aspects of what has been achieved in the reality within which a project operates.

SWOT analyses often are conducted as expert group reviews or brainstorming sessions in which informed experts jointly bring forth a description of status quo in the form of key conditions or elements, sorted into the four categories. Briefly, the procedure has three steps:

1. Establish a group of analysts, whose expertise and backgrounds differ.
2. Identify strengths, weaknesses, opportunities and threats relevant to the alternative decisions at hand, based on the brainstorming.
3. Summarize the results for each alternative in a four-cell table.

It's helpful if the first round of the process is dedicated to charting the principal aspects of stakeholder needs and prioritizations as well as to clarifying professional matters in economic, technical, institutional, environmental, political, social and other sectors.

The aspects or elements that then come forth can thereafter be classified more closely as to whether they are external or internal or if they are to be considered as positive or negative. Internal aspects usually are characterized by being mostly due to technical, economic and institutional factors, while external aspects often are predominantly ascribed to environmental, social and political conditions. An example of concretization into the four categories is shown in Figure 18.1.

In a SWOT analysis, the elements identified should result from information and dialogues among and analyses by the participating parties. In the formulation of the results, it's important that

1. the formulations are brief and to the point
2. whenever possible, strengths and weaknesses are related to critical success factors
3. the actual and the hypothetical are clearly distinguished from each other
4. the elements are based on level-headed, realistic evaluations.

The result is a rough overview of the location of the project's 'centre of gravity', that is, whether the situation is positive or negative and whether the principal problems are internal or external. The evaluation can be further amplified in various ways, such as by weighting the various elements or their assumed impacts, and then performing a simple multi-attribute evaluation. Furthermore, one might take a step in the direction of risk analysis by characterizing the elements according to their importance and the probability of realization.

The overview resulting from a SWOT analysis provides the basis for strategic choice, such as in a concept appraisal or in choosing tactical or strategic means in an ongoing process.

The strength of the SWOT method is that it is methodically consistent, that is it operates with:

1. an outcome space that is all inclusive, so systematic bias is avoided.
2. mutually exclusive categories, so there are no indistinct grey zones.

Alternative North

| Strengths | Weaknesses |
| --- | --- |
| • Existing residential and commercial properties are not affected<br>• Allows much flexibility in designing the new housing project | • Will require a new feeder road that will increase total project costs<br>• The new settlement will be located far from schools, shops and service institutions |
| **Opportunities** | **Threats** |
| • Allows future expansion in an otherwise unexploited area<br>• Absence of services can attract new businesses in the area | • Possible objections from local population against the use of a recreational area for housing settlements<br>• Uncertain market response due to the remote location |

Alternative East

| Strengths | Weaknesses |
| --- | --- |
| • Effective use of the area and infrastructure by expanding the existing housing complex<br>• Permission for expansion was granted Already when the existing settlement was established | • Will require expensive expansion of existing roads<br>• Existing industry will have to be relocated |
| **Opportunities** | **Threats** |
| • Increased population in the centre will utilize present overcapacity in the local school | • Relocation of industry is a sensitive issue<br>• Possible opposition to expansions from present residents |

Alternative South

| Strengths | Weaknesses |
| --- | --- |
| • Effective use of existing infrastructure<br>• Allows flexibility in designing the new housing estate | • Will ruin an existing popular recreation area<br>• The settlement will be cut off from the district centre |
| **Opportunities** | **Threats** |
| • Allow buildings to be located in the harmony with nature<br>• Could trigger new developments in this part of the district | • Strong opposition among residents against destruction of a park area |

*Figure 18.2* Three alternative concepts

This strength suits the method well to supporting group-based brainstorming, because to a great extent it rules out discussion of choice of categories as well as vagueness concerning their interpretation. The method is straightforward and inexpensive, while also being generally applicable to all types of projects and processes.

The weaknesses of the method are that its simple descriptions of reality in categories cannot contribute to illustrating the interactions between and dynamics in the processes studied. Consequently it can only be used as a first approximation to an analysis. Its result depends on the insight and understanding of the participants in the analysis and not least on their composition. If the key interest groups are not represented, the result is likely to have limited value and validity. If the result builds on a consensus-based dialogue between informed parties, the result of a SWOT analysis may be extremely valuable.

## 18.2 Example: Assessing sites for a housing development

A municipality contemplates establishing a new, large housing estate and has selected three alternative sites:

1. North: The land is deserted and will need a long access road, but otherwise will not affect other housing areas or business activities.
2. East: The site will be an expansion of an existing housing area, and it will require expansion of the existing road network and relocation of a small industrial enterprise.
3. South: The road network and infrastructure utilities are suitable, but the development will require that a small park and recreation area be rezoned to housing.

The project affects several interests in the municipality that may have differing views of the development and consequently wish to influence or work against it in various ways. They include the citizenry in general, future residents, land owners, interest groups, builders, business in general, and not least the media that will cover the plans and their implementation in the local press.

An assessment of the various interests concluded that the North alternative can be controversial due to the additional costs of road building, but most deem its location to be the best. The East alternative will meet resistance from both present homeowners and from the company that must relocate. The South alternative will meet resistance from the citizens in general, the media and the interest organizations, but probably is the least costly alternative.

The municipal planners wish to use a SWOT analysis to more closely examine the three alternatives. A working group is set up consisting of the leader of the planning and building service, the chief municipal officer, a road and transport expert, an environmental expert and two local council politicians.

The group meets and uses half a working day to identify factors within each of the analytic perspectives for each of the three alternatives. A simplified representation of the group's findings is summarized in the tabulations of Figure 18.2.

The group voted down the East alternative due to resistance from homeowners and business in the area. The South alternative is directly preferable, but probably would be the most controversial for the citizens of the municipality in general. Hence, the conclusion is to recommend the North alternative, despite its considerable additional cost for roadworks, because it is seen as a more forward-looking alternative that affords flexibility for further developments in the years to come.

As illustrated by this example, a SWOT analysis is only an aid to acquiring and classifying information. Consequently it has obvious limits. Its strength is that it provides a methodically consistent comparative framework for discussion that works well in groups. Clear basic terms, such as the goal, the perspective or the alternatives, stimulate the group members to constructive thought. The weakness is that the identified attributes are not prioritized, valued or weighted, so that the picture of the situation may easily be biased. This drawback can be overcome by further processing of the results, such as in a multi-attribute evaluation.

# 19
# Strategy Analysis – Logical Framework

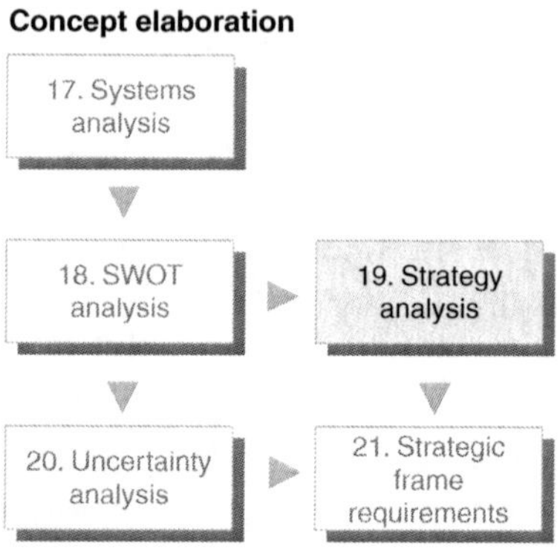


*The strategy analysis described in this chapter applies a simple analytical framework to give an overall presentation of project strategy and the key uncertainty factors that might influence its realization. Strategy analysis aims in part to elicit an overriding perspective for a project and in part to test the realism of the concept using intuitive probability assessment.*

## 19.1 Evaluating project strategies

Project development and management often smacks of a narrow project perspective in which overriding evaluation is of lesser interest. These matters are discussed in Chapter 2. In contrast, the whole perspective has long been in focus in the planning and implementation of international development projects funded by industrialized

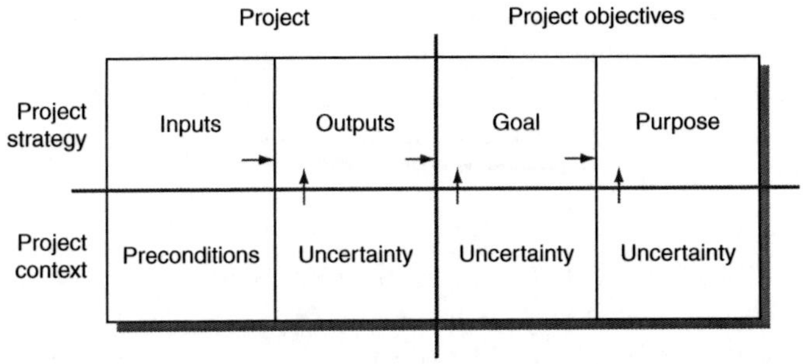


*Figure 19.1* A logical framework for appraisal of projects. One distinguishes between the project itself, the purpose of the project and the external conditions that can influence the project

countries. This probably is because decision makers feel that the uncertainty associated with development projects is considerable, particularly so for contextual uncertainty. Hence, an overview over the principal uncertainty components is essential as early as possible in planning. Consequently the United Nations, the OECD and the European Commission recommend that the so-called Logical Framework method be used in project concept appraisals (Samset 1999). Gradually many other actors in industrialized countries have adopted it. For example, Canadian authorities have adopted the method as a standard in public investment projects. It is used to develop and evaluate alternative project strategies and to analyze the uncertainty associated with projects.

The strategy analysis in this chapter applies a simplified logical framework to identify the principal components of a project, as shown in Figure 19.1. In it, attention is focused on clarifying and analyzing the project purpose as expressed in terms of its intended first order and second order effects. However, as shown, the detailing of the project itself is limited. It is described only in terms of the key outputs and the resources needed to realize them. This brevity reflects that the initial phase concern should preferably be with the reason for the project and for ensuring that the concept is relevant to it, but only to a lesser degree with questions that should be addressed later, such as choices of technology, organization, etc.

The method attaches importance to identification of the key uncertainty elements that can influence project implementation. The top row of the framework itemizes aspects of the project strategy that project management can directly influence, as distinguished from the bottom row of uncertainty components that are outside of management control. Accomplished project planning requires as complete an overview as possible of these aspects and elements at the earliest possible point of time.

A review of the contextual opportunities and risks will indicate whether the uncertainty components reduce or increase the probability of realization at each level of the project strategy. If the contextual uncertainty is found to considerably reduce the probability of realization, the project concept must be reconsidered, such as by changing the inputs and outputs to increase the chance of success.

The framework is methodically *consistent* in the sense that it (1) is all-inclusive: the matrix describes a global outcome space that can encompass all conceivable given events (an event is either actually factual or hypothetical, that is, its probability of realization is less than 100 per cent). An event is either internal to the strategy, that is within the scope of the project, or external. At the same time, the outcome space (2) is divided into four mutually exclusive categories (those within the strategy versus those outside it, and actual versus hypothetical events).

All components within the framework are in principle described in the same way, that is, in positive terms. This applies both to goals described as states (for example, a road is built) or uncertainty components described as assumptions (for example, road capacity is adequate to accommodate future traffic volume). When all components are described in such positive terms, they may be moved as needed within the framework without having to be reformulated. Various strategies or scenarios may be visualized in this manner. For example, one might discuss the probability of realization of goals at various levels and redefine those deemed unrealistic. One might expand a project by introducing new outputs or shrink it, as by augmenting one of its outputs to a goal, in which case other outputs will expire. A strategy also may be altered by bringing an external uncertainty component into the project and taking control of it, such as by designating it as an output. Thereafter, one can evaluate the resultant consequences for the total strategy. A likely consequence is that it will increase the chances of realization but also will entail additional costs to be included in the budget.

**Terms of the analysis**

1. All essential internal and external elements shall be identified.
2. All elements shall be stated as positive conditions.
3. Each uncertainty element is associated with a specific level of objective.
4. All outputs shall be 100 per cent attainable.
5. No uncertainty element can represent a risk that jeopardizes realization of the objective with which it is associated.
6. Realization of the project shall contribute noticeably to fulfilling the project purpose.

The components within the framework can be characterized in terms of importance and probability of realization. Thereafter, simple, intuitive evaluation may be made of the possibilities and risks associated with the various strategies.

As shown in Figure 19.1, each uncertainty element within the framework is associated with a particular goal level. One condition for accepting a project strategy is that no uncertainty element constitutes a risk so great that it jeopardizes the realization of the goal at the appurtenant level. Should the overall evaluation show that individual components have unacceptably low probability of realization or high risks, the project should be altered. Hence, the process is iterative. The matrix affords a framework and a means for analyzing and redesigning the concept. Systematic changes may be made within the framework to test various changes and provide a basis for choice.

The method is a simple objective-oriented management procedure principally suited to qualitative evaluation. It's often used in work groups in which key persons and experts analyze alternative project strategies based on their own experience, information from preliminary surveys, etc. In such situations, many inputs are based on subjective judgement. The normal prerequisite for an acceptable decision is that consensus underlies all conclusions.

One characteristic of the method is that it entails a process in which uncertainty gradually increases as the process progresses. This is in contradistinction to the traditional model of the course of a project, in which uncertainty diminishes as the project actors progressively gain control. This is because the perspective goes beyond realization of the

**Elements of the framework**

*Purpose*

- The overriding justification for the project, that is, the long-term objective to which the project is intended to contribute.

*Goal*

- The first-order effect of the project, that is, for the project target group or users. There should be only one goal. It should state the level of ambition against which the project subsequently will be evaluated, and should be a unifying motivational factor for the parties involved.

*Outputs*

- The results that the project shall have produced upon termination of the implementation phase.

*Inputs*

- The funding, staff and material resources necessary for realizing the outputs.

*Uncertainty elements*

- Specifies the outcome sought as the result of an uncertain condition or event.
- Both goals and uncertainty components should be expressed as independent events, and not causally linked in chains of two or more events.

outputs and involves carrying on after they are attained; see Chapter 4. This is in keeping with the current emphasis on user orientation and quality in projects. We must increasingly expect that requirements on projects will go beyond the contractor's perspective and the first-order effects for users and that external conditions will be taken ever more into consideration. This approach contributes to amplifying and clarifying uncertainty and thereby to foreseeing and preventing some problems that one may be left with after a project starts.

## 19.2 Basis for the LogFrame

The concept to be evaluated, that is, the content of the project matrix, can be developed in several ways. In this book, a way is outlined from idea to concept via systems analysis and SWOT analysis, as discussed in Chapters 17 and 18. This typifies a consistent, methodical approach in which one builds bit by bit, as shown in Figure 17.1. Systems analysis contributes an impartial outside-in approach to a problem and provides a description of a solution within a system in which the essential external parameters are also determined. As a continuation, SWOT analysis may be used to evaluate system strengths and weaknesses. The logical framework then is a continuation of the SWOT matrix, retaining the distinction between internal and external conditions and adding a new parameter of the probability of realization. In so doing, one takes yet another step in depth in the overall analysis of a concept. This is illustrated in Figure 16.1.

The logical framework also is well suited to straightforward evaluation of the systematic approach to and realism in existing concepts or project plans. In this case, one may simply identify the elements of the project structure and locate them in the upper part of the matrix, while the uncertainty components are located in its lower part. Projects often have complex, compound objectives that provide no clear bearing and also may have internal goal conflicts. Now and then, a designated output may actually be a goal and the other way round. Likewise, a designated goal often may be an uncertainty factor applicable to conditions outside the project mandate and the other way round. Such a review of an existing project usually clarifies consistency and realism and leads to appreciable improvements in project strategy.

The initial phase of concept development customarily entails mostly qualitative evaluation and is only inappreciably concerned with

When the LogFrame is used to develop concepts, it may be used in a sequence of several analytical steps as listed below. This is a light version of the approach presented in this book, as described in Chapter 16.

1. **Participation analysis** – an identification of the potential stakeholders and affected groups, their problems and interests and interactions among them.
2. **Problem analysis** – starting from the core problem, a problem tree is developed. It consists of chains of causes that lead to the problem, and chains of consequences that may be derived from the problem.
3. **Objectives analysis** – the problems in the problem tree are transformed to positive expressions of objectives, and the tree develops into an *objectives tree*.
4. **Strategy analysis** – on the basis of the objectives tree, sequences of goals that should be included in alternative strategies are chosen. Thereafter, one chooses evaluation criteria, evaluates strategies against each other, and thereby evolves a preferred strategy.
5. **Logical framework** – the elements of the chosen strategy are placed on a project matrix to clarify target levels and evaluate uncertainty and realizability. Some elements in the objectives tree will also appear in the matrix as uncertainty components.

*Source*: Norad 1999

quantifying magnitudes such as scope, cost or time. That said, as the evaluation of the concept progresses, one will of course increasingly quantify individual components of the strategy as well as the uncertainty factors in order to increase the precision of evaluation and suit the concept to the functional requirements and the relevant resource availability.

## 19.3 Expert judgement

Expert judgement, as described in section 13.2, is rudimentary in the sense that it entails elementary, often intuitive, probability assessments. However, it has great practical application as a first approximation to the development and evaluation of project concepts. It might be seen as an initial rough risk assessment of an envisioned project. As discussed in section 19.1 and corroborated by experience, such analyses are particularly effective when based mostly on qualitative information. But this isn't the same as unequivocal assumption. Relevant information is crucial in carrying through such analyses. Thorough descriptions and evaluations of problems and needs as well as of the interests and prioritizations of affected parties are vital. The same is true of conditions that conceivably may affect the implementation of a strategy. In the analysis, any information that is quantified may be epitomized in qualitative terms to focus on its fundamental content and not on its numerical magnitude.

We know that individual experience alone is not the best basis for reliable forecasts. Moreover, judgemental evaluation often reflects individual attitudes and preferences, and bias often is systematic and robust. We also know that forecasting based on the judgement of groups usually comes out better than that of individuals, even expert individuals (Surowiecki 2004). Perhaps more important, the systematic use of relevant empirical material and models often produces forecasts better than the judgemental evaluations of experts or groups. Notwithstanding, today surprisingly little is done to systematically learn from previous projects and to organize what has been learned so it may be made available to benefit new projects. Reinventing the wheel seems to be the rule rather than the exception. This inclination implies that there's a great and partly unresearched potential for improvement.

On the whole there's a need for preliminary surveys supplemented with knowledge gained in similar projects. Additionally excellent results may be attained using simple aids, provided the analysis is conducted cooperatively by well-informed people in a consensus-based process. Nonetheless in many cases such an approach is far better than the seemingly commonplace contemporary practice of not conducting a systematic initial evaluation.

The following example illustrates an application of the method in a project that has been in its front-end phase for two decades and at time of writing is presented to the politicians in a new, expanded format. The example is based on information from governmental studies and from extensive media coverage of the project.

## 19.4 Example: Building a tunnel for coastal ship traffic

The shipping tunnel project initially envisioned a tunnel for smaller vessels (up to 5,000 GRT) between fjord arms north and south of the Stad Peninsula that juts out into the North Sea between the ports of Måløy and Ulsteinvik on the west coast of Norway. The idea was put forth some 100 years ago, but first studied in 1990. The study concluded that it was unprofitable. Subsequently, for two decades, the idea was kept alive by local interests, despite having been rejected at the national level on the bases of repeated studies that had deemed the project to be socio-economically unprofitable. In 2007 the Norwegian Coastal Administration conducted a new study of the consequences of building an enlarged tunnel that could accommodate vessels such as the Coastal Express liners (up to 16,000 GRT).

Should it be built, the shipping tunnel would allow ships to avoid the tough Stad Sea that in poor weather is treacherous due to high waves caused by its being shallow with a rough sea bottom. The stretch of about four nautical miles was particularly dangerous for smaller vessels, which delayed voyages, as ships either waited for better weather or sailed long detours past the Stad Peninsula (Kystverket 2007). Larger ships have the option of sailing farther out from the coast, where wave conditions were better.

The tunnel was to be about two kilometres long and have a height of 50 metres. Such large dimensions indicate that extensive protective works would be required. The envisioned design was at the extreme edge of maritime experience, so unanticipated problems could well arise. Uncertainties concerning the geological conditions made construction cost estimation difficult.

As discussed in section 12.3, the grounds for the project were not clear. In the long term, it was believed that the enterprise would lead to more jobs and more population in the region. The expected short-term effect was held to be increased ship traffic and more regular cargo delivery as a result of improved safety. It also seemed possible that the coastal express route could be extended to connect two main towns, with the ships using the tunnel. As it might be a world's-first of its sort, the tunnel was believed to be a future tourist attraction. However, the extent to which various groups would use the tunnel and the spin-off effects of it were uncertain.

### Project strategy

The project strategy, expressed as a conceivable cause-effect chain, is illustrated in the top row of the matrix of Figure 19.2.

The original idea triggers a sequence of events, from the development of the concept and the decision process that results in an appropriation of funds from government. In turn, this brings about planning, construction and the final commissioning of the tunnel. Ships sail through the tunnel and new passenger vessel schedules are set up. Freight delivery regularity improves. This may open up new markets, enable new production and increase tourism that gradually will increase employment and population in the region.

Not all these elements are apparent in the strategy shown in the matrix. The project itself is limited to the construction and readying of the tunnel. Consequently the *outputs* are mostly constrained to blasting out and securing the tunnel and to installing equipment for communications, ventilation, operation and maintenance, etc. Tunnel operation accordingly is outside the scope of the project and hence is listed under the uncertainties in the lower row of the matrix.

The *goal* is associated with first-order effects for users, in this case the impact the tunnel has on ship traffic past the Stord Peninsula. Any resultant spin-off effects, in the form of upswings in business, tourism, employment and population, are regarded as second-order effects and are associated with the project's *purpose*. In major infrastructure projects, a lofty purpose, such as economic growth or greater prosperity, often are put forth. The difficulty with such lofty objectives is that they are overly ambitious and too general, in the sense that realization of them presupposes initiatives not only in sea transport, but also in other sectors. This will cause a problem, which is commonly termed attribution. This

| **Inputs** | **Outputs** | **Goal** | **Purpose** |
|---|---|---|---|
| 0.2 Billion £ | The shipping tunnel is constructed (1.8 km. and large cross-section) | More efficient sea transport in the region | • Increased employment in the region<br>• Population increase in the region |
| **Preconditions** | **Uncertainties** | **Uncertainties** | **Uncertainties** |
| 1. The project is considered economically viable<br>2. The Parliament appropriates fund for the project | 3. The budget is sufficient to produce agreed outputs<br>4. Geological conditions are as expected<br>5. Measures to ensure safety are as foreseen | 6. A major share of the traffic will use the tunnel<br>7. A speed boat service with anticipated number of passengers in operation<br>8. The traffic with small boats more than doubles<br>9. A major share of freight traffic North-South is channelled through the tunnel<br>10. The expected volume of freight is transferred from road to sea transport<br>11. The number of ship accidents is reduced to a third<br>12. The tunnel has sufficient capacity to cater for the demand<br>13. The tunnel is operated efficiently and without major accidents | 14. Economic activities in the region increases as expected<br>15. The number of tourists to the region increases as expected<br>16. Export of fresh fish to the European continent increases as stipulated<br>17. Regularity of freight transport increases as expected |

*Figure 19.2* Initial layout of a concept in a logical framework

means that it will be difficult, even impossible to demonstrate to what extent the observed changes can be attributed to the project as compared with other developments or confounding processes in society. Hence, such objectives are unsuitable as the project purpose.

Realism in the strategy described may be singled out and evaluated by asking the question: what is the conditional probability that the goal will be realized if the output is realized, that is, the shipping tunnel is built as assumed? In this case, by disregarding the uncertainty components in the bottom row of the matrix, the probability of realization seems relatively high. Doubt then principally concerns the extent to which the tunnel will be used by the potential user groups.

In the same manner, one might question the conditional probability of realizing the purpose, provided that the goal is realized. In this case, there's reason to suspect that the probability is limited. Consequently the tentative conclusion is that the realism of the concept remains vague, so the consequences of external, uncertain conditions need to be more closely examined.

## Uncertainty components

In this case, 17 uncertainty factors are listed and numbered in Figure 19.2 and discussed below. Two uncertainty factors are called preconditions and are associated with whether the necessary resources will be available to implement the project. Documentation of the socio-economic viability (1) should be a prerequisite for major infrastructure projects. But that alone is not sufficient, as other aspects also must be assessed if the Parliament appropriates funds for the project (2). At time of writing, the project remains in the pre-project stage, and these preconditions have yet to be fulfilled.

Three uncertainty factors are associated with realization of the outputs. The proposed budget (3) of NOK 1.7 billion is the basis for the calculation of profitability, yet the Norwegian Coastal Administration study pointed to uncertainty in that figure. The uncertainties concern geological conditions in bedrock (4) and the extent of preventive works (5) in so large a tunnel. But as this is the world's first facility of its sort, there probably are many other uncertain components not listed in the matrix.

Eight uncertainty components are associated with the goal, some by and large relate to operation of the facility, to the extent to which various user groups will use it and to the effect the project will have on maritime safety. The tunnel is designed to accommodate 84 per cent of the ship traffic that passes the Stad Peninsula. Needless to say, at so early a point of time, the nature of ship traffic is unknown, whether it will be large or small, even throughout the year or peaking only during seasonal bad weather, or whether peak traffic might strain capacity or cause delays. The financial assumptions for operations are not included here. But they are uncertain, not least because free use by shipping has been contemplated.

Four uncertainty factors are associated with the purpose and accordingly should be seen as prerequisites for realizing the goal. They concern employment and population, which to a great extent reflect the level of economic activity (14). Specifically, they are tourism (15), transport of fresh fish (16) and regularity of freight transport in general (17). Moreover, the realization of the purpose, as discussed above, will also depend on several other conditions external to the concrete project. These conditions are not included in the matrix.

Most of the uncertainty factors listed here obviously are important to the successful realization of the conceived strategy. Hence, a unified evaluation of the concept should consider all uncertainty components. It will be based on evaluations of the importance of and probability of realizing each element, followed by an intuitive evaluation of the conditional probability of realization of goals at each target level. A project with so many appreciable uncertainty components should ring a warning bell. Probably most obvious is that an appreciable cost increase will further weaken the project's already feeble socio-economic viability. The same is true of a possible overestimation of benefits. Should the assumptions not be fulfilled, the socio-economic viability will be still further weakened, as discussed in Chapter 9. This applies both to the question of the extent that the tunnel will be used and by whom as well as to the nature of the economic spin-off effects it may trigger.

A closer evaluation of the uncertainty of this project is described in Chapter 20.

# 20
# Rough Analysis of Uncertainty

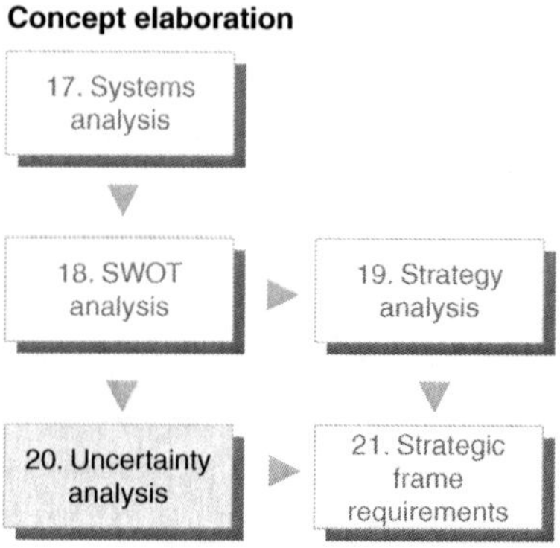


*A logical framework may be used to identify uncertainty factors that can affect project strategy but which lie outside of the project's mandate and control. The first step towards a risk analysis is to roughly sort these elements to find which may be fatal, which may embrace appreciable opportunities and which are the risk factors between these two extremes. This tells us quite a bit about the merit of the concept.*

## 20.1 Probability and effects

Uncertainty must be *identified* before it can be quantified and analyzed. Though there are many methods for analyzing risk, there are few methods for systematic identification of uncertainty (Williams 1995). This is yet another neglected sector in practical project work (Samset 1998). In that respect, the principal aids probably are case studies or scenario techniques. The logical framework method is a type of simple scenario technique

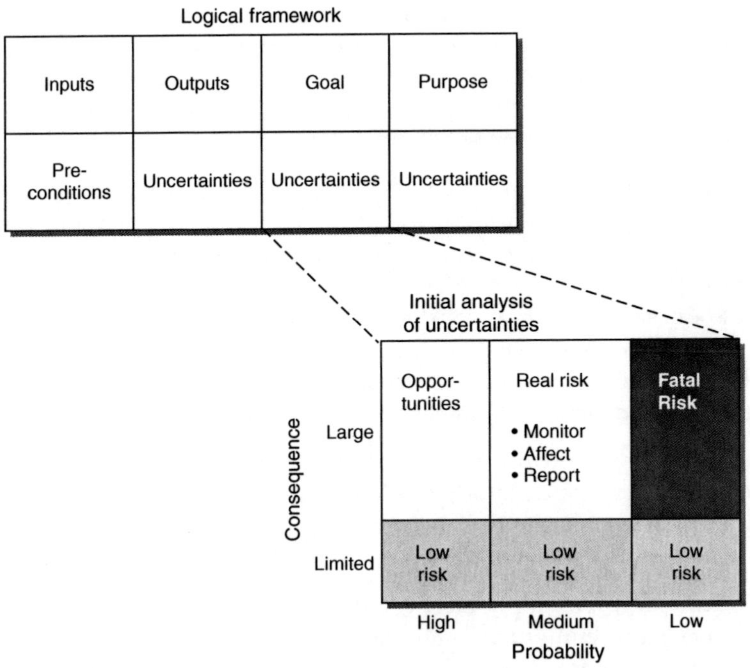


*Figure 20.1* In the first round, the crude categories of uncertainty components to be identified include any fatal risk elements as well as the greatest opportunities that may arise

that is used to describe and evaluate various strategies. In it, goals in strategies may be varied, and uncertainty components may be associated with specific goals to help develop a picture of project practicality and of how uncertainty may affect realization.

As discussed in Chapter 19, one then arrives at a strategy described in four target levels. The uncertainty components may be sorted in the framework according to the target levels they affect. All descriptions are of positive events, such as '*Demand for the product is as anticipated*'. The individual elements have varying degrees of influence on the project. Uncertainty may be classified in the form of expected consequence and probability of manifestation. In the first round, crude categories, such as limited/large and high/low, are used to picture the risks and opportunities of various groups. This is illustrated in Figure 20.1, which is a unified outcome space for an initial analysis, or crude sorting of uncertainty elements, divided into six categories.

The upshot of the concept development may be an abundance of uncertainty components. Hence, as a first step, each uncertainty component should be considered. Those found to have limited effect, shown grey shaded in Figure 20.1, presumably entail low risk, so they may be eliminated.

The remaining uncertainty components are those presumed to have considerable consequences for the project. They are divided into three groups, as shown in the figure. Consider first the group for which the probability of manifestation is low, shown in the rightmost column. These uncertainties have considerable consequences, here designated as fatal risks, shown uppermost in the right column. Should these elements arise, the strategy has to be redefined to reduce their effects. If that isn't possible, the strategy must be abandoned.

The other extreme comprises the uncertainty components for which the probability of manifestation is high, shown in the leftmost column. They comprise opportunities. Accordingly, they don't represent risks, but rather are part of the grounds for the concept in the final evaluation.

The remaining group of uncertainty components between these two extremes may be important and may manifest themselves with certain probabilities. They are the real risks, shown in the middle column. The individual and collective risks that these components represent should be evaluated against the project strategy. As a matter of course, these elements may be evaluated with regard to how they might be included and influenced in the project implementation phase. Later on, the elements may be more finely classified according to the severities of risk that they represent, as illustrated in Figure 20.2.

Even though this type of simple evaluation builds mostly on subjective judgement of consequences and probabilities, it often has helped guide a project process onto a sensible course at an early point of time.

Evaluations may be made at various levels. In innovative projects, in which uncertainty is great and available information is inadequate, systematic use of this type of simple qualitative methods doubtlessly is advantageous compared to the use of advanced quantitative methods. Of course, in familiar types of projects, implemented in predictable conditions and building on reliable, quantitative information, precise quantitative methods will be used to a greater degree.

The evolution of a successful project depends firstly on the nature of the available information, secondly on the assumptions and evaluations

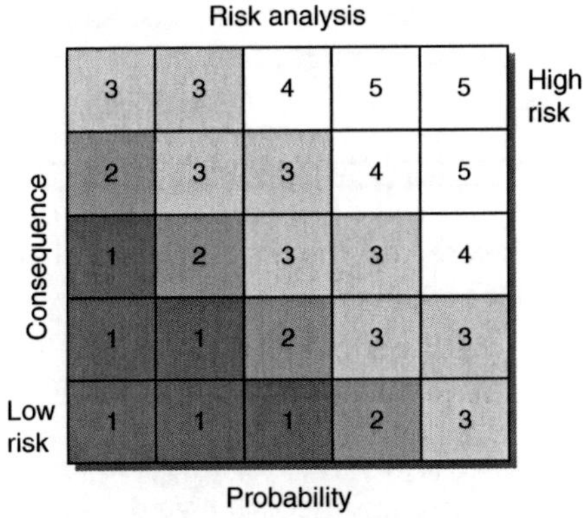


*Figure 20.2* More detailed classification of risks

made to express information in terms of utility and probability, and finally on the analysis and application of the information in the final formulation of the strategy. Like other social and administrative systems, projects have their own natural dynamics and are self-adjusting with respect to external influencing factors. Hence, quality assurance of the analysis of information is more difficult than quality assurance of the information underpinning the analysis. Consequently the trend in the uncertainty management of projects is towards simple data analysis methods. This is illustrated in the following example of section 20.2.

## 20.2 Example: Building a tunnel for coastal ship traffic

The triggering idea for the coastal ship tunnel project, described in section 19.4, was to improve fairway safety for appreciable parts of the coastal ship traffic past the Stad Peninsula on the west coast of Norway. After about 20 years of studies and political compromise, the project still is in the concept stage, chiefly because it has yet to be proven socio-economically viable. Figure 19.1 comprises a rough overview of the strategy including several uncertainty components that believably could affect its realization. These uncertainty components may be examined more closely to fully understand the risks they represent, see Figure 20.3.

The conclusion of the discussion of section 19.4 was that the concept was problematic due to numerous, appreciable uncertainty factors. The uncertainty components were sorted relative to the target levels that they influenced, but there was no further consideration of the risks they represented or which measures might have been implemented to reduce their relevant effects.

In this case, there's considerable factual information on the existing situation, but many judgements will still have to be based on assumptions. The following discussion is based on the draft report of the choice of concept study (Kystverket 2007) and on public debate as reported in the media.

### Low risk

A crude analysis of uncertainty may simply start with winnowing out the uncertainty components assumed to have consequences so negligible that they may be neglected. Thereafter the remaining uncertainty components may be assessed according to the probabilities that they will occur, as shown in Figure 20.3. As can be seen in the lower row, four uncertainty components have limited consequences. The first is the assumption that sailing through the tunnel will reduce the number of ship accidents (11). The risk is regarded low, as though probability is high, the consequences are small, because the accident rate already is low, due to improvements in ships and navigational aids. Recently in these waters, there have been only four accidents a year, and there have been no fatal accidents for the past 20 years.

The second is the expectation that leisure boat traffic will more than double (8). The reasoning here is that even if this happens, it will hardly have noticeable socio-economic impact. Moreover, the third is the question as to whether tourism will increase as expected (15). The reasoning here is that even though the tunnel will be a unique attraction, by itself it cannot be expected to trigger a major upswing in tourist volume. The fourth is an anticipation that the tunnel will bring about a shift of a substantial part of freight transport from road to sea (10). In the media debate on the project, many have doubted that such a shift will ever take place.

### Opportunities

As mentioned in section 19.1, all uncertainty components are expressed in positive terms as outcomes of uncertain situations. That is, if the probability of occurrence of a component is high, it represents more opportunity than risk. Hence, many of the uncertainty components of a viable concept should classify into its opportunities group. In the example of Figure 20.3, only three components classify as opportunities.

| | High probability | Medium | Low probability |
|---|---|---|---|
| Large consequence | **Opportunities**<br>17. Regularity of freight transport improves as expected<br>12. Tunnel capacity is adequate to meet demand<br>13. The tunnel operates efficiently with no major accidents | **Real risk**<br>4. Geological conditions are as expected<br>5. Measures to ensure safety are as foreseen<br>6. A major share of the traffic will use the tunnel<br>7. A speed boat service with anticipated number of passengers in operation<br>9. A major share of north-south freight traffic is routed through the tunnel<br>14. Economic activity in the region increases as expected<br>16. Export of fresh fish to central Europe increases as stipulated | **Fatal risk**<br>1. The project is considered economically viable<br>2. The Parliament appropriates funds for the project<br>3. The budget is adequate to produce agreed outputs. |
| Limited consequence | **Low risk**<br>11. The number of ship accidents is reduced to a third | **Low risk**<br>8. Leisure boat traffic more than doubles<br>10. The expected volume of freight moves from road to sea transport | **Low risk**<br>15. The number of tourists to the region increases as expected |

*Figure 20.3* Example of a shipping tunnel: A crude analysis of risk factors

The first is the assumption of improved regularity of sea freight transport (17). The reasoning here is that today in bad weather periods, some small ships risk having to stay in harbour, awaiting weather improvement. The in-harbour delays usually last from a few to 12 hours. Larger vessels that elect to avoid turbulent waters nearer the coast by sailing farther out also incur delay, as sailing a longer stretch takes longer. Assuming that both the small and large vessel groups probably will use the tunnel in bad weather periods, regularity will improve. The second is the assumption that tunnel capacity is adequate to meet demand (12). Current ship traffic counts indicate that this is a realistic assumption, even though it presupposes that only one vessel at a time will be in the tunnel (12). The third condition is the expectation that the tunnel will

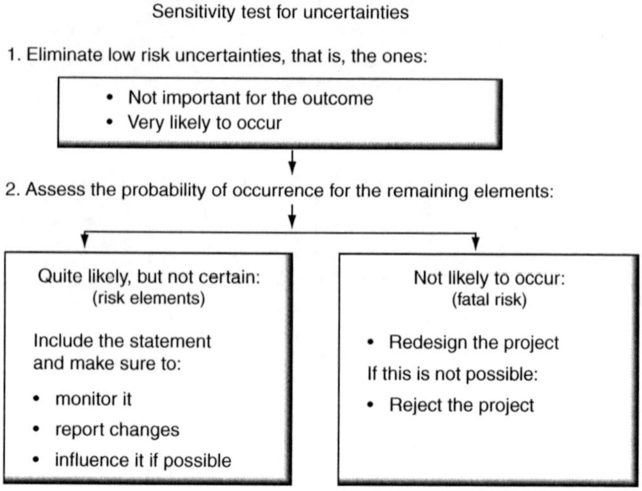


*Figure 20.4* Procedure for assessing uncertainties

operate efficiently with no major accidents (13). It seems reasonable to assume that this will hold with acceptable probability.

## Fatal risk

At the other extreme are the uncertainty components with low probabilities of occurrence. As the consequences of their occurrences already have been identified as major, these are the *fatal risks*. An acceptable project concept can have no fatal risks. In this example, three such risks have been identified.

The first concerns the extent to which the project is socio-economically viable (1), which is closely connected to whether the Parliament decides to fund the project (2). A favourable Parliamentary decision brings in a third component, whether the budget is adequate (3). The present Norwegian Coastal Administration study concludes is that the project isn't profitable in financial terms, but takes no stand on the degree to which non-financial consequences may alter viability. Another aspect is that socio-economic profitability depends on building costs, seen in the light of the cost estimates most likely being highly uncertain. Several involved in the media debate feel that the costs are grossly under-estimated. If this is the case, viability will be correspondingly low and one might question whether or not the project should be implemented. The approach used here gives us two general choices in the situation of being faced with a fatal risk. The first is to change the concept to reduce the risk. If that isn't possible, the concept must be abandoned. In the Coastal Administration study, several alternatives with differing tunnel locations and tunnel cross-sections were evaluated. None of the alternatives were found to be socio-economically viable. This implies that the only possible conclusion is to abandon the concept.

**Real risk**

*Real risk* lies between these two extremes, as shown in the middle column in Figure 20.3. Here are risk factors that individually are tolerable, but require risk management in the implementation phase. In other words, happenings related to these components are monitored and subjected to influence, with registration of changes seen. However, with a great number of real risks, the overall situation may be unacceptable. So the multitude of real risks may constitute a fatal risk.

This is easily seen in this example, because some of the uncertainty components listed are directly connected to matters decisive to the socio-economic viability of the project. Seven uncertainty components are listed. For example, the geological conditions will determine whether blasting (4) and securing (5) the tunnel will proceed as expected or will encounter problems. The upshot will influence costs. The study did not clarify this matter.

The remaining uncertainty components concern traffic volume and utility of the endeavour. Actual figures less than those projected will negatively influence viability. The first assumption is that a major of ship traffic will use the tunnel (6). The tunnel capacity is estimated to be equivalent to upwards of 84 per cent of the traffic round the Stad Peninsula. But many factors affecting volume are uncertain, including the degree of exploitation, which sectors of the ship trade will traffic it, whether use will be regular or sporadic in bad weather periods, etc. For example, the study assumed that the Coastal Express ships would traffic the tunnel, but media reports maintain that the relevant shipowners doubt that their ships will use it. Another uncertainty component is the assumed establishment of a coastal express service of viable volume between two main coastal towns (7). Whether there's an adequate traffic base is unclear. Moreover, a major share of the sea freight traffic is expected to go through the tunnel (9). It's also not clear as to whether these ships will sail into the fjords to avoid the waters around the Stad Peninsula or whether their owners will prefer that they sail farther out where conditions are less problematic. Another condition that also influences the socio-economic benefit is the extent to which the spin-off effects of the tunnel will include stimulation of local economic activity (14). This aspect has been much debated, and opinion on it varies. Finally there's the question as to whether the tunnel will trigger an upswing in the export of fresh fish to central Europe or whether transport will continue as now, by truck southwards. Opinion on this matter also varies.

The above aspects permit closer examination of the initial evaluation of the project concept of section 19.4. Over all, there are more risks than opportunities that might substantiate the project. In all, 10 risk factors that can negatively influence the project have been identified. Three of them are deemed fatal. Therefore, there are no grounds for financing the project.

The final decision of Parliament is nonetheless uncertain, as politics is not just about logic, but also about political prioritization and positioning. Therefore, the rational often has been voted down and conclusions shelved as a result of political compromise.

# 21
# Strategic Frames for Implementation

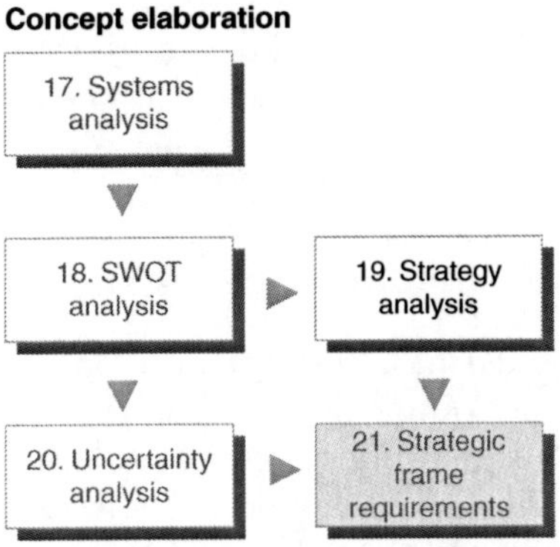


*The logical framework yields a description of the project concept in a strategic perspective. Uncertainty associated with a concept makes it difficult to realize projects as assumed. Hence, flexibility must be allowed in implementation. That said, the flexibility should not lead to excessive aberration in strategic guidance. So strategic frame requirements should be set up for those who implement a project.*

## 21.1 Strategic guidance and tactical flexibility

Two principal prerequisites for project success are that the front-end phase results in a sensible *strategy* and that the implementation phase affords the *tactical* flexibility needed to accommodate promising technical options in situations that may arise. This was discussed in Chapter 7.

The distinction between strategic guidance and tactical flexibility is significant in project management. In cases when a project is both financed and implemented by a single organization, conflicts of interest at the borderline between the strategic and the tactical are avoided. The organization itself can determine the extent to which tactical choices that depart from the project strategic guidance may be made. However, in many cases, the commissioner is not the same as the contractor. So, considerable conflicts of interest may arise between them, not least in the sharing of risk. The implementation of a project is influenced by internal conditions and by the surroundings with which uncertainty is associated. A choice made may result in desirable or undesirable results and consequently imply risk. The commissioner may choose to bear the relevant risk or may transfer it to the implementing party. A commissioner who opts for making tactical choices also incurs the relevant risks and must sustain any losses that arise. Likewise, a contractor allowed to make tactical choices must also bear the relevant risks. In such instances, the contractor normally will require a risk premium or a price differential to compensate for possible losses.

## 21.2 Contractual assignment of risk

Risk may be transferred in a contract or a clause in a contract. The commissioner and the contractor both wish to work together to implement the project. Both aim to reduce uncertainty. But they also have basic contrasts of interests. Simplified to the extreme, the commissioner aims to implement the project as initially assumed to the lowest possible price. Likewise, the contractor aims to maximize profit and consequently seeks to cut costs, perhaps to the detriment of quality. The way this divergence is handled is determined mostly by the nature of the contract between the commissioner and the contractor. The two extremes are the reimbursement contract and the fixed-price contract, as shown in Figure 21.1.

In a *reimbursement contract*, the commissioner pays an hourly rate and covers the costs incurred in implementing the project. The commissioner then enjoys the advantage of maximum leeway to influence the implementation and make changes on the way. But the commissioner then also hazards paying for all changes, mistakes made, low productivity and other conditions that increase costs. The contractor has no incentive to limit costs, so overruns might be appreciable for the commissioner. So the commissioner will need an extensive control facility that covers project costs, progress and quality. The contractor hazards neither loss nor the additional expenses of any unfortunate choices made by the commissioner. However, the contractor's potential profit is limited.

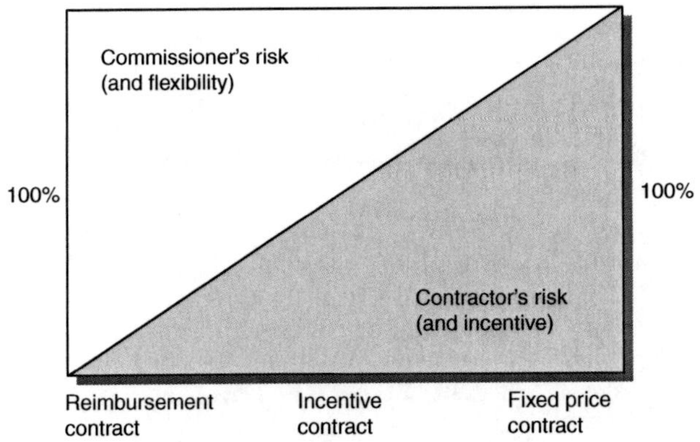


*Figure 21.1* The contractual assignment of risk has two extremes. The reimbursement contract provides the commissioner considerable influence but only a vague cost picture. The fixed-price contract assigns risk to the contractor. Between these two extremes is the incentive contract that divides risk between the commissioner and the contractor

The situation is the converse under a *fixed-price contract*. The commissioner transfers all risk to the contractor. The contractual price is an all-inclusive amount, usually based on the accepted bid from a round of bidding between competing contractors. The commissioner pays the agreed sum regardless of the costs that the contractor may incur in implementing the project. The contractor then suffers all loss should the price be too low or the costs higher than anticipated. But the contractor also may realize a considerable profit should costs be lower than anticipated.

Under a fixed-price contract, the commissioner cannot influence or change the project during its implementation, within the terms of the applicable contract. The contractor will have a strong incentive to cut costs. Hence, the commissioner risks low quality, unless quality is contractually specified in advance and can be verified. The commissioner also runs the risk of the contractor lacking the financial strength to cover losses that may arise in implementation, so that the project slows to a halt before completion, such as by a contractor declaring bankruptcy. In turn, this can markedly increase the cost of a project.

## 21.3 Strategic frames

In many cases, commissioners prefer fixed-price contracts so as to reduce risks and costs. The roles of the commissioner and the contractor then

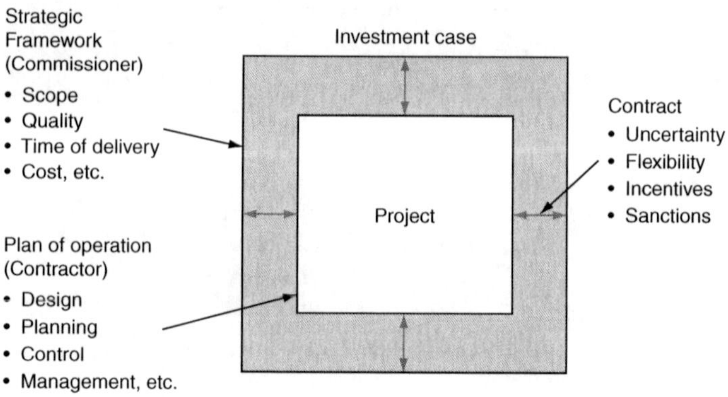


*Figure 21.2* Successful projects presuppose tactical flexibility with strategic frames in implementation. This requires clarification of the strategic framework conditions that apply to the contractor

become clear if the *project* is distinguished from the *strategic frame* within which it operates, as illustrated in Figure 21.2.

The commissioner has little or no freedom to influence implementation under the relevant contract and consequently will seek maximum precision and detailing of the strategic framework conditions. However, greater detail decreases the latitude for tactical manoeuvring and thereby reduces the chances of implementing the project as foreseen. The contractor most likely will stipulate the flexibility needed to implement the project, illustrated by the gap between the project and the strategic frame shown in Figure 21.2. The control system applied needs to be designed to ensure project conduct within the strategic frame yet permit exploiting flexibility.

The transfer of risk comes at the expense of costs, time and quality, borne by the commissioner. Both the commissioner and the contractor will be interested in a realistic stipulation of the risk increment early on in the concept phase. This can best be done using probabilistic or stochastic analyses. An example of probabilistic cost estimation is included in Chapter 22, and an example of probabilistic progress analysis is included in Chapter 25.

The above discussion concerns the principles of contractual agreements between commissioners and contractors. The principles are equally applicable in the public sector, as in investment cases between ministries and executing agencies, between national and local governments, between donor and recipient countries, etc. Investment cases and projects customarily are distinguished from each other. The investment case then may be regarded as a financial instrument used by the initiating commissioner in planning, initiating and implementing a specific project. The investment case is delineated by the strategic frame, in other words the overriding strategic description of what is sought within which financial order of magnitude. On the other hand, a project is the executing party's construction that is a complementary, planned set of activities that are necessary to attain a specified goal within a stipulated budget to a deadline.

The same is true in the private sectors whenever investors are principally involved in business cases and contractors consequently are involved in projects. Interdependency then arises in a chain of stakeholders that comprises the initiating/financing party, the managing party and the contractor and subcontractors, where responsibilities and risks should be assigned in ways most suitable to implementing the project. This is illustrated by the following example in international development aid.

## 21.4 Example: Building a university complex

A developing country requested financial aid and technical assistance to build capability and initiate research in monitoring and prevention of natural phenomena such as earthquakes and volcanic eruptions. An industrial country with the relevant expertise agreed to support the project. It is well experienced in joint initiatives in developing countries in which involvement in planning and implementation has been extensive. This approach has incurred administrative burdens and has driven up project costs. Consequently the donor country's policy is now to minimalize its involvement in the design, organization and implementation of projects. At the same time, it seeks assurance that projects are implemented as assumed.

In the recipient country, public investment projects often are considerably delayed and suffer cost overruns. Consequently a model is sought in which construction is done by a consortium comprising a major international building contractor and a group of local contractors. The relevant professional services will be provided by the existing professional community in the country in cooperation with research institutes and companies in the donor country.

A central question is which control parameters should be included in the strategic frame to ensure that the project is implemented in a manner acceptable to the donor country. Experience indicates that there should be few control parameters. The fewer they are, the more the recipient country can assume responsibility and the more the donor country can monitor and steer the project.

In this case, ideally, the number of control parameters may be reduced to less than ten, provided that the strategic steering document or agreement puts forth the following conditions:

1. The outputs and goals are specified and dated.
2. A concurrent description of the needs of the involved parties is compiled.
3. There's an overall project budget.
4. There are time schedules for construction and professional services.
5. Building construction shall be based on a recognized quality standard.
6. Design shall be by a qualified architectural company with relevant experience.
7. The involved parties and the extent and duration of their professional involvement shall be stated.
8. Follow-up and quality control shall be done by a qualified, independent entity.

Provided that these conditions are set at realistic levels, the entire project can be handled via a responsible party in the recipient country, in this case jointly with a corresponding institution in the donor country, and a consortium of suppliers without much involvement by the financing party. The donor country will require that these strategic requirements not be exceeded and will intervene should they be. Provided that the costs of handling risk are realistically stipulated, it should be possible for the institution to implement the project without cost overruns, and the chances of the financing party realizing the project are correspondingly high.

Use of this type of frame steering addresses a considerable, cost escalating problem commonplace in development projects, that control, quality assurance and administration of such projects have often been provided by high-paid experts from donor countries, permanently stationed in recipient countries to follow up projects.

# 22
# Top-Down Probability-Based Cost Estimation

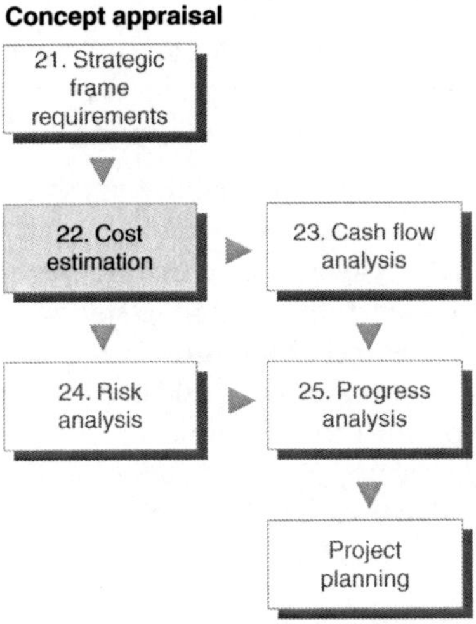


*Compiling cost estimates for major projects can be exhaustive, time-consuming and expensive. Nonetheless experience indicates that estimate precision can be poor. So the less comprehensive probability-based cost estimate is an attractive alternative. It is based on expert evaluations in teams, who can rapidly arrive at relatively reliable cost estimates.*

## 22.1 Resources and precision

Cost calculations normally are based on fixed cost estimates.[1] A cost calculation may be a simple overview at a high aggregation level with

*Table 22.1* Two types of costs estimation

| Deterministic calculation of cost | Stochastic cost estimation |
|---|---|
| • 'Bottom-up'. Adding up detailed level cost components | • 'From above'. Cost breakdown based on stochastic estimation |
| • High level of detailing | • Detailing used to reduce variance in estimates |
| • Based on existing/projected prices | • Based on systematic estimation |

only a few items.[2] If so, the uncertainty of the result normally is considerable. A cost calculation also may be meticulously detailed. That reduces uncertainty. But for major projects, the computation often is exhaustive and expensive. It's also extremely rigid in the sense that considerable revision may be required should fundamental assumptions be changed in the project concept. Hence, early on in the concept phase, detailed cost overviews often are counterproductive.

An alternative is to perform a probability-based cost calculation, also known as stochastic cost estimation. It starts with a simple cost calculation at a high aggregation level, where the project is broken down only in its major few components. In addition to stating the expected costs of the individual items, the uncertainties of each are indicated. Thereafter the components where estimates are considered most uncertain are further detailed, step by step, until their assumed uncertainties are reduced to acceptable levels. Experience with such procedures indicates that they rapidly and inexpensively can yield cost estimates that subsequently prove to provide relative good pictures of actual costs (see Table 22.1).

Stochastic cost estimation may be carried out using mathematical and statistical calculation, as in the example of this chapter. But it's usually carried out using Mote Carlo simulation, as discussed and used in Chapter 25. In both cases, the starting point is that each individual item in the calculation can be expressed in terms of a probability distribution of known mean and spread (see Figure 22.1). The costs are summed according to statistical rules for independent variables.[3] The spread is an expression of the uncertainty of an estimate. The sum of the means of the estimates gives the most likely expected value, and the spread is expressed in terms of the standard deviation of the probability distribution of the aggregate.

Stochastic cost estimation comprises a systematic approach to evaluating economic problems that embrace uncertainty. It is particularly

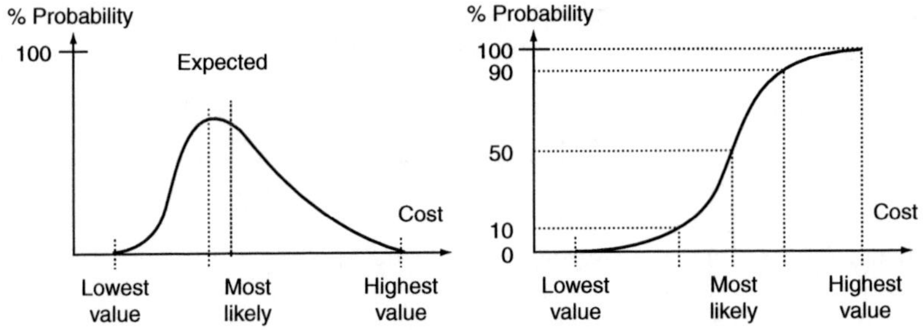


*Figure 22.1* In stochastic cost estimation the total is based on estimates of the items and the assumption that their values assume probability distributions. Input values are the lowest, most likely and the highest value in the distribution. On this basis the expected value and standard deviation is determined (the curve to the left). The total cost for the project is presented in terms of a probability distribution where the cost and corresponding probability of occurrence is stipulated, as in the cumulative distribution to the right, where 10%, 50% and 90% probabilities of occurrence are plotted

suited to estimation early on in a project, before details are immersed in total engineering. Its procedure may be divided into six steps.

1. Define what the estimate is to include, that is, the estimate object.
2. Divide the estimate object into principal items that are assumed to be independent of each other.
3. Estimate the magnitude of each item by assessing the costs, that is, a lowest value (minimum), a highest value (maximum) and a most likely value. See Figure 22.2.
4. Calculate or estimate the expected value and spread of each individual item and the sum of the individual sub items, that is, the expected total cost as well as its spread.
5. Consider the items having the largest spreads and divide them up into independent sub items.
6. Repeat steps 3 and 4 until the spread of the total cost is deemed reasonable or acceptable or when further improvement cannot be made by dividing up the estimate.

Valid statistical calculation in cases like this requires that the items of the estimate are independent, so the cost picture should be divided to ensure that is the case to the degree possible. Fine detailing increases the chance of dependence between items, so the risk of overlooking uncertainty increases with the degree of detailing.

Experientally some conditions may influence all or most items in an estimate, such as the weather for certain types of projects, labour status, quality level, project management, etc. These are called general aspects. Compensatory factors are used throughout the calculations to systematically adjust the estimate for general aspects.

## 22.2 Example: Building a shopping centre

A centrally located shopping centre is to be built to serve several small communities. The project also requires building access roads and a car park to serve the centre. Early on in the appraisal of various concepts, there's not enough information to support a deterministic cost estimate. Instead a method for successive stochastic calculation is used to generate an initial overall estimate of project costs. Experience in previous shopping centre projects indicates that final costs often exceed initial budgets. The total price for similar projects has been NOK 50 to 200 million. The process and the estimate follow below, step by step.

### Define and delimit the project

A realistic estimate presupposes a clearly defined project and an overview of the principal conditions that may influence planning and implementation. The persons involved in the analysis must uniformly understand the extent and quality of the components of the project. This requires preliminary work to acquire information, define components and precisely define the applicable limits.

### Assemble an expert group

The analysis will be based on planning meetings of a group of experts who together work out the cost estimates to be included in the overall estimate. The figures that they put forth will be based on a combination of subjective assessments and consensus in the group. The group should be a broad composite of people who:

- have relevant expertise
- are experienced in similar projects
- can assess the project from various aspects
- represent different interests relative to the project

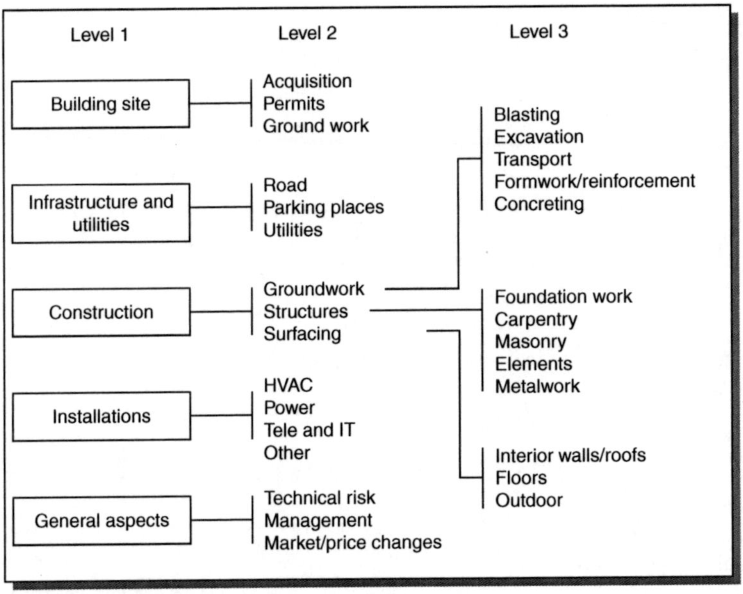


*Figure 22.2* Splitting up a project into its constituent items

The planning meetings are led by a facilitator who is independent of the parties in the project. The facilitator should lead discussion and be impartial concerning content but should ensure that the process is correctly carried through.

## Split up the object of calculation

The estimate entails splitting the project up into items that form a *complementary* ensemble covering all parts of the project. At the same time, the items must be *mutually exclusive* with no latitude for overlap.

This is illustrated in Figure 22.2. At the top aggregation level, designated Level 1, there are only four concrete cost items in addition to a compensatory item covering general aspects that may influence other items to increase or decrease overall cost. Normally several such compensatory items may be included in an analysis. But for simplicity in this example, there's only one such item.

In Figure 22.2, Level 1 items are split up into sub items at Level 2. In turn, the Construction sub items of Level 2 are split up further into specific

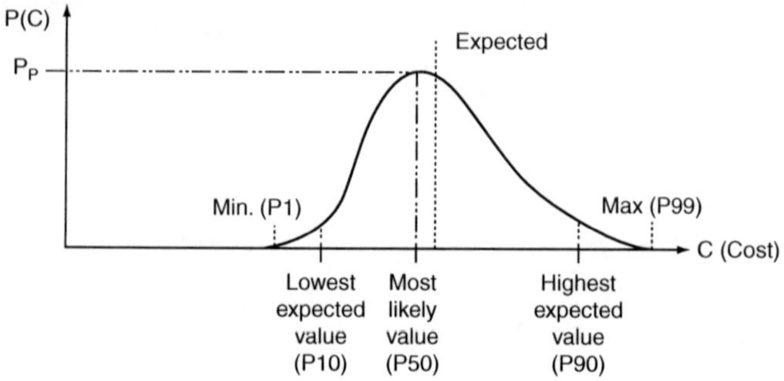


*Figure 22.3* The cost estimates are of the lowest, most likely and highest values in a skew distribution

tasks at Level 3. That said, the picture of the project is still without much detail.

### Cost approximation

The principal task of the expert group is to collectively agree upon the most realistic cost estimates. The estimate for each item comprises a range of three cost values:

1. Minimum – the lowest expected cost value
2. Maximum – the highest expected cost value
3. The most likely cost value. This is equal to the value customarily used in a deterministic estimate.

The values are used in an approximation to delineate a probability distribution for each cost estimate. The computational model customarily assumes a skewed distribution as shown in Figure 22.3. Consequently the calculated expected value usually is slightly higher than the most likely value.

Simulation or statistical models are used to include the uncertainties of the individual estimates. The models are not explained further here, as they are described in the literature (Austeng and Hugsted 1995; Lichtenberg 2000). The following numerical example illustrates their principle.

### Initial estimate

The computational model yields an expected value and a standard deviation for each item, according to the relevant type of probability

*Table 22.2* Rough estimates and corresponding output values

| Step 1: Initial estimates | Cost estimate | | | Expected value | Standard deviation | Variance |
|---|---|---|---|---|---|---|
| | P10 | Likely | P90 | | | |
| 1 Building site | 5 | 15 | 25 | 15 | 4 | 16 |
| 2 Infrastructure/ connections | 5 | 8 | 15 | 8.8 | 2 | 4 |
| 3 Construction | 10 | 20 | 40 | 22 | 6 | 36 |
| 4 Installations | 20 | 35 | 80 | 41 | 12 | 144 |
| 5 General aspects | 10 | 20 | 50 | 24 | 8 | 64 |
| | | 98 | | 110.8 | 16.25 | 264 |

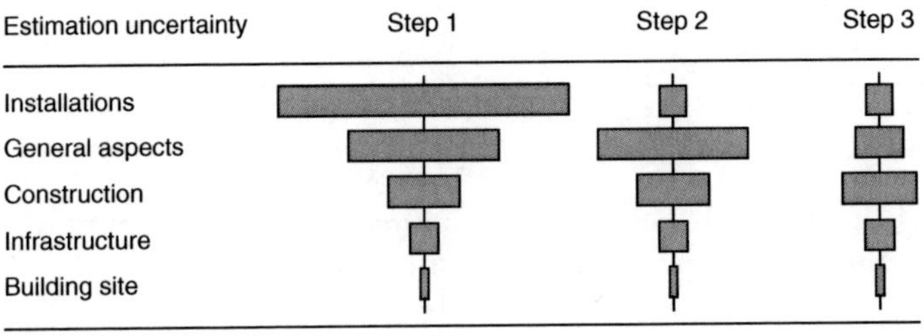


*Figure 22.4* Prioritization list (tornado diagram). Variances of the estimates in the first three steps of the estimation are shown

distribution. The following example uses a skewed continuous probability distribution (Erlang distribution)

The expected value is EV = (P10 + 3*Likely + P90)/5
The standard deviation SD = (P90 – P10)/5

The cost estimates are in NOK million.

Subsequent to the first step of the process, that is the analysis at Level 1 in Figure 22.3, if the expert group's estimates are summed to a most likely cost, the deterministic cost will be NOK 98 million. However, the stochastic estimate yields an expected value of NOK 110.8 million. The standard deviation is calculated for each item on the basis of the lowest expected, most likely and highest expected values (Step 4 above). The variance is the square of the standard deviation. The calculated variances are shown in Figure 22.4. As can be seen, the uncertainties of

*Table 22.3* Detailing of estimates, Step 2 and corresponding output values

| **Step 2: Detailing** (Item 4 is split into four parts) | **Cost estimate** Min | Likely | Max | **Expected value** | **Standard deviation** | **Variance** |
|---|---|---|---|---|---|---|
| 1 Building site | 5 | 15 | 25 | 15 | 4 | 16 |
| 2 Infrastructure/ connections | 5 | 8 | 15 | 8.8 | 2 | 4 |
| 3 Construction | 10 | 20 | 40 | 22 | 6 | 36 |
| 4 Installations | | | | 42.2 | | 13 |
| 4.1 HVAC | 5 | 10 | 15 | 10 | 2 | 4 |
| 4.2 Power | 10 | 15 | 20 | 15 | 2 | 4 |
| 4.3 Tele and IT | 10 | 15 | 20 | 15 | 2 | 4 |
| 4.4 Other | 0 | 2 | 5 | 2.2 | 1 | 1 |
| 5 General aspects | 10 | 20 | 50 | 24 | 8 | 64 |
| | | 105 | | 112 | 11.5 | 133 |

items 4 (installations) and 5 (general aspects) are far greater than those of the other items. The standard deviation of the total estimate is:

$$\text{Standard deviation} \quad SD = Var^{1/2} = 264^{1/2} = \text{NOK } 16.25 \text{ million}$$

This represents about 15 per cent of the expected value. Accordingly an effort is made to reduce the spread of expected values by going into more detailing of some individual items.

## Detailed estimate

Consequently the next step is to focus on the cost item having the greatest variance, in this case item 4, installations, by breaking it down into four parts, as listed in Table 22.3.

As shown in the columns of Table 22.3, the result of the breakdown is to reduce the variance appreciably, in this case from 144 to 13. The total expected value now increases to 112, and in this case the standard deviation is reduced to:

$$\text{Standard deviation} = 133^{-2} = \text{NOK } 11.5 \text{ million}$$

This is about 10 per cent of the expected value. The effect in terms of reduced uncertainty of the total estimate for item 4 is illustrated in Figure 22.4.

*Table 22.4* Detailing of estimates, Step 3 and corresponding output values

| Step 3: Detailing (Item 4 is split into four parts) | Cost estimate | | | Expected value | Standard deviation | Variance |
|---|---|---|---|---|---|---|
| | Min | Likely | Max | | | |
| 1 Building site | 5 | 15 | 25 | 15 | 4 | 16 |
| 2 Infrastructure/ connections | 5 | 8 | 15 | 8.8 | 2 | 4 |
| 3 Construction | 10 | 20 | 40 | 22 | 6 | 36 |
| 4 Installations | | 42 | | 42.2 | | 13 |
| 5 General aspects | | | | 42.2 | | 13 |
| 5.1 Technical risk | 10 | 15 | 30 | 17 | 4 | 16 |
| 5.2 Management | 0 | 1 | 10 | 2.6 | 2 | 4 |
| 5.3 Market price changes | 0 | 3 | 10 | 3.8 | 2 | 4 |
| | | 104 | | 111.4 | 9.6 | 93 |

## Further detailing

The estimate is detailed further by reducing the uncertainties in the estimates of the individual items so that the total estimate lies within acceptable limits. Consider item 5 in Table 22.4, the general aspects that are broken down into three sub items, each with a cost estimate at Level 3 in Figure 22.2. The breakdown reduces the variance from 64 to 24. The result of the estimate in this round is that the expected value goes down to NOK 111.4 million, while the standard deviation goes down to NOK 9.6 million, corresponding to about 9 per cent of the expected value. This is illustrated in Figure 22.4, in which the original tornado diagram at Step 1 approaches a slender column at Step 3 that shows regular low uncertainties in its estimates.

## 8. Evaluate results

The overall estimate for the project is illustrated in the cumulative probability distribution of Figure 22.5. As can be seen from the curve for Step 3, the expert group estimate of NOK 111.4 million suggests an outcome space between about NOK 80 and 140 million. The total cost will be less than NOK 123 million with a probability of 90 per cent. At the same time, it's 90 per cent probable that the total cost will be greater than NOK 96 million.

This method includes several simplifications and builds on experiential data as well as subjective and collective judgement instead of facts.

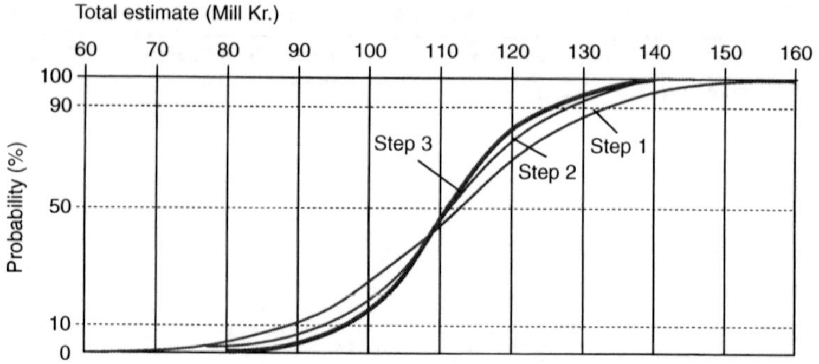


*Figure 22.5* S-curve showing the cumulative probability for the possible outcomes of the total cost

Experience implies that input data error normally is greater than calculation error. Consequently emphasis should be placed on the acquisition of information and the composition of the expert group. The communication process itself between participants, is essential, experience with this type of stochastic estimation demonstrates that the utility may be great even though the degree of detailing is small. The method is used first and foremost in cases in which:

1. the project basis is incomplete or uncertain
2. a quick cost estimate is needed
3. several alternatives are to be evaluated

The method principally supplements other methods and is suitable as a first approximation to clarify the need for further inquiry. In most cases, Monte Carlo simulation is used to process data. The procedure is the same as described above, but data processing is iterative and entails sampling random values from each cost element and summing them to a total cost. The values are sampled according to the probability distribution associated with each element. This is repeated, often several thousand times in the computer. The result is a probability distribution of total expected values, such as that shown in Figure 22.5. The application of Monte Carlo simulation is further illustrated by an example in Chapter 25.

# 23
# Assessing Profitability

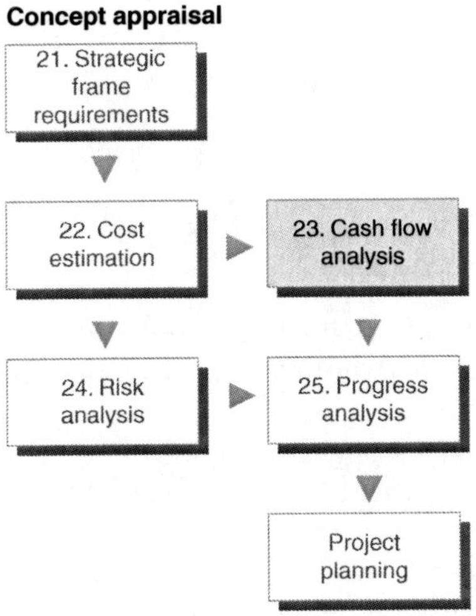


*Once probabilistic cost figures are available, the next step is to calculate anticipated income to portray profitability. This chapter comprises a brief overview of frequently used cost-benefit criteria and of profitability calculation.*

## 23.1 Expressions of costs and benefits

Evaluating profitability[1] is central in the choice of concept. Needless to say, project profitability can be proven only retrospectively. But in the front-end phase, profitability may be appraised, mostly on the bases of assumptions and judgement. Hence, there's often a need for stochastic

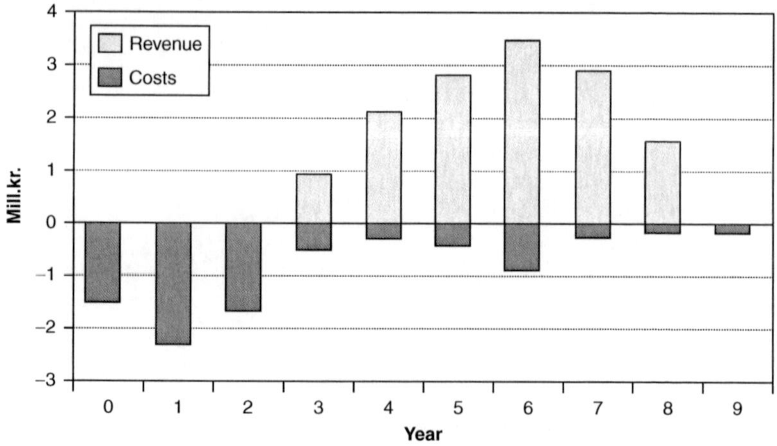


*Figure 23.1* Cash flow over the lifetime of a project

analyses that can derive meaningful figures for costs and benefits from probability distributions.

Profitability evaluations usually build on knowledge or on assumptions of a project's anticipated future cash flow, or inflow of income and outflow of expenses over time. The expenses consist mostly of investments usually made in a project's implementation phase as well as the operational costs and other running expenses in the operational phase. Income flows in over a longer period of time, after the investments are made, as shown in the bar chart of Figure 23.1. The cash flow is the annual difference between income/revenue and expenses.

The figures behind the bar chart are listed with explanations in Figure 23.2. They may be used in various ways to calculate project profitability. Briefly, the most commonly used profitability criteria are:

- Net cash flow
- Payback period
- Yield on investment
- Discounted investment
- Net present value (NPV)
- Internal rate of return (IRR)

Net cash flow — Investment — Payback period

| Year | Sum | 0 | 1 | 2 | 3 | 4 | 5 | 6 | 7 | 8 | 9 |
|---|---|---|---|---|---|---|---|---|---|---|---|
| Revenue | 13,6 | | | | 0,9 | 2,1 | 2,8 | 3,4 | 2,9 | 1,5 | |
| Costs | –8,3 | –1,5 | –2,3 | –1,7 | –0,5 | –0,3 | –0,4 | –0,9 | –0,3 | –0,2 | –0,2 |
| Cash flow | 5,3 | –1,5 | –2,3 | –1,7 | 0,4 | 1,8 | 2,4 | 2,5 | 2,6 | 1,3 | –0,2 |
| Discounting factor % | | 1 | 0,93 | 0,87 | 0,82 | 0,76 | 0,71 | 0,67 | 0,62 | 0,58 | 0,54 |
| Discounting cash flow | 2,2 | –1,5 | –2,15 | –1,48 | 0,33 | 1,37 | 1,71 | 1,67 | 1,62 | 0,76 | –0,11 |

Net present value (NPV) — Discounted investment

*Figure 23.2* Undiscounted and discounted cash flow in a project. Amounts in NOK million

Profitability may be roughly estimated without discounting, that is, without adjusting for the fluctuating values of capital over time. For example, a simple estimation may be made to calculate *net cash flow* by adding up contributions over time and assuming that a project is profitable if its cash flow is positive. However, this gives a flawed picture for a long-term project. The net cash flow in the example of Figure 23.2 is NOK 5.3 million, which implies that the project is profitable on the basis of such a simple procedure.

A correspondingly simple criterion is the calculate *the payback period*, that is, the elapsed time before the cash flow sums to zero. The shorter the payback period, the more profitable the project is assumed to be. This criterion gives no indication of the yield of the project. In the project of Figure 23.2, the investment over the first three years amounts to NOK 5.5 million. Adding the subsequent annual cash flow contributions indicates that the investment is paid back in five years.

A third criterion that indicates what may be expected of a project is the investment yield, expressed as the *benefit/cost ratio (BCR)*. The yield in Figure 23.2 is the difference between income and expenses, that is 13.6 – 8.3 = NOK 5.3 million. The investment is NOK 5.5 million. So the non-discounted yield on investment is 5.3/5.6 = 0.96, which implies low profitability.

Discounted cash flows are used in profitability calculations of projects that last several years. The annual discount rate in the example of Figure 23.3 is set at 7 per cent over duration of the project. The discount factor is calculated as $1/(1 + r)^n$ where r is the discount rate and n is the

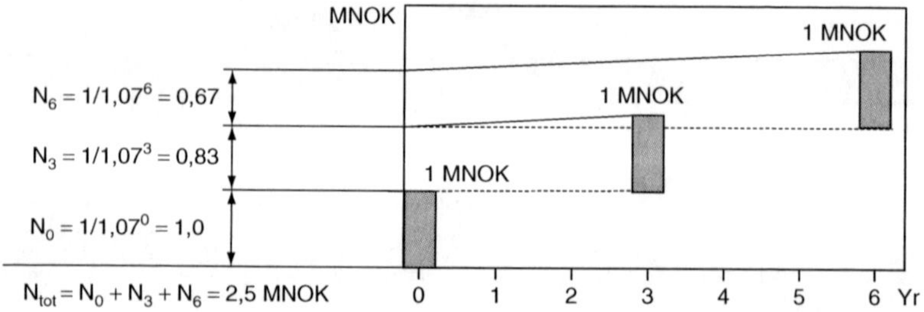


*Figure 23.3* Net present value (NPV) of an investment of NOK 3 million paid back over six years at a discount rate of 7%. The NPV of a future investment corresponds to the amount that must be deposited in a bank at 7% interest so it may be available at the time of investment. In this case, the NPV of the investment is NOK 2.5 million

number of years from year zero for the calculation. The discount factor indicates how much the value of future cash flows must be reduced relative to the value in year zero.

Considering the effect of discounting, the discounted yield is NOK 2.2 million and the discounted investment is NOK 5.13 million. So the *discounted yield on investment* is 2.2/5.13 = 0.42, substantially lower than the non-discounted figure.

The *net present value* (NPV) is a profitability criterion often used for appraising long-term projects. The NPV is defined as the discounted present value of a sequence of cash flows over the lifetime of the project, based on the discount rate chosen. If the discount rate is set equal to the market rate, the NPV will show a value increase attained by the project compared to investment in instruments with yields corresponding to the market rate. The NPV also is a direct expression of the profit that the project will show. The criterion for profitability is that the NPV is positive. A project is unprofitable if its NPV is negative.

This is equivalent to saying that a project is attractive if the yield on money invested is greater than the discount rate. In other words, the discount rate is an expression of the minimum yield required of the investment in a project. In the example of Figure 23.2, the NPV is calculated at NOK 2.2 million, which is positive and indicates that the project is profitable over time.

The NPV is easy to use and expresses the absolute value of the yield, such as in monetary units. However, the NPV does not indicate the yield relative to investment. That may be calculated using the discounted yield on investment, as discussed above, or *the internal rate of return* (IRR) of the project, which measures relative profitability, that is, yield per monetary unit invested.

The IRR is the interest rate that gives a zero NPV. It's a direct expression of the anticipated yield of a project. Seeing that the IRR is independent of the magnitude of the cash flow, it is amenable as a general criterion that may be used to compare the profitability of projects of varying sizes. Consequently the IRR is the most used profitability criterion.

Regardless of the profitability criterion chosen, the figures used should be subjected to probability assessment. In Chapter 22, a method was described to calculate probabilistic cost estimates in projects. Likewise, a probabilistic calculation of project income may be used in a probabilistic expression of profitability, such as the expected value of the NPV expressed in a probability distribution.

Further discussion of project profitability appraisals is beyond the scope of this book; further details are available in the literature, such as Bøhren and Gjærum 1999.

# 24
# Risk Analysis

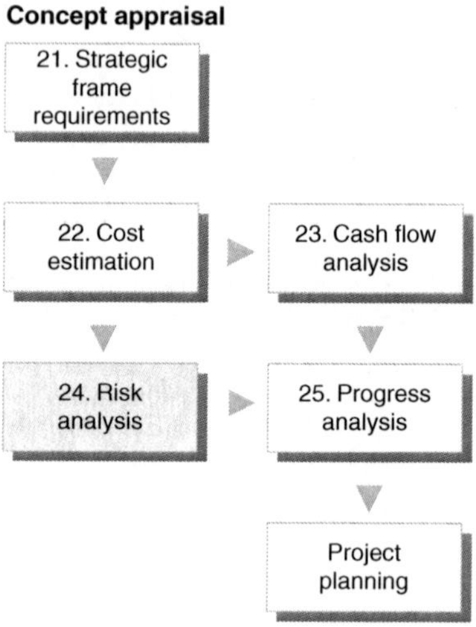


*All projects involve risk in the sense that the result is not exactly as expected. Many aspects affect risk. Some of them cannot be foreseen. Risk is associated with the degree of uncertainty associated with a project. The degree of certainty that contributes to reducing risk is based either on knowledge of and experience with other projects or on the ability of project management to handle uncertainty. This means that risk may be regarded to be a function of the uniqueness of the project and the experience of the project organization.*

## 24.1 Quantified expressions of expected value

In general, risk is defined as a function of two parameters, the probability of an event happening and the consequence of the event should it happen, that is:

$$\text{Risk} = f\cdot(\text{probability, consequence})$$

Once the magnitudes of the two parameters are known, the risk function gives the degree of risk. Of the many conditions entailing risk that affect projects, only a few are worth considering. They may be identified in an analysis that permits their ranking.

The simplest definition of risk is the expected value, that is, the product of probability and consequence. True, this aggregate expression of risk yields figures that can be ranked, but at the same time it suffers loss of perspective of risk. A drawback of using the expected value alone is that a risk with a low probability of occurrence may be ignored, even though its consequence may be extensive, perhaps catastrophically so, because the product of the two parameters is small. The impact of nuclear reactor accidents is an example. Such projects may have fatal consequences for thousands, or perhaps hundreds of thousands of people. So even though the probability of an accident is very small, its risk cannot be ignored.

In complex systems in which many independent situations interact, the risks of the individual situations are usually analyzed, but the risk of simultaneous occurrence of several independent situations usually is not, because the probability of its occurrence is very small. But such unlikely events must be viewed in terms of the consequences of such compound failures. Whenever the consequences may be extensive, it's wrong to ignore the risk, even though its expected value is negligible. For example, the gas tragedy of December 1984 at the pesticide plant at Bhopal, India, was due to 30 failures that occurred simultaneously. The probability of the happening was extremely small, but nonetheless it occurred and caused more than 10,000 deaths and more than 100,000 injuries. The Chernobyl nuclear reactor accident of April 1986 was caused by six human errors. If they had not occurred simultaneously, the accident would not have happened.

## 24.2 Risk matrix

The qualitative aspect of a risk may be illustrated in a risk matrix, since this provides a two-dimensional view of consequence and probability where these are ranked. The matrix provides a picture of the nuances of risk relative to each other and independent of the risk calculation

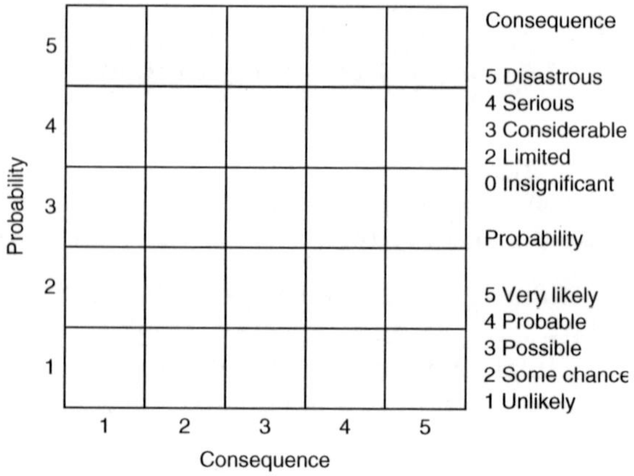


*Figure 24.1* The risk matrix provides an overview of risk level and the magnitude of the principal parameters determining risk

based on the above equation. It also depicts the risk profile of a project subjected to several risks and may also be used to spell out whether risks are acceptable or unacceptable, as in the examples above.

A simple risk matrix is shown in Figure 24.1, in which both probability and consequence are ranked in five levels. This is the same matrix as that of Figure 20.2, used for the crude categories of uncertainty components. In this case, the matrix comprises an outcome space of 25 cells. Risk expressed in expected value will range from low in the bottom left to high in the upper right cell of the matrix. The matrix is a sort of map showing the locations of risks relative to each other. It portrays the risk profile and is a useful tool, among other things for enabling an overall view and for selecting the risk factors that should be further analyzed.

## 24.3 Identifying risk factors

Many tools and techniques are available to identify risk factors. The systems analysis of Chapter 17 focuses on needs and requirement specifications. The SWOT analysis of Chapter 18 focuses on the internal weaknesses and external threats associated with a project concept. The strategy analysis of Chapter 19 uses a logical framework to chart uncertainty factors. Scenario techniques may also be employed to analyze a project in the time dimension, from various perspectives, and risk factors may be identified in various ways, such as by viewing the project concept and the strategy as problems, systematically from various aspects, such as environmental, organizational, socio-economical or financial. Such matters are beyond the scope of this book and won't be further discussed here.

## 24.4 Classifying risk

Classifying risk requires a means of quantifying probability and consequence. This is true, regardless of whether risk is expressed in expected value or in another way. Yet, quantifying the parameters of probability and consequence may be difficult. *Consequence* may be expressed in many ways and units that cannot easily be compared, such as monetary units, time, damages, workload, etc. Ideally a common parameter would be desirable in project evaluation. But as for cost-benefit analyses, not everything can be expressed in monetary terms. There are many examples of validity problems in cases where analysts have tried to express various consequences in monetary terms, because they involved spurious assumptions that could not be tested.

Moreover it's often difficult to express the probability of occurrence of an event in reliable, quantitative terms. Hence, such expressions of probability are often based on experiential data and judgement. In this book, which deals with the initial appraisal in the front-end phase of projects, the discussion is limited to simple qualitative approach, as depicted in Figure 24.1, in which both probability and consequence are characterized at the ordinal level and divided into classes. Hence, quantitative risk analysis methods will not be discussed here.

## 24.5 Risk policy

A risk policy is necessary to provide rules or guidelines for deciding what to do when faced with risk. The simplest risk policy might be to rank risk elements according to their calculated expected values and set an upper limit for acceptable risk. A more advanced policy might be to aggregate the effects of risk elements, such as by using influence diagrams or Monte Carlo simulation. This permits simulating the effects of various risks within the overall picture. A third variant, between these two extremes, may be to make do with a simple classification of risk elements and then compare it with a risk policy that differentiates between various types of risk and states what should be done with each of them.

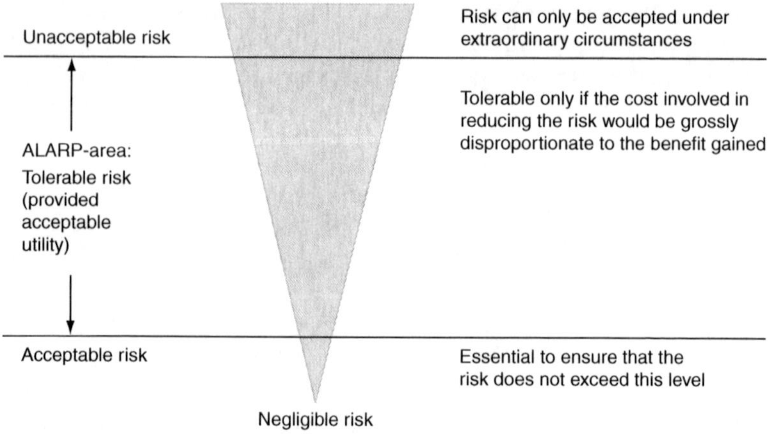


*Figure 24.2* As Low As Reasonable Possible (ALARP) principle as a basis for risk policy

The risk matrix is a simple, useful tool for such an approach. For example, the differentiation may be according to the degree of risk, as illustrated in Figure 24.2, which distinguishes between unacceptable, tolerable and negligible risk. As indicated in the figure, a tolerable risk is associated with an assessment of cost by reducing the risk relative to the benefit gained. Acceptable risk is partly associated with the expected value and partly with the consequence of a given event.

But the differentiation may also be associated to a particular risk, such as by having differing criteria for tolerance of financial risks, environmental risks and institutional risks. For example, an unacceptable risk could be defined as one that might result in financial overruns, create politically difficult situations or injure people. One might accept that a risk that results in lesser damages can be tolerated, provided that the costs of reducing the risk are much higher than the loss incurred when the damage occurred. For example, risk up to a certain level may be deemed acceptable in a project implemented jointly with reputable institutions. Or one might elect to ignore risk associated with lesser pilot projects, because the consequences are curtailed or because it is inherently valuable as a small-scale test of the uncertainty and consequence of a full-scale project implemented later.

A risk policy also may be determined by the division of the risk matrix outcome space. This is illustrated in Figure 24.3, in which a risk adverse

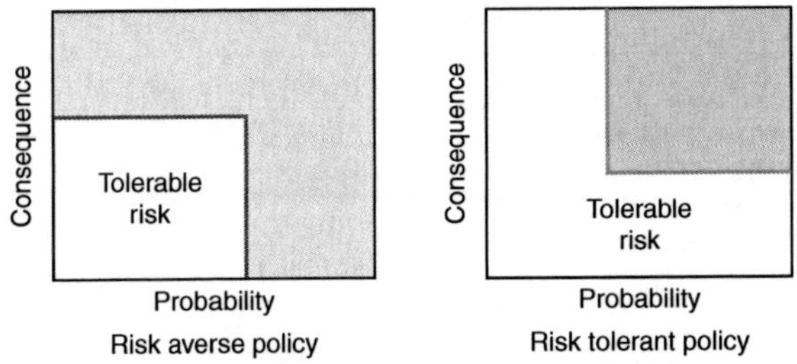


*Figure 24.3* The risk matrix as used to provide an overview of the risk profile of a project

policy sets upper limits to acceptable consequence and probability, and a risk tolerant policy accepts outcomes when one of the parameters is high but the other stays within a given limit.

## 24.6 Example: Developing and implementing an IT system

A project is organized for the development and delivery of an administrative computer system to a large public agency. The project is responsible for detailing needs, supporting concretization of the requirement specification, developing the software meeting that specification, acquiring hardware from a supplier, testing software and training the user organization staff in use of the system.

A review of the uncertain aspects of the process concluded that 13 aspects of it must be further evaluated. The review expresses the per-unit probabilities of occurrence of these aspects along with their consequences ranked on a severity scale from 0 to 10, as listed in Table 24.1 along with the associated risk of each.

A simple approach might be to rank the events according to risk and set an upper limit for tolerable risk, such as by stating that risks greater than 0.3 won't be tolerated. In this case, this would involve closer examination of five risk elements to see what might be done with them. The five include risk elements 1 and 2, which may arise, should needs or requirements change on the way so that software no longer is compliant. The same is true of numbers 12 and 13 concerning the users' lack of preparation and user training, as well as number 7, delayed income from ongoing projects. The remaining eight risk elements concerning personnel and hardware are considered tolerable.

*Table 24.1* Estimated risks of 13 anticipated events

| | | Probability | Consequence | Risk |
|---|---|---|---|---|
| 1 | Software not in compliance with requirements | 0.2 | 2.0 | 0.40 |
| 2 | Specified requirements may be changed | 0.3 | 1.5 | 0.45 |
| 3 | Delayed delivery of hardware | 0.1 | 0.25 | 0.03 |
| 4 | Hardware not compatible with software | 0.05 | 0.5 | 0.03 |
| 5 | Hardware supplier goes bankrupt | 0.05 | 2.0 | 0.10 |
| 6 | Lack of funds to cover salaries and expenses | 0.05 | 1.0 | 0.05 |
| 7 | Income from ongoing projects delayed | 0.3 | 2.0 | 0.6 |
| 8 | Personnel shortage | 0.1 | 2.0 | 0.2 |
| 9 | Lacking capacity to train new employees | 0.15 | 1.5 | 0.23 |
| 10 | Insufficient expertise to solve essential problems | 0.1 | 3.0 | 0.3 |
| 11 | New hardware not compatible with present system | 0.05 | 3.0 | 0.15 |
| 12 | The client is not sufficiently prepared | 0.2 | 3.0 | 0.6 |
| 13 | Difficulties in training the client to use new procedures | 0.1 | 4.0 | 0.4 |

Another approach would be to construct an influence diagram and calculate an aggregate expression for the probability of manifestation or the unified risk under various assumptions. Even with a relatively simple problem such as this one, there will be numerous interdependencies between the various risk elements, as shown in the influence diagram of Figure 24.4, in addition to the uncertainty associated with the estimations of probabilities and consequences of the various risk elements. Consequently problems will be encountered in attempting to conduct the modelling, simulation and interpretation of results in a meaningful analysis that can have practical application.

A third approach may be to describe the problem in a simple risk matrix as illustrated in Figure 24.5, in which the probability and consequence are both ranked in five classes. The matrix indicates that low-risk

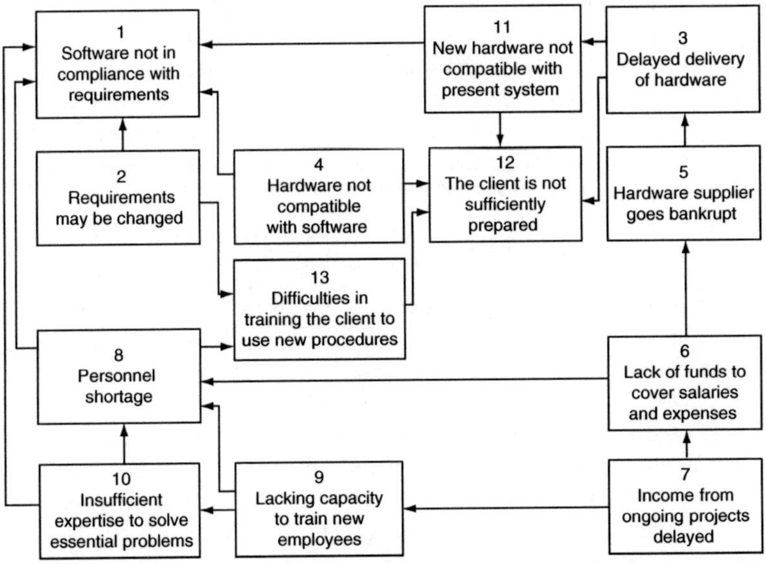


*Figure 24.4* The influence diagram shows links between various risk elements

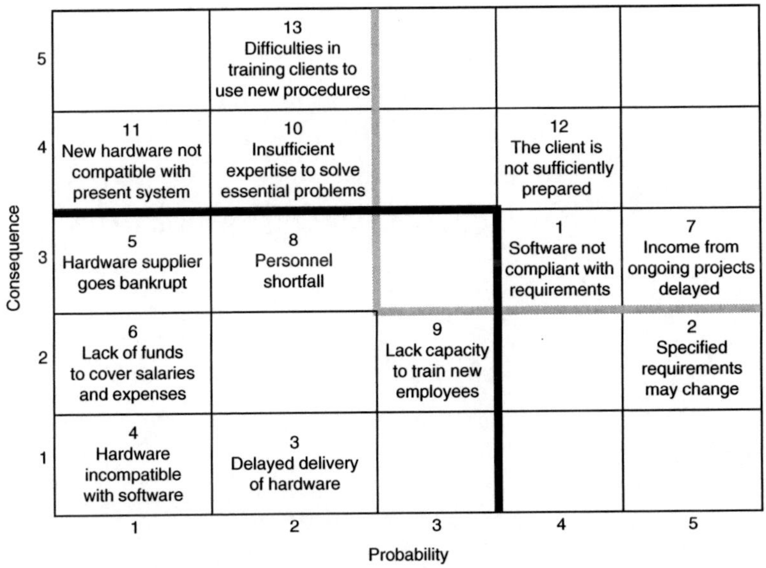


*Figure 24.5* Risk matrix applying to the same project as illustrated in the influence diagram. In the example discussed, a risk-tolerant approach evaluates only the risk elements outside the grey border as unacceptable, while a risk-averse approach evaluates all risk elements outside the black boarder as unacceptable

elements outnumber high-risk elements. It also brings out a qualitative aspect of the risk elements. For example, on one hand, it shows that changes in the requirement specification on the way (element 2) are highly probable but will have relatively small consequences. On the other hand, the difficulty in training users (element 13) is less probable but has a greater consequence. The risk is the same in both cases. This should have consequences for which initiatives are prioritized.

The risk elements considered will depend on the risk policy or the prevailing attitude as to which risks may be accepted. For example, a risk-tolerant attitude may make do with consideration of the elements that lie outside the grey border in Figure 24.5, that is (12) insufficient user preparation, (7) delayed income from ongoing projects, and (1) software compliant with requirements. A more risk averse attitude may result in consideration of the seven additional risk elements outside the black border in Figure 24.5, that is, (13) difficulties in user training, (2) active follow-up of changes in needs and requirements, (10) staff professional expertise and (11) ensuring that hardware is compatible with the system already in place.

# 25 Probability-Based Progress Analysis

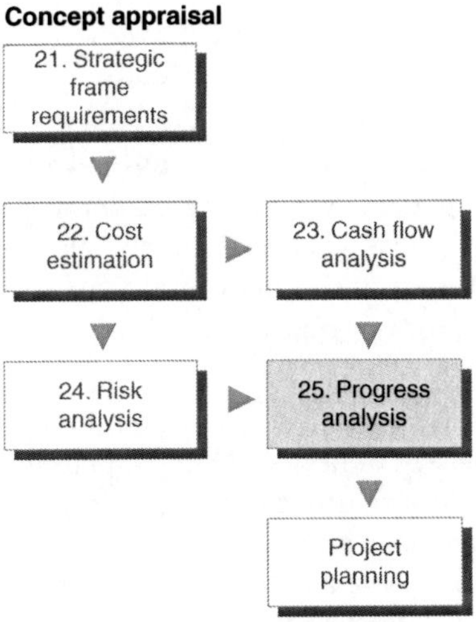


*The parameter of time is decisively significant in concept appraisal. One approach is to use straightforward, deterministic network scheduling. Common software tools enable probability-based analyses that provide the bases for more flexible pictures of a project's progress in time and of the uncertainties associated with the analysis.*

## 25.1 Improved network analysis

Progress in projects is burdened with uncertainty. To a considerable extent, the root causes may be written back to project planning, organization and management. The approaches to reducing uncertainty include acquiring relevant information and systematic analyses of processes. Network scheduling is customarily used for these purposes. In it, a project or process is described in a network diagram that shows the activities and the links between them. The diagram may be used to calculate the time a process takes, from when it starts until it ends.

Since network scheduling was first used in the mid-1950s, several related techniques of it have evolved. They may be roughly classified in three groups:

1. Simple deterministic analysis in which the individual activity durations are assumed to be known. An example is the Critical Path Method (CPM) in which the earliest completion date is calculated without regard to uncertainty. The network diagram is used to identify the activities critical in the calculation, that is, those that lie along the project's critical path.
2. Deterministic methods that include simple evaluation of uncertainty. The first such method was the Program Evaluation and Review Technique (PERT) developed in the early 1960s in the US. In it, for example, the shortest and longest durations of each activity of the project are included to support assumed implementation time under various assumptions.
3. Stochastic methods in which the expected durations of the individual activities are expressed in probability distributions. As opposed to PERT, which calculates uncertainty only along critical paths in a project, a stochastic analysis will take account of parallel paths in a network. These methods provide an estimate of the most likely duration, the shortest duration and the longest duration, together called a triple estimate. These values are used to calculate the expected value of the duration and the spread for each activity. The expected values are arithmetically summed, and the spreads are geometrically summed. The resultant expression is then total implementation time for the entire process, expressed in a probability distribution. Triple estimates may also be used as bases for simulation, as in the following example.

Network analysis is a vital tool for project management, particularly in large, complex projects and in the coordination of many projects. Information technology has made it possible to take the step from deterministic calculation to probabilistic computation, and there are many suppliers of relevant software programs.

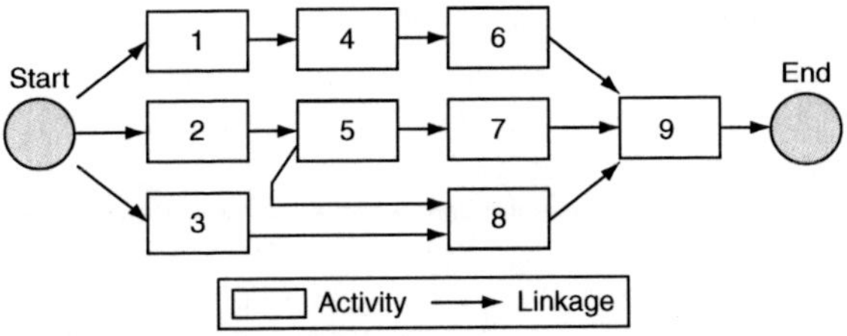


*Figure 25.1* Diagram for network analysis

A simple network analysis diagram of sequential and parallel activities is illustrated in Figure 25.1. In a stochastic analysis, all paths in the network must run unbroken from a start point to an end point, as shown in the figure. As shown, there are connections between activities, for example, activities 5 and 8 begin at the same time, but activity 8 can begin only after activity 3 ends.

A principal assumption in probabilistic progress analysis is that the activities in the network are stochastically independent.[1] They can well be logically dependent, but the duration of each activity must be independent of the durations of all other activities. Consequently care must be taken in dividing up the plan into activities. Whenever co-variation occurs, the causes of dependency must be eliminated from the plan.

In place of concrete activities, collective activities may be introduced in the network to represent the effects of general uncertainty. The general aspects are overriding cross-cutting issues within or external to the project that may influence its implementation.

Whenever a network includes parallel activities, a deterministic analysis concludes that the longest path through the network determines the time of finishing. However, taking uncertainty into consideration for each of the activities implies that the longest path may not be known, particularly when the paths are about the same length (nearly critical).

Stochastic network analysis builds on the assumption that the duration of each individual activity can be expressed in a probability distribution. Usually the distribution is skewed, such as the Beta distribution. The total, that is the implementation time for the entire project or process, depends on the sums of the effects of several such probability distributions. Hence the result is assumed to be a Normal (Gauss) distribution. The result of the analysis is described using a *cumulative* Normal distribution (S-curve), as shown in Figure 25.5. The uncertainties associated with each activity are expressed in tornado diagrams, as shown in Figure 25.3 and discussed in section 22.2. The analysis is illustrated in the following example of section 25.2.

The basic data in stochastic progress estimation are in practice based to a great extent on evaluation by panels of experts who arrive at triple estimates for the lowest, most probable and highest expected values for the elements included in the analysis, as described in Chapter 22. In most cases, data processing involves simulation.

The Monte Carlo method performs a large number of recursive network calculation in which random values of individual elements are taken from the associated probability distributions. Hence, it isn't necessary to consider the assumption of stochastically independent elements. The method can model connections, such as by describing co-variation between various activities.

This suits the method well to straightforward modelling of the effects that various events may have on a project. Two drawbacks of extensive use of co-variation in simulation are that the limits to what may be modelled may be exceeded and that models may lose their practical worth, as discussed in Chapter 13.

## 25.2 Example: Linking a town to the mainland

The example is of a major project to provide a road connection to a town on an island in an archipelago off the coast.[2] Natural conditions, including distances between the islands, bottom conditions, sea currents, etc., have led to three solutions being put forth, a suspension bridge, a subsea tunnel and a pontoon bridge, see Figure 25.2. The pontoon bridge is a new, previously untried construction.

The main part of the project comprises the three sub-projects that will be implemented simultaneously. The sub-projects also include access roads at both ends, to tie the entire roadworks together. Even before the sub-project planning started, a realistic finishing date for the project was sought. The visionary question was: when shall the King be invited to come clip the ribbon?

The initial estimate is made on the bases of expert judgement, in a procedure resembling that described in Chapter 22 for probabilistic cost estimation. A group is put together of experts extensively experienced

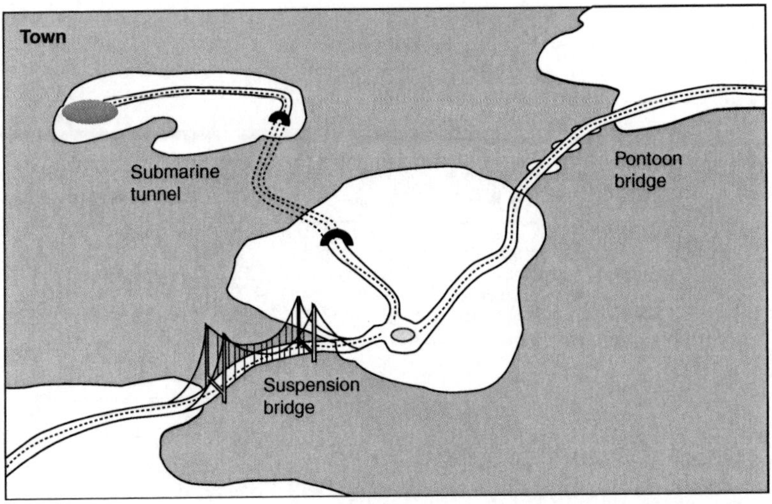


*Figure 25.2* Road connection to a town at the mouth of a fjord

in similar projects. They are familiar with local conditions, business, decision-making agencies, climate, etc. The group starts by dividing the whole project up into principal activities, and thereafter jointly arrives at a triple estimate of the duration of each activity. These estimates also express uncertainties in the durations. Should the uncertainty of any one activity be excessive, it may be subdivided into lesser activities that may be individually analyzed to reduce uncertainty.

A simplified network diagram providing an overview of the project is shown in Figure 25.3. It includes five principal activities, designated A to E. Additionally there's an activity F that reflects the general uncertainty associated with the project. The bases for agreeing on a triple estimate for the duration of 'activity F' is a thorough discussion of the types of uncertainty it might include, such as:

- Delays due to ship drift
- Fire engineering conditions
- Geological conditions
- Uncertainties associated with technologies, particularly the pontoon bridge
- Wind, weather and ocean current conditions

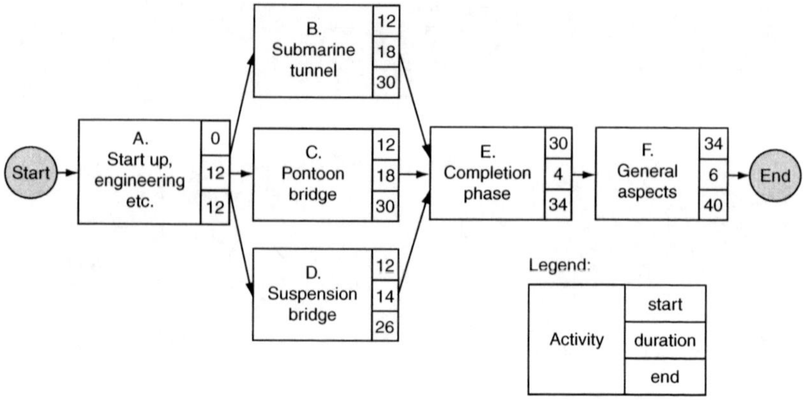


*Figure 25.3* Simple network diagram for deterministic calculation of implementation time

- Security problems that may arise
- Political decisions
- Quality assurance
- Uncertainty concerning the project organization
- Effects of applicable working time regulations

There's also a long list of conditions over which the project has no control and of which the experts don't know the effects.

In the network diagram of Figure 25.3, the durations of the individual activities are set up for a simple deterministic analysis. Moreover, the start and finish times of each activity have been calculated. As can be seen, Activity E, the completion phase, starts after Activity C, the pontoon bridge that takes 30 months, finishes. The diagram illustrates a deterministic analysis that results in an estimated duration of 40 months for the whole project.

The figures are listed in Table 25.1 in the 'most likely duration' column. The table also lists the lowest estimate (P10) and highest estimate (P90) of the triple estimate for each activity. These figures are related to probability distributions, as listed in the rightmost column of the table.

The results of a Monte Carlo simulation with 1000 recursive calculations are listed in Table 25.2. As can be seen in the table, data regarding the estimated durations is recorded at five levels, which are for 0, 10, 50, 90 and 100 per cent probability of realization. The simulation doesn't

*Table 25.1* Estimated durations: Input values from expert review

| | | Estimated duration (months) | | | Type of distribution |
|---|---|---|---|---|---|
| | | Lowest (P10) | Most likely | Highest (P90) | |
| A | Engineering | 8 | 12 | 14 | Lognormal |
| B | Submarine tunnel | 10 | 18 | 26 | Normal |
| C | Pontoon bridge | 4 | 18 | 40 | Triangular |
| D | Suspension bridge | 6 | 14 | 24 | Triangular |
| E | Completion | 2 | 4 | 7 | Triangular |
| F | General aspects | –6 | 6 | 36 | Triangular |
| | | 14 | 40 | 97 | |

*Table 25.2* Estimated durations: Output values from simulation

| | | Estimated duration (months) | | | | | | |
|---|---|---|---|---|---|---|---|---|
| | | Basis | Lowest | 10 % percentile | Expected | 90 % percentile | Highest | Standard deviation |
| | Start | 0 | 0.0 | 0.0 | 0.0 | 0.0 | 0.0 | 0.0 |
| A | Engineering | 12 | 7.8 | 10.8 | 11.8 | 13.6 | 18.2 | 1.4 |
| B | Submarine tunnel | 30 | 20.0 | 24.7 | 28.8 | 33.8 | 42.5 | 3.5 |
| C | Pontoon bridge | 30 | 13.6 | 22.7 | 31.8 | 43.7 | 53.7 | 7.8 |
| D | Suspension bridge | 26 | 15.5 | 21.3 | 26.4 | 31.7 | 37.5 | 4.0 |
| E | Completion | 34 | 26.0 | 32.5 | 37.8 | 48.0 | 57.9 | 5.1 |
| F | General aspects | 40 | 24.8 | 37.9 | 50.2 | 65.4 | 86.2 | 10.4 |
| | End | 40 | 24.8 | 37.9 | 50.2 | 65.4 | 86.2 | 10.4 |

include any stochastic correlations between parallel activities, and the values used are taken from the distributions listed in Table 25.1.

The simulation yields an expected duration of 50.2 months with a standard deviation of 10.4 months, or about 20 per cent. This indicates that the uncertainty of the estimate is relatively large. The uncertainty is illustrated more exactly in the tornado diagram of Figure 25.3, in which variance is used to reflect uncertainty. As can be seen in the tornado diagram, the general aspects comprise the greatest component of uncertainty. These

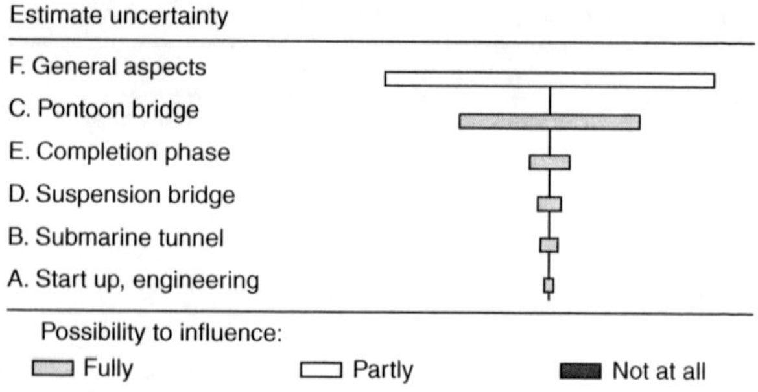


*Figure 25.4* A tornado diagram to illustrate the uncertainties of estimates

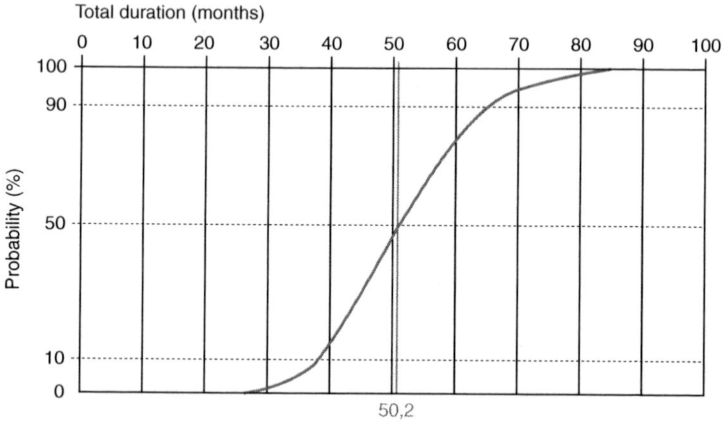


*Figure 25.5* Probability distribution for a project's total implementation time

aspects are partly susceptible to influence. The estimate for the pontoon bridge also is extremely uncertain. It also is susceptible to influence.

The next step to ensure a more certain result may be to distinguish between the parts of the general aspects that are more susceptible to influence and those that are less susceptible, accordingly rework the network diagram, and then calculate new triple estimates for each of them. The pontoon bridge sub-project can be divided up into smaller activities for a more certain time estimate. The relevant procedure is described in Chapter 22.

The answer to the initial question of when should the King come is indicated in Figure 25.5, which is the cumulative probability distribution for total duration. The expected value is 50.2 months. That is, with 50 per cent certainty, the project can be expected to be completed slightly more than four years after its start. To be fairly certain, the opening can be postponed a year, to 65.4 months after the project starts. Then it is 90 per cent certain that the project will be finished, which should be sufficient to invite the dignitary to clip the ribbon.

However, to take consideration of everything that can go wrong with the project, it all may take 86.2 months, slightly more than seven years.

# 26
# Evaluating Projects

*Projects are evaluated at various points of time during implementation or after they are finished. In some cases, a project may be evaluated after a serious problem has arisen, to find out what might be done about it. In other cases, the aim is to learn from what has gone on in a project, for better or worse. In the front-end phase, evaluation is used to a lesser degree, to appraise the worth of a project concept. This chapter comprises a closer examination of the two project examples of Chapter 2.*

> *If it happens once it is ignorance, if it happens twice it's neglect, if it happens three times it is policy.*
>
> —*Anon*

## 26.1 The moment of truth

This book is concerned with what can be done to increase the chances of success in projects. As the focus is on the front-end phase, the problem to be addressed is hypothetical and the perspective normative. We may refer to and reflect upon the causes of failure in other similar projects. But we can only recommend measures that can prevent recurrence, as we have no guarantee that will happen.

One of the problems addressed in this book is the circumstance that many projects are insufficiently studied early on. Technical solutions often are chosen before needs are charted. Sometimes one starts with the wrong question, and sometimes one finishes with the wrong answer. And sometimes both the question and the answer are wrong.

Another problem is the surprisingly strong and persistent trend of planners and decision makers to overestimate the benefit of an enterprise or initially underestimate its cost or both. The earlier in the decision process, the greater the discrepancy from what is finally adopted. Of course, this increases the chances of choosing the wrong project and dramatically increases the risk of project error.

The moment of truth for a project, that is the point of time at which it can be verified to what extent it is successful, comes long after it has been implemented. Success is not just a question of delivering the agreed outputs upon completion of a project. There's a broader evaluation of viability and utility in the long term. These matters were introduced in Chapter 2 and illustrated by two considerably different projects, the building of the new National University Hospital in Oslo and the torpedo battery in Northern Norway.

For some sample projects, the moment of truth comes formally at the time they are evaluated. An evaluation includes a thorough analysis of the worth and merits of a project. For major public-sector projects, the emphasis is on evaluation conducted by independent experts. But most projects are not subjected to formal evaluation.

Many believe that evaluation should preferably be at a sufficiently late point of time so one can verify the outcome and evaluate viability and utility. This is called *ex post* evaluation. Some wits have borrowed the medical term *post mortem* to characterize such evaluation. This implies that such an evaluation has limited value because it comes too late to do anything about a situation. The patient is already dead.

Hence, it makes much sense to evaluate up front, as the possibilities of influencing the process are greater the earlier they are contemplated. If this happens in the front-end phase before the decision to finance is made. Of course, the problem is that one faces a hypothetical situation in which the lack of information compels relying on experience or judgement, or at worst, on uneducated guessing.

## 26.2 Types of evaluation

Figure 26.1 provides an overview of various types of evaluation. There are two main categories. In some cases, evaluations are used to examine and change ongoing processes. This is called *formative* evaluations. In other cases, the aim is to establish the performance or achievements, such as at the end of a project. These are called

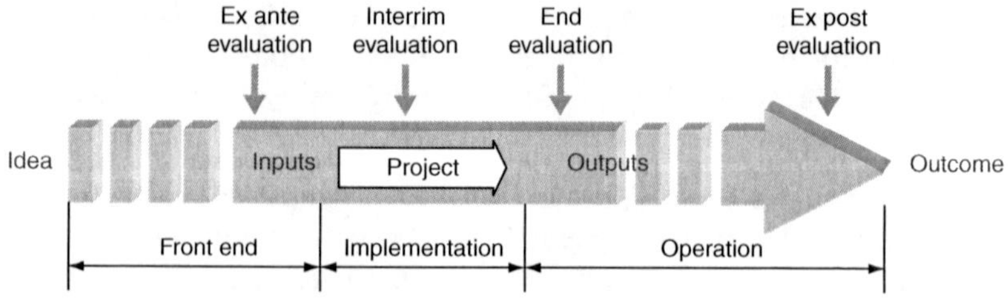


*Figure 26.1* Evaluation at different stages of a project

*summative* evaluations. A well-known analogy is the following: When the cook tastes the soup – it is formative. When the guest tastes the soup – it is summative.

Evaluations are made at four different stages of the project cycle. The first two are essentially formative, and the last two summative:

- *Ex ante evaluation* is an early evaluation of the project concept. It aims to support the decision of whether or not to finance the project and go ahead with it. It should have a broad view of the project, much as should subsequent evaluations, in order to ensure that it is economically viable, is relevant in relation to user needs, and is likely to be sustainable.
- Evaluations of ongoing projects are called *interim evaluations*, and usually are made midterm in the implementation period or at the end of a distinct phase. They usually help guide management or are in response to requests or pressure from stakeholders or the public. Interim evaluations typically focus on operational activities, but also may take a wider perspective and possibly may consider long-term effects.
- *End-evaluations* aim to establish the situation when the project is terminated and to identify possible needs for follow-up activities. They are made as a formal exercise and focus essentially on the production of project outputs in terms of quality, timing and cost as well as on the extent to which formally agreed objectives have been or are likely to be achieved.
- *Ex-post evaluations* are made after the project is terminated. Their main purpose is to assess the lasting impact the project may have had or is likely to have. This may require analysis in a broad socio-economic perspective. The motive might be to draw lessons that could be useful for similar projects in the future. In most projects, formal ex post evaluations are not made.

## 26.3 An evaluation model

The evaluation model on which the discussion of Chapter 2 is based is the objectives-oriented evaluation recommended by international bodies such as the UN, OECD and the European Commission. The recommended evaluation includes a project's *efficiency, effectiveness, impact, relevance* and *sustainability*. The relationships between these evaluation criteria are illustrated in Figure 26.2.

The evaluation of project *efficiency* is a question of the degree to which resources used have resulted in a delivery of agreed outputs. The customary parameters will be the extent and quality of a delivery, as well as the costs incurred and time spent. The reference will be the agreed outputs as well as what is reasonably attainable, such as with respect to other similar projects or to benchmark information. For example, in a building project, the resources may be expressed in terms of money, manpower, materials, equipment, etc. In a building project, for instance, the delivery principally is the building. Efficiency can be expressed as the degree to which the delivery conforms to the agreed specifications, considering use of resources, as well as in comparison with the efficiency attained in similar projects.

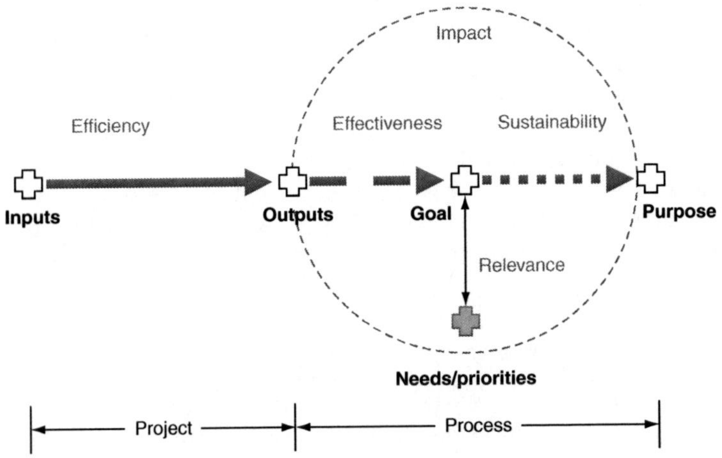


*Figure 26.2* Evaluation criteria in a goal-oriented evaluation according to a Log-frame model

*Effectiveness* is related to the goal, or in other words, that which was planned as the first-order effect of the project. This is the formal evaluation. It's usually supplemented with an evaluation of the effect as viewed relative to what would be reasonable in light of what the project has delivered (that doesn't necessarily correspond to the agreed output) and compared to effects attained in similar projects. In a building project, effectiveness may be expressed in the terms of user response, including extent of use, how suitable the building is for its intended purpose and how well it reasonably compares to similar projects.

Evaluation of the project's *impact* goes beyond the expected first-order effect and also includes long-term effects foreseen. Additionally there are all other positive and negative effects that can be attributed to the project, regardless of whether or not they were expected. They may include economic or institutional effects as well as social, environmental or any other effects that reasonably may be said to be caused by the concrete project. Verification of effects may entail an extensive, expensive search that all the same may be useful for accumulating lessons learnt to benefit future projects. For example, the evaluation of a building project can go beyond user response to include social consequences of settlement, business or other aspects that can be attributed to the project, as well as negative upshots such as changes in cost levels, conflicts with neighbours and other interests, etc.

An evaluation of the *relevance* of a project goes beyond effectiveness and instead assesses the worth or a goal or a strategy. A project is relevant if and only if the formally agreed goal is in accordance with related needs and prioritizations in society. So this is a test of whether the map agrees with the ground. Should the economy change or a new technology be developed, a product may no longer be needed in a market or a project may no longer be relevant. A lack of relevance most likely will also lead to low effectiveness. The explanation for low effectiveness in a building project might be found by asking whether the project is relevant. Perhaps the building was built for a market sector in which users have other priorities. Or it may have been built at the wrong place, at the wrong time or otherwise have been incongruous.

An evaluation of the *sustainability* of a project assumes a broad time frame and raises the question of how long the envisioned effect of a project will last after implementation is completed. Not least this applies to questions of profitability and positive cash flow, which again are tightly linked to project relevance. The sustainability of

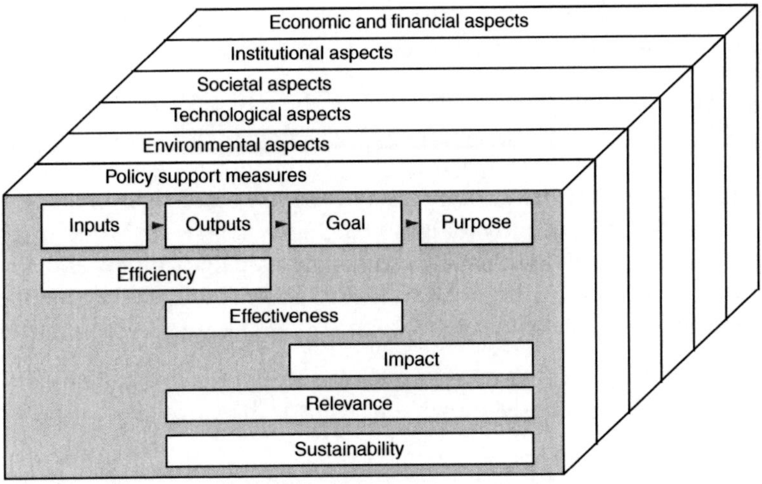


*Figure 26.3* Evaluation criteria are related to project strategy. Moreover, whenever necessary, multidisciplinary evaluations must be made, as of economic, social, environmental factors, etc

a building project may be directly evaluated in terms of whether income is greater than expenses, or indirectly in terms of how well the building is maintained, whether funds are allocated for future rehabilitation, etc.

According to this evaluation model, a successful project is one that was implemented according to plan, has produced the anticipated effect in the short and long terms, has no marked negative impact, is in accordance with needs and prioritizations in society and which carries on independently throughout its anticipated life cycle. When conducting an evaluation, the five evaluation criteria are considered in relation to strategy as discussed above, but must also take into consideration different aspects of the context in which the project operates. The analysis then becomes three-dimensional, as illustrated in Figure 26.3.

## 26.4 Ex ante evaluation

The above evaluation model customarily is used *ex post*, which means that it considers actual results after the completion of a project or a process. But it may be even more valuable if performed *ex ante*, which means in advance, before results are available, as in the front-end phase.

The question then is whether the amount of information available early on is sufficient to apply the five evaluation criteria.

For evaluations of *efficiency*, doubtlessly the costs of a project and the nature of its delivery are reasonably well understood at an early stage. But there's doubt as to whether cost estimates are realistic and the conditions of implementation will allow that outputs are produced as anticipated. Consequently gauging efficiency isn't worthwhile in the front-end phase. Not least the complications facing planners and decision makers in estimating realistic costs clearly indicate that the basis for evaluating efficiency usually is poor.

The same is true of *effectiveness*. Undoubtedly the first-order effects sought usually are clearly known, but realistic forecasting also is notoriously flawed.

Early estimates of *impacts* are even more difficult. Undoubtedly experiential knowledge may be acquired by studying similar projects. But we face conditions that are difficult to forecast and arguably require imagination and guesswork beyond our capabilities.

However, the situation for *relevance* differs. Common sense and user surveys, as well as knowledge of markets, laws and regulations permit us to form an early, accurate picture of whether an initiative is relevant. That we also are notoriously poor at this sort of early evaluation is not due to it being impossible, but rather to it not being done to a sufficient extent.

Finally forecasting future *sustainability* is also difficult. However, the question is closely related to whether an initiative is relevant. Moreover, early on, we usually can realistically analyze cash flows.

Consequently the answer to the initial question is that with modest effort, we can gain a good picture of whether a project is relevant and sustainable, but should not consider evaluating the other three criteria. The good news is that relevance and sustainability are precisely the attributes that determine whether a project will be successful or not in the long term. Therefore, this may be a minimalistic answer to the question this book raises, or a quick-and-dirty approach to front-end phase evaluation, in which the benefits are great compared to the cost.

Finally let's review the examples of Chapter 2. First, consider the building of the new National University Hospital, with its appreciable cost overruns and delays. What could have been said early on about its relevance and sustainability?

There's no doubt that the project was relevant. The National Hospital is the country's largest. It has the country's foremost specialists in many medical fields and also is a vital educational institution. The relocation of the Hospital from the centre of the city to its periphery eases access and also frees the valuable area of its former location for urban development. Here it's a matter of improving the operating environment of a well functioning institution, so clearly the project was relevant. Moreover it's obviously sustainable, as there's no doubt that public funding will ensure operations in years to come. Together, these considerations afford a solid basis for further planning and decision making. With this sort of certainty at the start, most projects would be successful in the long run.

Second, consider the torpedo battery up North that was abandoned soon after it was built. Here the concern is with a realistic defence scenario that in part builds on perceptions of the international political situation and military threats and in part on weapons technologies. Since the end of the Cold War, the political situation has changed dramatically and positively. There's no doubt that adequate information on these changes was available more than ten years before the decision to finance the project was made. Moreover it's obvious that uses of newer defence technologies, such as missiles, made this type of facility completely outdated and superfluous. In this case, the conclusion should have been that the project concept wasn't relevant so no agency would be willing to finance its operation. Here there's no excuse; the project should have been turned down.

This means that in relevance and sustainability, the hospital scored high and the torpedo battery low. In Figure 26.4, the two projects are compared as they might in ex-post evaluations. Topmost in the figure are so-called spider diagrams for the projects, in which the five evaluation criteria are ranked from zero to one. Hence, the area within the pentagon is a visualization of the worth of the project. The hospital scores maximum in relevance and sustainability, while the torpedo battery scores zero for both criteria.

Under the spider diagrams are diagrams of strategic and tactical performance, as in Figure 7.1. As can be seen, the tactical performance of the torpedo battery was successful. However, that's immaterial, as

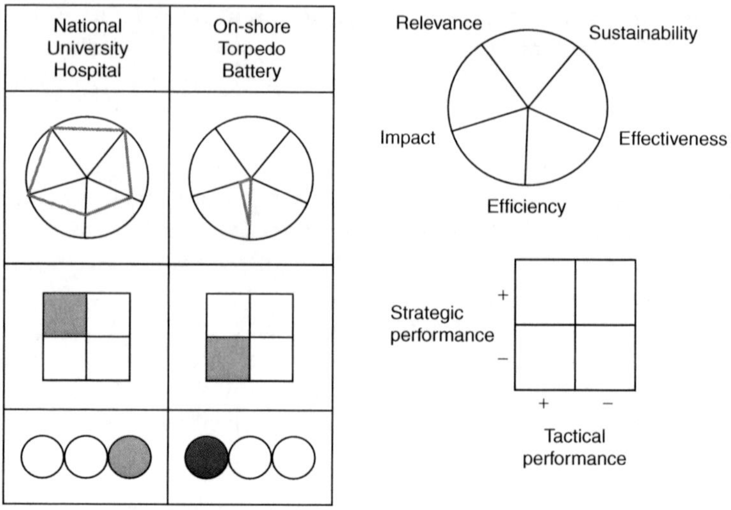


*Figure 26.4* Summary evaluation of two projects. The uppermost circle indicates scores of five evaluation criteria, the two-by-two matrix squares indicate tactical and strategic performances, and the shaded circles indicate the summary conclusions that one project is successful and the other unsuccessful

it failed strategically. The hospital was strategically successful, and the problems of its tactical implementation were deemed marginal.

In the lowermost row of Figure 26.4, the top aggregation levels of the two projects are compared. The traffic light for the hospital project is green (here grey) while that for the torpedo battery gets a red signal. Provided that these conclusions build on firm foundations of information and evaluation, they afford solid bases for sensible decision making.

# 27
# Boondoggles and White Elephants

*The mistakes we make and the projects that fail to produce what was expected are not in vain if we take the opportunity to learn from them. Some argue that failures are essential to making progress. The issue seems to be that there is much to be improved upon in systematically bringing forth lessons from the past to improve future performance.*

> *It is better to learn from others' mistakes than from one's own experience.*
>
> —*Otto von Bismarck*

## 27.1 Some project cases

The term *Boondoggle* is used to describe a project that wastes time and money, or one that generally is known to be futile long before it is shut down. The word is said to have been coined in the early 1930s by Robert H. Link, an American scoutmaster, for the braided leather lanyard made and worn by Boy Scouts. Hence, in the Great Depression of the 1930s, when millions of jobs were given to the unemployed in the US to get the economy moving again, it was applied to projects involving the teaching of simple manual skills, regardless of their ultimate benefit.

As described in Chapter 2, the torpedo battery in Norway is one such project. It was completed as designed and then closed down by Parliament one week after it was officially opened. Its concept was politically and technologically obsolete, so the project was of no real value to the country.

Another such project was the Anglo-French Concorde supersonic passenger airliner. In all, 20 aircraft were built. The first flew in 1969, and the

14 commercial service aircraft flew for 27 years until 2003, even though the income from the venture was insignificant compared with the actual cost of the project. Though clearly not its intent at the outset, the project proved that the advantages of supersonic flight were insufficient for it to compete with the low fares made possible by far more cost-effective subsonic aircraft.

The term *White Elephant* refers to a burdensome or costly possession considered to be without use or value. It originates from the story that the kings of Siam were accustomed to make a present of one of these animals to courtiers who had rendered themselves obnoxious, in order to ruin the recipient by the cost of its maintenance (Oxford English Dictionary). It is used to characterize projects that turn out to be wasted or where the costs (particularly costs of upkeep) are out of proportion to their usefulness.

The Millennium Dome in London, completed in 1999 at the cost of some 700 million pounds to celebrate the turn of the millennium, is one such project. It was badly thought out, badly executed, and left the government with an embarrassing question of what to do with it afterwards.

The list of project non-fulfilments is long. In the 1970s, a water supply project in Zambia was initiated to provide wells with hand pumps for the rural population living near the Zambezi River. After a slow start and a considerable investment of funds in infrastructure and institutional development, external evaluators concluded that abundant water was available year round on the river plains, so there was no need for the project. However, in view of the sizeable investments already made, the donor decided to continue the project. After 25 years the final evaluation concluded that the funds wasted could have been used to give each and every household in the target area an annual minimum salary in each of those years, or the water consumed could have been delivered free of charge in bottles imported from the donor country.

Everything seemed to have gone wrong in the project. There was no need for the water supplies in the target area. The project set out to strengthen a government institution's ability to build this type of infrastructure in the area. However, the government was beyond bankruptcy and would not have been able to keep the institution unless it was fully funded by external donors. Moreover the institution was inefficient, so much so that a private contractor could have finished the job much sooner at a far lower cost. Even so, this would have solved no problems, as water supplies were not relevant to user needs, and there was neither capability nor willingness to maintain the facilities. When the donor withdrew after 25 years, the institution broke down and its investments were pointless.

The five evaluation criteria discussed in Chapters 2 and 26 reveal why the project was a fiasco:

- *Efficiency* was low, as it took 25 years to expensively produce what could otherwise have been done in five at a far lower cost.
- *Effectiveness* was unacceptable, because the project had hardly any effect in terms of increased consumption of potable water.
- The *impact* was negative, because the project benefitted the dominant ethnic group and marginalized others, causing conflict and inequality.
- It was not *relevant,* as it did not respond to the perceived needs of user groups.
- It was not *sustainable,* because neither the government nor the users could afford it.

Hindsight enables us to clearly see the ludicrous aspects of such projects. This may not be possible up front. The two principal questions raised in this book are: (1) why aren't such obvious mistakes avoided up front?, and (2) what is needed to prevent such mistakes in the future? The answer to the first question is that it probably is impossible to avoid mega flops. Moreover as Jeffrey Pinto points out, such examples provide us with valuable experience.

> Much as a child learns to walk through trial and error, standing and falling relentlessly until the process becomes ingrained, so too does technology typically advance through the knowledge gained from disaster ... We gain wisdom every bit as much from failure as from success; we often discover what works by finding out what does not.
> (Kharbanda and Pinto 1996)

The answer to the second question is what this book is about. Kharbanda and Pinto go on to point to the paradox that we spend enormous amounts of money to plan and implement projects, but far too little to critically evaluate and learn from their experiences. In other words, we fail to systematically search for such information and feed the insight gained into new projects at their earliest stages.

There always will be white elephants and boondoggles. That said, there are ways to avoid some of the more predictable surprises. And there is proof that it may be worthwhile. As observed in this book, there is a human penchant for at least three counterproductive scenarios:

- People tend to choose an initial concept and stick with it.
- Incremental improvements of an inferior solution often are preferred to fundamental changes that would be better.
- Inertia is irrepressible: once initiated, a project is nigh impossible to stop.

This underscores the importance of getting the initial choice of concept right, which is also the basic theme of this book: Look before you leap; it's easier than you think. Also, the upside is obviously greater than the downside. The potential reward is high, because:

- The window of opportunities usually is larger than envisioned and probably is mostly unexplored.
- There usually is abundant evidence from similar projects that we can learn from.
- A broad perspective and systematic inquiry of relevant information at an early stage usually proves useful.

## 27.2 Analysis and decision to improve quality at entry

At the same time, arriving at the right solution to a problem is not only a question of reason, but also of chance. The making of an investment case is a lengthy process with many stakeholders involved, each with their own perspectives, views, priorities, and degrees of influence. A small thought experiment illustrates the situation, as shown in Figure 27.1 as a simplified representation of a project in terms of a decision tree, from project inception to completion.

The initial idea is the starting point for a sequence of steps that lead to the final choice of the project concept. For simplicity of illustration, we don't allow for any fuzziness, so the idea is said to be either the right one or wrong. The next step is the decision process, as it was illustrated in Figure 15.2, as a series of iterative steps evolving under the influence of analysts and decision makers. It ends up in a final decision that determines the choice of concept, which again is either right or wrong.

| Percentage Right/Wrong | Chance of success(%) |
|---|---|
| 20/80 | 4 |
| 50/50 | 25 |
| 80/20 | 64 |

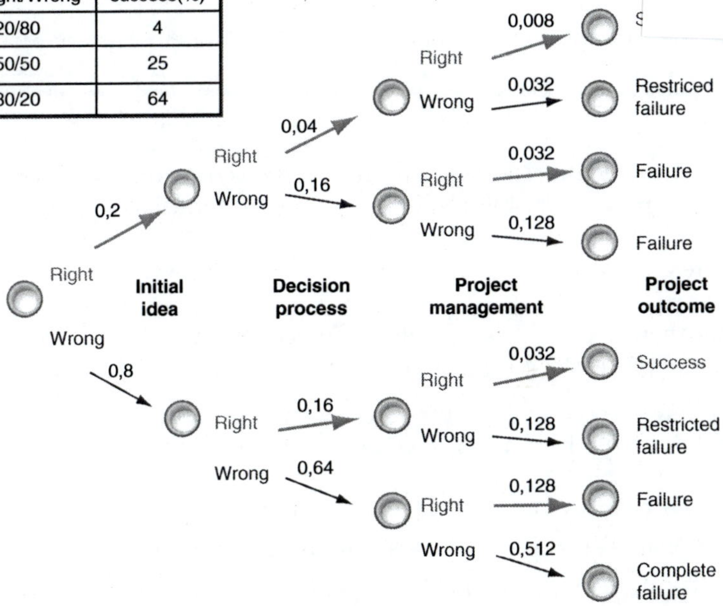


*Figure 27.1* Decision tree with possible outcomes in a project

The project is now implemented and also at this stage, there are two alternatives: either it is right or wrong in terms of its progress, costs and the quality of outputs.

There are eight possible outcomes. The question then is to what extent will the project be a success or failure in these eight cases, as illustrated in Figure 27.1. So there are eight answers:

1. Everything is done right, the idea, decisions and project management. The project will be a success.
2. The concept is right but badly implemented. The project is a restricted failure.
3. Decision makers get the concept wrong, but it is well implemented. The project still is a failure.
4. The concept is wrong, and it is badly implemented: clearly a failure.
5. The idea is the wrong one, but decision makers turn it around, so the project is well implemented and consequently successful.

6. The concept is right, but badly implemented. The project is a restricted failure.
7. The concept is wrong, but well executed. Nonetheless the project is a failure.
8. Everything is done wrong. The project is a complete failure.

Now imagine that there is a 20 per cent probability of getting it right at each step. The probabilities are apportioned as shown in Figure 27.1. The overall chance of success is then a meagre 4 per cent. Correspondingly if there is a 50–50 chance of success at each step, there is only 25 per cent chance of success overall. In the other extreme case, when we assume that there is an 80 per cent chance of success at each step, the overall chance of success is only 64 per cent.

Of course, this sort of simplified calculation is unrealistic. But it's useful in illustrating the problem encountered. It suggests that

1. Our chances of success are easily restricted.
2. Much of success or failure is determined up front.
3. The initial idea and the decision process clearly and decisively better or worsen the outcome.
4. Contemporary focus on project management seems disproportionate in comparison with the impact it may have on a project's success or failure.

These conclusions are of course based on pure speculation. Reality is more complex, as evidenced by the result of decades of research on project management and performance. The preliminary findings from an in-depth study of 25 large public investment projects shed some light on the issues discussed in this book. The study focused on the type of problems encountered in the projects and the extent to which these problems could be attributed to the quality of analysis and decisions up front. About half the projects were considered to be successful and half of them to have failed.

It found that as many as 12 out of 13 of the failed projects actually were not relevant to the problem identified or the needs expressed in the market, further that there was a lack of justification and realistic objectives in decision documents, and finally that alternative concepts had not been examined to any significant extent up front. These are grave problems that could have been sorted out by analysts and planners and for which there clearly was considerable potential for improvement. The situation differed in the successful projects, where all but one project were considered relevant to the needs as initially perceived.

The problems of underestimated costs and overestimated needs and benefits up front, as discussed in Chapters 8 and 9, were more evenly distributed in the two groups of projects. Such misestimates arose in about two-thirds of the projects, which suggest that the potential for improvement is considerable.

In terms of decision making, all the failed projects were characterized as negatively affected by what is called 'major predictable surprises' (see section 6.6), in the sense that decision makers were aware of but did not act to remedy the problems. And finally, one of the main findings was that in half of the cases, sound advice had been overruled by political preferences that adversely affected outcomes. Again it is a question of advice versus decision making, or of rationality versus chance. Solving the latter type of problems may be even more difficult than improving analysis. But an increased awareness of the problems as well as more transparency and openness, as discussed in Chapter 15, certainly is called for.

And now we are back where we started: Aside from all other aspects of a project, the acid test of whether it will be a success or a failure seems to be the extent to which it is *relevant* and *sustainable*. If analysts and decision makers joined forces to ensure that their project provided an adequate response to the problem in question and that its operation would be sustained in the future, there would be fewer boondoggles and white elephants in our man-made jungle called civilization.

# Notes

## 1 Attributes of a Project

1. This is of course nothing entirely new. Throughout history, many major tasks have been project type undertakings. There was no Pyramids Ltd. for serial manufacturing of pyramids. After the Second World War, there was a boom in reconstruction and other projects, and a number of methods and techniques were introduced to improve planning and project management. This was the beginning of a trend and, of course, not the start of anything entirely new.

2. Based on 31 separate studies from the period 1959–86, covering more than 4000 projects.

3. Does cost overrun result from poor planning or weak management? In a technologically innovative off-shore oilfield development project in the North Sea, a paradoxical situation arose after it was completed with excessive cost overrun: should the board be dismissed because of a cost increase of three billion dollars, or be rewarded because the project cost was about two billion dollars below the cost of comparable projects?

4. Traditional literature on strategy presupposes that the future to a certain degree can be foreseen, either deterministically or in terms of a number of scenarios. The task then is to adapt to these future conditions and thus outperform competitors. At present, the alternative view might be more in focus: how the organization as such could influence reality or the market, in other words, create its own future.

5. This is quite obvious. Traditional strategic planning aims to increase predictability and robustness by managing details and control as many variables as possible. However, since reality is not fully predictable, and all variables cannot be controlled, our attempts at detailed management might result in the opposite effect, that is, a reduced ability to manage.

6. The tendency might be to avoid a critical view of uncertainty at an early stage, particularly in projects that are paid for by the public. As we all know, it is often easier to ask for forgiveness than for permission. This seems to be common to the extent that we can talk of a situation with normalization of deviance (Pinto 2006). How many cultural projects would not have been implemented if the initial cost estimate was realistic?

7. There is a tendency to try to make our predictions more rational and credible by formalizing them in theories and models. The problem is often that fundamental assumptions and preconditions built into the models are left out or remain unchallenged. The models will then tend to provide us with systematic bias rather that insight and knowledge.

## 3 Three Perspectives on a Project

1. In some cases, each of these parties might be represented by several individual stakeholders, who, in certain cases, are also legally or financially independent of each other. Therefore, not only do conflicts of interest arise between the different groups, but also within the groups themselves. In some cases considerable problems might occur just because of internal changes of personnel. It is easy to forget that we deal not only with organizations, but also with the representatives of these organizations, who not always act in a coordinated manner.
2. Because of different priorities among stakeholders, it may often be difficult to state with certainty to what extent there is a need for large public investment projects, or make valid comparisons between alternative projects. Needs and priorities may be expressed indirectly through demands in the market. However, people may for instance not have the economic ability or purchasing power to express their needs in the form of market demand. Needs may also be expressed by initiatives from public authorities or specific groups in society.

## 5 Uncertainty, Risk and Opportunities

1. Which of these cross-cutting issues are essential will of course vary from project to project.
2. This may of course be ascribed to healthy scepticism. In persuading decision makers to consider a project proposal, opportunities are certainly emphasized, if not exaggerated, far more than threats. Experienced decision makers know this, which in turn may lead to the logical fallacy that all opportunities are at least already considered in the concept outline. So only negative risk aspects remain.
3. Note that the total risk is not the same as the sum of the sub-risks. That said, there may be some strong correlations between them, so the effects of a risk element can have both positive and negative consequences for other elements in the project as a whole.
4. We may be able to reduce the uncertainty that is associated with knowledge, the so-called epistemic or systematic uncertainty – but will still remain with the uncertainty associated with chance, the so-called aleatoric or statistical uncertainty.
5. Unrealistic assumptions can have severe consequences. For the Oslo Airport express train, the assumption of tunnelling in nearly perfect rock led to a considerable cost increase. In a similar example in Japan, the driving of a submarine tunnel came not into rock but into argillaceous sediment, so special techniques had to be developed to freeze the clay and then drive and cast the tunnel. This led to colossal cost overrun and delay of the project.

## 6 Possibilities of Foreseeing

1. One of the first and most known was 'Limits to Growth', compiled in the early 1970s at the Massachusetts Institute of Technology. It modeled the consequences of increasing exploitation of global resources over the next 100 years.

2. It's easy to drown in information, which itself can provoke paralysis. This is quite obvious in open-book exams. The more students are allowed to bring to the exam, the less they rely upon their own knowledge of the subject. Instead of using what they know, they sit, frantically searching the literature until the time is up. So their answers can in fact be poorer than had they relied on their own knowledge at the outset.

## 7 Strategic Guidance and Tactical Flexibility

1. For example, choice of concept normally varies, depending on our perception of uncertainty and the likelihood for changes on the way. Great uncertainty normally makes flexible or robust concepts more interesting, even though at the outset they may cost more than solutions optimized for fixed sets of conditions.

2. Not least, it's evident that the importance of obvious contextual conditions are overlooked, even though they may involve considerable additional cost. For example, the cost depends strongly on factors such as whether a tunnel will be driven through uniform shale or through silt and sludge, whether an opera house is to be built on rock or on loam, whether the result will function within a well-defined infrastructure or require additional infrastructure, building, etc.

3. This applies to a yet greater degree when contextual conditions can have impact on choice of concept and implementation. For example, the large gas pipeline across Alaska was delayed by several years, in part because the requirements of the burgeoning environmental movement were not taken into account. Retrospectively it's clear that many of the environmentalists' requirements could have been accommodated inexpensively in the concept development. Moreover the project was planned as if there were a well-developed infrastructure on site. In reality, it was in the wilderness, which required flying in equipment, fuel and provisions by helicopter. This had a colossal effect on time used as well as costs incurred.

4. Regrettably there's a pervasive belief that if specifications are compiled to the most minute detail, everything will go as planned. The paradox of this view is that most people dislike detail specification by their superiors, yet many people have no scruples in specifying details to their subordinates and colleagues.

5. The essence here is to evaluate more than one concept, more than one approach, more than one tool, etc. In methodology, this is called triangulation. In studying a problem, various perspectives or vantage points are chosen, precisely because of the realization that it's impossible to understand

a problem from a single starting point. Complex problems require complex approximations, not just to see different aspects of them, but also to be able to change approaches on the way should things initially overseen become apparent.

6. Criticism of strategy in practice now has gained support from several and in part unexpected quarters. For one, Henry Mintzberg, one of the greats of strategic thought, wrote a book entitled *The Rise and Fall of Strategic Planning* (Mintzberg 1994). In it, he contends that work with strategy has become a ritual in organizations and accordingly involves more 'witchcraft' than anchoring in reality. Consequently little is done to execute or follow up strategy.

## 8 The Problem of Cost

1. This is an imprecise statement of estimation as uncertainty is associated with all figures. Consequently the confidence interval also is stated, as it is an indicator of the estimate error margin. A confidence interval gives an estimated range of values that with a specified probability includes the unknown value of a parameter. The probability is expressed in percent. A confidence interval of 95 per cent means that the interval includes the parameter with a probability of 95 per cent.
2. Parenthetically the additional subsequent costs of changing an already well-designed, functioning road system of the adjoining shoreline area far exceeded the budget for the Opera and were felt by many to be completely unnecessary.
3. The difference between budget and final cost is erroneously designated by some as strategic misrepresentation (Flyvbjerg et al. 2003). It concerns the tactical implementation of a project, not the strategic choice made.

## 10 What is a Concept?

1. Of course, this is an oversimplified conceptual model. In practice, the various stakeholders will have partly differing opinions on what comprises the problem, the needs, the desired goal and the effect. That which is a problem for one may be an advantage for another. Hence the expression 'one man's meat is another man's poison'.

## 12 Objectives and Their Formulation

1. The origin of the term SMART is not known, but it usually is attributed to management consultant Peter Drucker (1909–2005), who first put forth its concepts in 1954 in his seminal book *Project Management*. Since then, there have been many versions of the keywords. For example, the first letter S may be taken to mean Significant, Stretching or Simple, in addition to Specific.
2. Of course, this depends slightly on what is meant by education. Some will contend that work experience is education for life.

## 13 Methods and Analyses in the Front-End Phase

1. In the front-end phase, the scope of possible alternatives will be at least as interesting as the details of one alternative. As is well known, creativity theory builds on the assumption that a diversity of alternatives creates quality.
2. A challenge is to find what sorts of experts should be involved. Should we engage experts from one discipline only, or perhaps also invite some at the periphery of the field or in supporting disciplines. Problems of some complexity will require the contributions of several disciplines to find the most suitable solution. Needless to say, one should build on both theoretical and practical knowledge.
3. Of course, one must distinguish more or less perpetual information, such as physical data, from less durable information, such as financial figures.

## 15 Front-End Assessment and the Decision to Finance a Project

1. One of the first was the 'Limits to Growth', compiled in the early 1970s and based on a simple system dynamics model to simulate the effect of increased exploitation of global resources for the next 100 years. The model now is available as an example in off-the-shelf computer simulation programs. Anyone can see that it's almost impossible to define values for and relationships between parameters in the model that provide some sort of credible picture of development. The authors probably took greater pains to manipulate the model to produce such results than to develop the model itself.
2. Simulation has become popular, not necessarily because it increases analytical precision, but because it has a considerable educational effect. The fact that the conclusion results from several thousand computations and can be presented in the form of smooth curves and exact numbers seemingly increases credibility for the target group.
3. The Ministry of Finance requirement for external quality assurance of major public investment projects entered into force in 2000.

## 16 Three Steps in Front-End Assessment: Definition, Development and Appraisal of Concept

1. Studies of managerial uses of decision information have shown that many managers first decide on the basis of their own experience and intuition, perhaps after having conferred with persons they trust. Thereafter available information is used to support the decision, not as a basis for making a decision.
2. There's always a central question of how much shall be subjected to detailed study. In general, if all parts are equally important, the total analysis is no better than the weakest analyses of a part. Consequently there must be some

reason for nonetheless analyzing some parts of a project concept more thoroughly than others. Is it due to tradition, or is it easier to analyze a particular area, such as when good information amenable for analysis is available, or is the analyzed area crucial to success, or what?

## 17 Systems Analysis

1. The context could be Social, economic, institutional, technical, environmental or political.

## 22 Top-Down Probability-Based Cost Estimation

1. Also called the *deterministic* estimate. A deterministic estimate is based only on fixed figures and assumptions.
2. For example, engineering, ground works, construction and construction management in a building project.
3. This is the principal weakness of the method, because the elements in the estimate often are not statistically independent variables.

## 23 Assessing Profitability

1. In this chapter, the problem to be addressed in the example is limited to evaluating financial viability. Whenever economic viability is to be evaluated, external effects must be included in the estimate. Such effects are discussed in Chapter 9.

## 25 Probability-Based Progress Analysis

1. That is, there is no co-variation, or the correlation coefficient is zero.
2. The example is from *Tidsplanlegging under usikkerhet* (Progress planning with uncertainty) (Klakegg 1994).

# Reference List

APM (2004), *Project Risk Analysis and Management Guide*, second edition, Association for Project Management, UK.

Andersen, Bjørn, et al. (1999), 'PS 2000 Oppsummering, Et sammendrag av forskningsprogrammet Prosjektstyring år 2000', NTNU, Trondheim.

Austeng, K. and Hugsted, R. (1995), 'Trinnvis kalkulasjon', Institutt for bygg- og anleggsteknikk, NTNU.

Austeng, Kjell, et al. (2006), Usikkerhetsanalyse – Kontekst og grunnlag, Concept rapport nr. 10, Concept programmet, NTNU, Trondheim.

Bazerman, Max H. and Watkins, Michael D. (2004), 'Predictable Surprises: The Disasters You Should Have Seen Coming, and How to Prevent Them', Harvard Business School Publishing Corporation, US.

Berg, Peder, et al. (1999), 'Management of Public Investments' (in Norwegian), Norwegian Ministry of Finance, Oslo.

Bøhren, Øyvind and Gjærum, Per Ivar (1999), 'Prosjektanalyse', Skarvet forlag, Oslo.

Christensen, S. and Kreiner, K. (1991), 'Prosjektledelse under usikkerhet', Universitetsforlaget A/S, Oslo.

Eden, C. and Ackermann, F. (1998), *Making Strategy: The Journey of Strategic Management*, Sage publications, London.

Forrester, Jay (1985), 'System Dynamics', MIT Press, US.

Flyvbjerg, Bent, Bruzelius, Nils and Rothengatter, Werner (2003), 'Megaprojects and Risk: An Anatomy of Ambition', Cambridge University Press, UK.

Gladwell, Malcolm (2005), *Blink. The Power of Thinking Without Thinking*, Penguin Books Ltd, US.

Goodwin, Paul and Wright, George (1996), *Decision Analysis for Management Judgment*, John Wiley & Sons, Inc., London.

Hagen, K. P. and Pedersen, K. R. (2009), 'Samfunnsøkonomisk lønnsomhetsanalyse: Alternativkostnader og valg av nullalternativ', (Economic Analysis: Alternative Costs and the Choice of the Zero Option), research note, Norwegian School of Economics and Business Administration, Bergen, Norway.

Hansson, Sven Ove (2003), Konsten att vara vetenskaplig, Kompendium, Filosofienheten, Kungliga Tekniska Högskolan, Stockholm.

Heijden, Kees van der (1996), *Scenarios: The Art of Strategic Conversation*, John Wiley & Sons, UK.

Heijden, Kees van der (2009), 'Scenarios Planning'. In T. Williams (eds), *Making Essential Choices with Scant Information*, Palgrave Macmillan, UK.

Hellevik, Ottar (1991), Forskningsmetode i sosiologi og statsvitenskap, Universitetsforlaget, Oslo.

Holst Volden, Gro (2009), 'Nullalternativet i KS 1 – analyser' (Zero Option in Qualitative Assurance Analysis), research note, SINTEF, Trondheim, Norway.

IMEC, Miller, R. and Lessard, D. (1999), *The Strategic Management of Large Engineering Projects*, MIT Press, US.

Jessen, Svein (1995), 'Konsekvensanalyse i praktisk prosjektarbeid', Tano A/S, Oslo.

Jouvenel B. de (1967), *The Art of Conjecture*, Basic Books, Inc., New York.

Kharbanda, O. P. and Pinto, J. K. (1996), 'What made Gertie Gallop? Lessons from Project Failures', Van Nostrand Reinhold, US.

Kystverket (2007), 'Konseptvalgutredning Stad skipstunnel', Utkast 2. november 2007, Kystverket, Oslo.

Lichtenberg, Steen (1990), 'Projektplanlægning i en foranderlig verden', Polyteknisk forlag, Lyngby, Danmark.

Lichtenberg, Steen (2000), *Proactive Management of Uncertainty Using the Successive Principle: A Practical Way to Manage Opportunities and Risks*, Polyteknisk Forlag, Lyngby, Danmark.

Lovins, H. and Lovins, A. (2007), *How Not to Parachute More Cats*, Rocky Mountain Institute, Colorado, US.

Løwendahl, B. and Wenstøp, F. (2002), 'Grunnbok i strategi', NKS forlaget, Oslo.

Merkhofer, M. W. (1987), 'Quantifying Judgmental Uncertainty: Methodology, Experiences, and Insights', *IEEE Transactions on Systems, Man and Cybernetics*, Volume 17, Issue 5.

Minken, H., et al. (2009), 'Konseptvalgsutredninger og samfunnsøkonomiske analyser' (Concept Appraisals and Economic Analysis), The Institute of Transport Economics (TØI), Oslo.

Mintzberg, H. (1994), *The Rise and Fall of Strategic Planning*, Prentice Hall, Hertfordshire.

Morra, L. G. and Thumm, U. R. W. (1997), *Evaluation Results 1995*, The International Bank for Reconstruction and Development, Washington DC.

Morris, P. W. G. and Hough, G. H. (1991), *The Anatomy of Major Projects: A Study of the Reality of Project Management*, John Wiley & Sons, Chichester.

NOU (1997), 'Nytte-kostnadsanalyse. Prinsipper for lønnsomhetsvurdering i offentlig sektor', Governmental white paper, Norwegian Ministry of Finance, 27.

Næss, Petter (2004), Bedre behovsanalyser. Erfaringer og anbefalinger om behovsanalyser i store offentlige investeringsprosjekt, Concept rapport nr. 5, NTNU, Trondheim.

Næss, Petter et al. (2005), Bedre utforming av store offentlige investeringsprosjekter. Vurdering av behov, mål og effekt i tidligfasen, Concept rapport nr. 9, Concept-programmet, NTNU, Trondheim.

Olsson, Henny and Sörensen, Stefan (2003), *Forskningsprosessen. Kvalitative og kvantitative perspektiver*, Gyldendal Akademisk, Oslo.

Olsson, Nils (2005), 'Project Flexibility in Large Engineering Projects', PhD thesis, Norwegian University of Science and Technology, Trondheim.

Olsson, Nils, et al. (2008), Investorers vurdering av prosjekters godhet, Concept rapport nr. 20, Concept programmet, NTNU, Trondheim.

Pinto, J. K. and Slevin, D. P. (1988), 'Project Success: Definition and Measurement Techniques', *Project Management Journal*, Vol. XIX, No. 1, February.

Pinto, J. K. (2006), 'Organizational Governance and Project Success: Lessons from Boston's Big Dig', Presentation at the International Symposium on Project Governance, Norwegian University of Science and technology, Trondheim.

PMI (1996), *A Guide to the Project Management Body of Knowledge*, Project Management Institute, US.

PMI Standards Committee (2008), *A Guide to the Project Management Body of Knowledge*, fourth edition, Project Management Institute, US.

Samset, K. (1998), *Project Management in a High-uncertainty Situation: Uncertainty, Risk and Project Management in International Development Projects*, Norwegian University of Science and Technology, Trondheim.

Samset, K. (1999), *The Logical Framework Approach (LFA): Handbook for Objectives-oriented Planning*, fourth edition, Norwegian Agency for Development Cooperation, Oslo, Norway.

Samset, K. (2003), *Project Evaluation: Making Investments Succeed*, Tapir Academic Press, Trondheim, Norway.

Samset, K. (2006), 'Design of High-Uncertainty Projects in International Aid', paper presentert på konferansen 'PROMAC 2006', Sydney.

Simon, Herbert (1979), *Models of Thought*, Yale University Press, US.

Slevin, D. P. and Pinto, J. K. (1989), 'Balancing Strategy and Tactics in Project Implementation', *Sloan Management Review*, pp. 33–41.

Starbuck, W. H. (ed.) (1993), *Handbook of Organizational Design*, two volumes, Oxford University Press, UK.

Surowiecki, James (2004), *The Wisdom of Crowds: Why the Many Are Smarter Than the Few*, Little, Brown/ Doubleday, US.

Teigen, Karl Halvor (2006), Skjønn og skivebom. Hvordan vi bedømmer usikkerhet, Foredrag, Norsk Senter for Prosjektledelse, Oslo.

Williams, T. (1995), 'A Classified Bibliography of Recent Research Relating to Project Risk Management', *European Journal of Operational Research*, 85, pp. 18–38.

World Bank (1996), *Evaluation Results 1994*, The International Bank for Reconstruction and Development, Washington DC.

Wright, George and Ayton, Peter (eds) (1987), *Judgmental Forecasting*, John Wiley & Sons Ltd, UK.

Øien, K., Hoknes, P. R., Rosness, R. and Klakegg, O. J. (1996), 'Håndbok for gjennomføring av ekspertvurderinger', Prosjektstyring år 2000, SINTEF, Trondheim.

# Bibliography


Adams, John (1995), *Risk*, Routledge, UK.

Altshuler, Alan and Luberott, David (2003), *Mega-Projects: The Changing Politics of Urban Public Investment*, Brookings Institution Press, Washington DC.

Andersen, Bjørn (2007), En verktøykasse for analyse i prosjekters tidligfase, kapittel i Concept studie nr. 17, 'Beslutninger på et svakt informasjonsgrunnlag', NTNU, Trondheim.

Ashley, D. B., Lurie, C. S. and Jaselskis, E. J. (1987), 'Determinants of Construction Project Success', *Project Management Journal*, Vol. XVIII, No. 2, June.

Austeng, Kjell, et al. (2006), Usikkerhetsanalyse – Kontekst og grunnlag, Concept rapport nr. 10, Concept programmet, NTNU, Trondheim.

Austeng, Kjell, et al. (2006), Metoder for usikkerhetsanalyse, Concept rapport nr. 12, Concept programmet, NTNU, Trondheim.

Austeng, Kjell, et al. (2006), Usikkerhetsanalyse – Feilkilder i metode og beregninger, Concept rapport nr. 13, Concept programmet, NTNU, Trondheim.

Ayton, P. and Wright, G. (1994), *Subjective Probability*, John Wiley & Sons, London.

Bacon, R. W., Besant-Jones, J. E. and Heidarian, J. (1996), 'Estimating Construction Costs and Schedules: Experience with Power Generation Projects in Developing Countries', World Bank Technical Paper No. 325, The World Bank, Washington DC, US.

Baird, B. (1989), *Managerial Decisions under Uncertainty: An Introduction to the Analysis of Decision Making*, John Wiley & Sons, US.

Bazerman, M. H. (1994), *Judgement in Managerial Decision Making*, John Wiley & Sons, UK.

Bendor, J. (1985), *Parallel Systems: Redundancy in Government*', University of California Press, US.

Bennett, Deborah (2004), *Logic Made Easy*, Penguin Books, London.

Berntsen, Stein and Sunde, Thorleif (2002), Styring av prosjektporteføljer i staten. Usikkerhetsavsetning på porteføljenivå, Concept rapport nr. 1, NTNU, Trondheim.

Borge, Dan (2001), *The Book of Risk*, John Wiley & Sons, Inc., UK.

Brekke, Kjell Arne (2004), Realopsjoner og fleksibilitet i store offentlige investeringsprosjekt, Concept rapport nr. 8, Concept programmet, NTNU, Trondheim.

Chapman, C. and Ward, S. (1997), *Project Risk Management. Processes, Techniques and Insights*, John Wiley & Sons, UK.

Chong, Yen Yee and Brown, May (2000), *Managing Project Risk. Business Risk Management for Project Leaders*, Prentice-Hall, US.

Christiansen, D. and Wallace, S. (1996), 'Option Theory and Modelling under Uncertainty', Department of Managerial Economics and Operation research, Norwegian University of Science and Technology, Trondheim, Norway.

Claessens, S. (1993), *Risk Management in Developing Countries*, The International Bank for Reconstruction and Development, Washington DC.

Clemen, Robert and Reilly, Terence (2001), *Making Hard Decisions with Decision Tools*, Duxbury Brooks/Cole, US.

Cooke, Roger M. (1991), *Experts in Uncertainty: Opinion and Subjective Probability in Science*, Oxford University Press, UK.

Dalen, Dag Morten, Lædre, Ola and Riis, Christian (2003), Statlig styring av prosjektledelse. Empiri og økonomiske prinsipper. Concept rapport nr. 2, NTNU, Trondheim.

Dixit, Avinash and Skeath, Susan (1999), *Games of Strategy*, WW Norton & Co., New York.

Dodson, E. N. (1993), *Analytic Techniques for Risk Analysis of High-Technology Programs*, General Research Corporation, RM-2590.

Douglas, M. and Wildavsky, A. (1982), *Risk and Culture: An Essay on the Selection of Technological and Environmental Dangers*, University of California Press, US.

Drevland, Frode, et al. (2006), Usikkerhetsanalyse – Modellering, estirriering og beregning, Concept rapport nr. 11, Concept programmet, NTNU, Trondheim.

Field, Mike and Keller, Laurie (1998), *Project Management*, The Open University, UK.

Galbraight, J. R. (1979), *Designing Complex Organizations*, Adison-Wesley, Reading, MA.

Gigerenzer, Gerd and Todd, Peter M. (1999), *Simple Heuristics That Make Us Smart*, Oxford University Press, Inc. UK.

Gigerenzer, Gerd (2007), *Gut Feelings: The Intelligence of the Unconcious*, Allen Låne, Penguin Books, UK.

Gottschalk, Petter and Wenstøp, Fred (1985), 'Kvantitativ beslutningsanalyse for ledere og planleggere, Del I og II', Universitetsforlaget.

Grey, S. (1995), *Practical Risk Assessment for Project Management*, John Wiley & Sons, New York.

Gullvåg, Ingemund (1990), Rasjonalitet, forståelse og forklaring. Innføring i argumentasjonsteori, logikk og vitenskapsfilosofi, Tapir Akademisk Forlag, Trondheim.

Henden, Gisle (2004), 'Intuition and Its Role in Strategic Thinking', PhD Thesis, Norwegian School of Management, Oslo.

Hendricks, Vincent F. (2006), *Thoughts 2 Talk. A Crash Course in Reflection and Expression*, available at www.formalphilosophy.com, Automatic Press.

Husby, Otto, et al. (1999), 'Usikkerhet som gevinst. Mulighet – risiko, beslutning, handling. Styring av usikkerhet i prosjekter', Norsk Senter for Prosjektledelse, Oslo.

Jessen, Svein Arne (1998), 'Mer effektivt prosjektarbeid i offentlig og privat virksomhet', TANO Aschehoug forlag.

Jordanger, Ingemund (2006), Positiv usikkerhet og økt verdiskaping, Concept rapport nr. 14, Concept programmet, NTNU, Trondheim.

Jouvenel, B. de (1967), *The Art of Conjecture*, Basic Books, Inc. Publishers, New York.

Kahneman, D., Slovic, P. and Tversky, A. (1982), *Judgement under Uncertainty: Heuristics and Biases*, Cambridge University Press, London.

Karlsen, J. T. (1998), 'Mestring av omgivelsesbasert usikkerhet: en empirisk studie av prosjekter', PhD dissertation, The Norwegian University of Science and Technology, Trondheim.

Kammen, Daniel M. and Hasselzahl, David M. (1999), 'Should We Risk It? Exploring Environmental, Health, and Technological Problem Solving', Princeton University Press, US.

Keeling, Ralph (2000), *Project Management in an International Perspective*, Macmillan Business, UK.

Klakegg, O. J. (1993), 'Trinnvis-prosessen', Institutt for bygg- og anleggsteknikk, NTNU.

Klakegg, Ole Jonny (1994), 'Tidsplanlegging under usikkerheit', Universitetet i Trondheim, NTH, Institutt for bygg- og anleggsteknikk.

Klakegg, Ole Jonny (2004), Målformulering i store statlige investeringsprosjekt, Concept rapport nr. 6, Concept-programmet, NTNU, Trondheim.

Klein, Michel R. and Methlie, Leif B. (1995), *Knowledge-Based Decision Support Systems with Application in Business*, John Wiley & Sons, US.

Larsen, Stein V., Holte, Eilif and Haanæs, Sverre (2009), Beslutnings-underlag og beslutninger i store statlige investeringsprosjekt, Concept rapport nr. 3, NTNU, Trondheim.

Lewis H. W. (1997), *Why Flip a Coin? The Art and Science of Good Decisions*, John Wiley & Sons, Inc., UK.

Lichtenberg, Steen (1990), 'Projektplanlægning i en foranderlig verden', Polyteknisk forlag, Lyngby, Danmark.

Marshall, D. and Ritchie, B. (1993), *Business Risk Management*, Chapman & Hall, London.

Miller, R. and Lessard, D. (2000), *The Strategic Management of Large Engineering Projects. Shaping Institutions, Risks, and Governance*, Massachusetts Institute of Technology, US.

Mintzberg, Henry, Ahlstrand, Bruce and Lampel, Joseph (2005), *Strategy Bites Back: It is Far More, and Less, than You Ever Imagined...*, Prentice Hall, UK.

Myking, Eystein (2001), 'Monte Carlo simulering vs. suksessiv kalkulasjon', Prosjektledelse nr. 1, pp. 25–7, Oslo.

Nicolas, John M. (2001), *Project Management for Business and Technology: Principles and Practice*, Prentice-Hall, US.

Norad (1999), *The Logical Framework Approach (LFA): Handbook for Objectives-Oriented Planning*, Norwegian Agency for Development Cooperation, Oslo, Norway.

Odeck, J. and Brudeseth, Å. (2003), Statens Vegvesen: Generelt god kostnadskontroll, men tunnelprosjektene sprekker, Samferdsel, nr. 8.

Olsson, Nils (2004), Hvordan trur vi at det blir? Effektvurderinger av store offentlige prosjekt, Concept rapport nr. 7, Concept programmet, NTNU, Trondheim.

Petroski, Henry (1999), *Remaking the World. Adventures in Engineering*, Vintage Books, New York.

PMI (1996), *A Guide to the Project Management Body of Knowledge*, PMI Standards Committee, Project Management Institute, US.

Priemus, Hugo, et al. (eds) (2008) *Decision-Making on Mega-Projects: Cost–benefit Analysis, Planning and Innovation*, Edward Elgar Publisher, UK.

Raftery, R. (1994), *Risk Analysis in Project Management*, E & FN SPON, London.

Rolstadås, Asbjørn (1997), *Praktisk prosjektstyring*, Tapir Forlag, Trondheim.

Samset, K. (1992), 'Contents Analysis of a Sample of Evaluation Reports and Project Reviews', Norwegian Ministry of Foreign Affairs. Separate Study to Evaluation Report I.93, Internal Learning from Evaluations and Reviews.

Samset, K. (1999), *The Logical Framework Approach (LFA): Handbook for Objectives-Oriented Planning*, fourth edition, Norad, Oslo.

Samset, Knut, Berg, Peder Andreas and Klakegg, Ole Jonny (2006), 'Front-End Governance of Major Public Projects', paper presented at the 6th Annual Conference of the European Management Academy, Oslo.

Samset, Knut (2007) 'God dag mann hostesaft. Kvalitativ informasjon og misforståelser som beslutningsunderlag i prosjekter. Logikk, semantikk og presisjon', Prosjektledelse, Nr. 1, pp. 21–7.

Samset, Knut (2008) 'Major Weaknesses in Large Infrastructure Projects and How to Overcome These'. In Hugo Priemus, et al. (eds) *Decision-Making On Mega-Projects. Cost–benefit Analysis, Planning and Innovation*, Edward Elgar Publisher, UK.

Savvides, S. (1994), 'Risk Analysis in Investment Appraisal', *Project Appraisal*, Vol. 9, No. 1, March, pp. 3–18.

Solheim, Hege Gry, et al. (2003), Konseptutvikling og evaluering I store statlige Investeringsprosjekt, Concept rapport nr. x, NTNU, Trondheim.

Sunnevåg, Kjell, J. (red.) (2006), Beslutninger på svakt informasjonsgrunnlag. Tilnærminger og utfordringer i prosjekters tidlige fase, Concept rapport nr. 17, Norges teknisk-naturvitenskapelige universitet NTNU, Trondheim.

TerraMar (1996), *Risk Management*, company guidebook, Norway.

Torp, O. and Kilde, H. S. (1996), 'Usikkerhet som styringsparameter ved prosjekt-gjennomføring', NTNU, Trondheim, Norway.

Torp, Olav (red.) (2007), Kostnadsusikkerhet i store statlige investeringsprosjekter; Empiriske studier basert på KS2, Concept rapport nr. 15, Concept programmet, NTNU, Trondheim.

Trikalk (1994), Dataprogram for trinnvis kalkulasjon. Universitetet i Trondheim, NTH, Institutt for bygg- og anleggsteknikk.

Warberg, Erik N. (2007) Kontrahering i prosjektets tidligfase; Forsvarets anskaffelser. Concept rapport nr. 16, Concept programmet, NTNU, Trondheim.

Williams, T. M. (1997), 'Empowerment vs Risk Management?', *International Journal of Project Management*, Vol. 15, No. 4, pp. 219–22.

Williams, T., Samset, K. and Sunnevaag, K. (2009), *Making Essential Choices with Scant Information, Front-End Decisions in Major Projects*, Palgrave MacMillan, UK.

Wright, George and Ayton, Peter (eds) (1987), *Judgmental Forecasting*, John Wiley & Sons Ltd, UK.

Wright, George (2001), *Strategic Decision Making. A Best Practice Blueprint*, John Wiley & Sons Ltd, UK.

# Index

Page numbers in **bold** refer to figures, pages numbers in *italic* refer to tables


accountability 76
Alaska 266
Alignment 104–106
ambiguity 145–6
amendments 34–6, **35**
analyses, front-end phase 18–9
analysis paralysis 137
anarchistic type decision model **155**, 156
Association for Project Management, PRAM-guide 50
assumptions 52, 61, 131, 202–3, 265

basis alternative, the 101
Bayesian assessment **132**, 133–4
benchmarking 151–2
benefit/cost ratio (BCR) 84–5, 227
Berg, Peder, et al. 115
Bhopal, India, gas tragedy 231
Bøhren, Øyvind 229
boondoggles 257–8, 260
Borneo, Dayak people 86–7
bounded rationality model 18–9
brainstorming sessions 183
broad planning perspective 24–6
budgets 5, 7–8, 77, 198, 267
building project, stakeholder analysis 108–10, **108**, *109*
business case, the 11, 91, 99

Calculation Method 152–3
Campus in Trondheim (CiT) project 119–20, **121**
Carson, Rachel 89
cash flow 226–8, **226**, **227**
cash flow analysis 36–7, **36**, 165
causality 125, 146–7
cause-effect chains 26, **87**, 94, 96, **97**, 114, 122–3, **123**, 124, **125**, 126, 147
certainty, front-end phase 15
Chernobyl nuclear reactor accident 231
client satisfaction 11
cognitive biases 135
commissioners 21, *21*, 210, 212–3; perspective *23*, 24, 29, 37; time perspective *29*
common need 101
communication 153–4
communication theory 64
competitors 107
complex systems, dynamic simulation models 55
complexity 39, 40, **44**, 46–7, **48**, 70
complexity theory 69
computational phase 135
concept assessment 9, 160, 165; cost estimation 165; profitability appraisal 165; progress analysis 166; project planning 166; risk analysis 165–6
concept definition 9, 90, 99, 160, 161, 162; systems analysis 162–3
concept development 9, 34, 93, **93**
concept elaboration 160, 163; strategic frame requirements 164; strategy analysis 163–4; SWOT analysis 163; uncertainty mapping 164
concepts 11, 26–8, 90, 99; alternatives 97–100, **98**; appraisal tools 159–60, **161**; cause-effect chains 94, 96, **97**; choice of 25, 97–103, 260, 266; design 27; formulation 27, 30; hierarchy **28**; identifying 94; lack of consideration 68; layout 26; mini-concepts 102–3; objectives 27, **28**; and

concepts – *continued*
problems 97–8, **98**, 101; qualitative assessment 157; and strategic choice 90–4, **91**, **92**, **93**; strategic failure 12–8; the zero option 94, 101–3
Concorde 257–8
conflict 107, 110
consensus-based assessment 64–5
consequence studies 107
consultant sector 160
context setters 111–2, **111**
contextual conditions 266
contractors 21–2, *21*, 210, 212; front-end phase 30–1; perspective 20–1, 22–3, *23*, 29; tactical concerns 22
contracts 24
control parameters 214
cost calculations 215–8; deterministic *216*; stochastic 216–8, *216*, **217**
cost overruns 5, 10, 12, 76–82, **79**, **80**, **81**, 264
cost-benefit analysis 83, 233
costs and cost estimation 4–5, 77, 78, 165; and accountability 76; amendment 35; approximation 220, **220**, *221*; calculations 215–8, *216*, **217**; confidence intervals 267; contextual conditions 266; control 77; and delays 37; detailing 222–3, *222*, *223*; deterministic 7, 269; efficiency 88; errors 224; expert group 218–9; final 267; front-end phase allocations 67; front-end phase budget increase 77; implementation phase 81–2; information 62–5, **63**; initial 220–2; probabilistic 212, 242–3; probability distribution 223–4, **224**; and profitability 225–6; project constituent items 219–20, **219**; project definition and delimitation 218; rise 78; shopping centre example 218–24, **219**, **220**, **221**, *221*, *222*, *223*, **224**; standard deviation 222; stochastic 216–8, *216*, **217**, 225–6, 269; strategic underestimation 78–82, **81**; tactical cost estimation 82; top-down probability-based 215–24, *216*, **217**, **219**, **220**, **221**, *221*, *222*, *223*, **224**; totals **217**; uncertainty 7–8, 49, 78, **79**, 216, 221–2, **221**, 267; underestimation 77–8, 78–82, 263; variance 221–2, **221**, 223
creativity theory 268
critical need 101
Critical Path Method (CPM) 240
crowds 112

decision bases 134
decision makers 19, 265
decision making 19, 61, 260–3, **261**, 268. *see also* finance decisions; outcome space 40–1, **41**, **42**; risk policy 41–2, **42**; uncertainty in 38–42, **40**, **41**, **42**, 54
decision theory 64
definition phase 34
Delphi techniques 172
demand analyses 96–7
determinism 69
deterministic analysis 240
deterministic estimates 7, 269
deviance, normalization of 264
discontinuities 56, 57–8, **58**; predictable 58–60, **59**, 260, 263
discounted cash flow 227–8, **227**
discounted yield on investment 228
diversification 50
Downey report 100
Drucker, Peter 267
durations, estimation 244–7, *245*
dynamic simulation models 55

earthquake emergency centre, Mexico 72
Eastern Europe, quality assurance systems 73
economic analysis 103
economic viability 85, 103

effectiveness 10–1, 14, **16**, **106**, 251, 253, 259
effects 86–9, **87**, 101; project alignment 104–6, **105**
efficiency 10–1, 14, **16**, 251, 253, 259
Eiffel Tower, Paris 91–2, **92**
Eisenhower, Dwight D. 7, 68
emergence 69
Empire State Building, New York 15–6
energy system choice 173–81, **173**; alternatives 176–7, *177*; comparative framework 174, **174**; evaluation 179, **179**; identification of needs 175, *175*; performance appraisal 177–8, *178*; requirement specification 175–6, *176*; system definition 174; system description 180–1, **180**
entry phase 33
environmental impact 89
European Commission 189
evaluation: criteria 251–3, **252**, 253–6, **255**, 259; effectiveness 251, 253, 259; efficiency 251, 253, 259; end 250, **250**; Ex ante 250; ex ante **250**, 253–6, **255**; ex-post 250, **250**, 253; formative 249; impact 251–2, 253, 259; interim 250, **250**; model 251–3, **252**; relevance 252, 253, 256, 259; success 248–9; summative 250; sustainability 252–3, 254, 256, 259; types of 249–50, **250**; value of 259
event uncertainty 49
exchange rates 50
execution 33, **33**
expert group reviews 183
experts 131, 268; cost estimation 218–9; judgement 134–5, 136, 194–5
explanatory phase 135

facts 131, 132
failure, causes of 262–3
finance decisions 149–51; communication 153–4; decision basis 153; information base 150, 151–2, **152**; methods and analyses 152–3; quality assurance 154–7, **155**, **156**; reality check 154
financial sustainability 88
findings, precision 8–9
fixed-price contracts 211, **211**
flexibility 44
foreign currency 50
framework conditions, adapting to 70
framework plans 44
France 91–2
frequentist assessment 132–3, **132**, 136
front-end assessment 36–7, **36**, 158–9; tools 159–62, **161**
front-end phase analysis 132–3
funding, approval 13–4
future, creating the 264

GIGO, garbage in–garbage out 8–9, 150
Gjærum, Per Ivar 229
goals 23, 25, 26, 27, 29–30, 53, 75, 91, 93; achieving 3–5, **5**; amendments 34–5; conflicting 67; formulation 128–9; hierarchy 120, **121**, 128; project alignment 104; qualitative 126; setting 96–7; statements 117–8
Goodwin, Paul 136
governance 31
governance frameworks 100
gradual changes **59**

half life of information 64, 136–137
hearings 107
heuristics 135

identification phase 34
impact 10–1, 13, 14, **16**, 251–2, 253, 259; assessment 25, 96–7, 108
implementation phase 8, 22, 30, 34, 37; contextual uncertainty 47; costs 81–2, **81**; resource allocation 67; stakeholders interests *31*

incentive contracts **211**
inception phase 101
individual judgement **132**, 135–6
influence diagrams 233, 236, **237**
influence versus interest grids 110–2, **111**
information 130–1; base 151–2, **152**; cost/benefit 62–5, **63**; data choice 152; flow 151, **152**; half-life of 64; hierarchies 144, 147–8; increase in volume 138; lack of exact 8–9; precision 64, 142–3, **143**, 144; and predictability 54, 60–1; qualitative 128, 131, 138–40, **139**, **140**, 141, 148; quality 64; quantitative 131, 138–40, **139**, 142, 148; relevance 63; reliability 141–3, 143, **143**, 148; sources 151–2; and uncertainty 43–5, **43**; validity 136–7, **137**, 141–3, **141**, 143–5, **143**, *144*, 148
initial phase 158
initiators 20
institutional conditions 89
internal rate of return (IRR) 229
international development agencies 99
intuition 136
investment cases 90–1, **91**
investment projects 19, 113–4, 115, 262–3

Japan, submarine tunnel project 265
judgemental data 8, 130–131
judgemental evaluation 194

key players **111**
Kharbanda, O. P 259

legislation, compliance with 88
Lesotho, small-scale industries 73
Level of ambition 27, 28, 116, 117, 122, 123, 126
life-cycle perspective 29–31, **29**, *31*, 34
Limits to Growth model 266, 268
Link, Robert H. 257
Lofoten road connection project 125, **125**, 128
log frame analysis 128
logic 146
Logical Framework method 189–92, **189**, **197**, 200–1, **201**, 232; basis for 192–4; components 190–1; concept layout **197**; consistency 190; elements 192; Stad shipping tunnel project example 195–9
long-term perspectives 7

management 72
market analyses 25
Merkhofer, M. W. 135
Mexico, earthquake emergency centre 72
Millennium Dome, London 258
Mintzberg, Henry 267
Monte Carlo simulation 152–3, 172, 216, 224, 233–5, 242, 244–5

National Defence Reserve Conference, 1957 7
needs 104–6, **105**, **106**, 263
needs analysis 34
neighbours 107, 108–10, *109*, 112
net cash flow 227
net present value (NPV) 228–9, **228**
network analysis 166, 239–42, **241**, 243–4, **244**
network scheduling 240
normalization of deviance 264
North Sea, off-shore oilfield development project 264
Norwegian combat aircraft project 120, 122–3, *123*, 126

objectives 6, 10, 113–6; analysis 193; assessment 28; cause-effect chains 114, 122–3, **123**, 124, **125**; conflicting 114; definition 113; formulation 114, 117–9, 119, 122, 124, 125, 128; hierarchies 22, **28**, 113–4, 116–7; hierarchy design **127**;

identifying 119–25, **121**; linked 116–7; multiple 114; parallel 117; probability assessment 126–9; project alignment 104–6, **105**, **106**; project with fleeting justification 120, 122–3, *123*; project with no obvious justification 124–5, **125**; purposeless project 125; specification 118; statements 119–20, 122, 124, 125; structure 27; top-heavy subproject 119–20
operational phase 30, *31*, 34, 37
operations 3–4
opportunities 39, 39–40, **40**, 41
Organization for Economic Co-Operation and Development (OECD) 10, 87–8, 189
Oslo airport express rail line 84–5, **84**, 97, 265
Oslo Opera House 78–9, 93
outcomes 72–4, **74**; possible 261–2, **261**; success indicators **18**
outputs 26; probability assessment 126; success indicators **18**

participation analysis 193
payback period 227
performance 114; appraisal 177–8, *178*; strategic and tactical 10–1, 12–8, **12**, 256
perspectives, focus 22–3, *23*
phases 32–7, **33**, 37. *see also* individual phases
Pinto, J. K. 11, 259
planning 7, 9, 33, **33**, 34, 67, 75. *see also* strategic planning; assumptions 47; concept assessment phase 166; front-end phase 18–9; long-term 69; scenario 61–2; tactical flexibility 68–71
players 111, **111**
policy support measures 88
political priorities 19
pre-appraisal phase 34
precision: findings 8–9; information 64, 142–3, **143**, 144; word usages 145–6
predictability 264; complex events 55; and discontinuities 57–8, **58**; and experience 194; factors affecting 52–4; foreseeing 51–2; and information 60–1; models and theories 264; predictable discontinuities 58–60, **59**, 260, 263; simple events 54–5; trends 56–7, **57**
preparation 134–5; and success 66–7
pre-project study 66, 158, 160, 166
price 30–1
prioritization **28**, 53, 105–6, **106**
probabilistic assessment 144
probability 38, 146, 147, 202–3, **261**, 262; assessment 54–5, 126–9, 144; conditional 198; cost estimation distribution 223–4, **224**; estimates 133; risk analysis 230–1, 232, 233, 236; subjective 139, **140**
problem analysis 193
process, project 29–30
profitability 165, 225–9, **226**, **227**, **228**
Program Evaluation and Review Technique (PERT) 240
progress analysis 166, 239–42, **241**; linking a town to the mainland example 242–7, **243**, **244**, *245*, **246**
project activity 24, 68, 159
project alignment: needs, objectives and effects 104–6, **105**, **106**; stakeholder analysis 106–12, **108**, *109*
project concept 6, 8, 11, 18, 25, 26–28, 37, 62, 70, 136, 154, 162, 189, 190, 206, 255, 260
project contractor see project manager
project efficiency 251
project goal 23, 29
project governance 31
project inception 137, 260
Project life cycle **43**

project management 5, 8, 11, **17**, 25, 33, **33**, **44**, 45, 71, 72, 74, 115, 166, 209, 240
*Project Management* (Drucker) 267
Project Management Institute, PM-BOK 50
project management studies 22
project managers 7, 20, 22, 45, 47, 70
project performance 16
project phase 32–34, 35, **46**, 160
project profitability 225, 226
project risk management 50
project stakeholders 20
project strategy 53, 71, 122, 191, 196–198
project success 17, **17–18**, 31, 67
project utility 85
projects: attributes 3–5, **5**; costs 4–5; definition 4, 11; examples 4; numbers 3; perspective 21; size 4; temporary 3
purpose 24, 30
pyramids, building of 264

qualitative information 128, 131, 138–40, **139**, **140**, 141, 148
quality assurance 25, 73, 101, 154–7, **155**, **156**
quality at entry 31, 32, 36–7, 260–3
quantitative information 131, 138–40, **139**, 142, 148

rational-decision model 18
rationalism 18, 146–7
realism 154, 198
reference concept, the 101
regional development 27
reimbursement contracts 210, **211**
relevance 10–1, 13, 14, 14–5, **16**, 252, 253, 256, 259, 263
resources, allocation 27, 115
*Rise and Fall of Strategic Planning, The* (Mintzberg) 267
risk and risk analysis 38, 44, 50, 128, 159, 165–6; classification 202, 203–8, **203**, **205**, 233; and complexity **48**; consequences 230–1, 232, 233, 236; contractual assignment of 210–1, **211**, 212; definition 38–9, 230–1; factor identification 232–3; fatal **205**, 206–7; IT system example 235–8, *236*, **237**; low 204, **205**; As Low As Reasonable Possible (ALARP) principle 234, **234**; matrix 231–2, **232**, 234–5, **235**, 236, **237**, 238; outcome space 40–1, **41**; outcomes 39; policy 233–5, **234**, 238; probability 230–1, 232, 233, 236; quantifying 230–1; real **205**, 207–8; responsibility for 30; severity scales 235, *236*; Stad shipping tunnel project example 203–8, **205**, **206**; total 265; transference of 5, 30–1; unacceptable 234
risk matrix 231–2, **232**, 234–5, **235**, 236, **237**, 238
risk policy 41–2, **42**

scenario analysis 61
scenario planning 61–2
scenario techniques 232–3
*Scorpion*, USS 133–4
Second World War 264
self-organization 44
*Silent Spring* (Carson) 89
simulations 55, 268
Slevin, D. P. 11
small-scale industries, Lesotho 73
social aspects, appraisal of 88–9
societal systems 55, 56
SpaceShipOne 94, **95**
Stad shipping tunnel project 124–5, **125**, 126–8; budget 198; concept 195–6, **197**; fatal risk factors **205**, 206–7; low risk factors 204, **205**; opportunities 204–6, **205**; project strategy 196–8, **197**; real risk factors **205**, 207–8; uncertainty analysis 203–8, **205**, **206**; uncertainty factors 198–9, 203–4
stakeholders 6, 20–2, *21*, 71; analysis 106–12, **107**, **108**, *109*, **111**; interests 22–4, *31*, 265, 267; perspectives 22–4, *23*;

power 111–2; priorities 265; role 21, *21*
statements: goals 117–8; objectives 119–20, 122, 124, 125; word usages 125–6
statistical analysis 132
steering documents 115–6
stochastic cost estimation 216–8, *216*, **217**, 225–6, 269
stochastic network analysis 241–2, **246**
strategic assessments 67
strategic choice, and concepts 90–4, **91**, **92**, **93**
strategic depth 67
strategic frame requirements 164; assignment of risk 210–1, **211**, 212; strategic frames 211–3, **212**; strategic guidance and tactical flexibility 209–10; tactical flexibility **212**; university complex example 213–4
strategic frames 211–3, **212**
strategic guidance 66–8, 209–10
strategic perspectives 7
strategic planning 7, 8–9, 66, 68, 264, 267; limits 71–5, **72**, **74**
strategic underestimation 78–82, **81**
strategy analysis 163–4, 188–92, **197**; expert judgement 194–5; Logical Framework method 189–92, **189**, 192–4; Stad shipping tunnel project example 195–9
subcontractors 29
subjectivist assessment **132**, 134–5, 136
subjects **111**, 112
success 10–9, **12**, 262; definition 16; evaluation 248–9; indicators 16–7, **16**, **17**, **18**; measurement 15–7, **17**; and perspective 22; and preparation 66–7
success criteria 10–1, 14, 15–7, **16**; case studies 12–8, **16**, **17**, **18**
sustainability 10–1, 13, 14, 15, **16**, 88, 252–3, 254, 256, 259, 263
SWOT analysis 42, 128, 163, 182–7, **183**, **185**, 192, 193, 232; housing development example **185**, 186–7; procedure 183–4; results 184; strength 184, 186, 187; weaknesses 186, 187
Sydney Opera House 22
systems analysis 162–3, 192; alternatives 176–7, *177*; comparative framework 174, **174**; definition 169; evaluation 179; identification of needs 175, *175*; model 170–1, **171**; performance appraisal 177–8, *178*; process 169–72, **170**; process example 173–81, **173**; requirement specification 175–6, *176*; steps 172; system definition 174; system description 180–1, **180**
systems theory 69

tactical cost estimation 82
tactical flexibility 68–71, 71, 209–10, **212**
tactical performance 7, 256
technocratic decision model 154–6, **155**
technology, choice of 89
termination phase 34
time perspectives *29*, 30
time span 6
torpedo battery project, Norway 13–4, 19, 249, 254, **255**, 256, 257
trends 56–7, **57**; interpretation 60; and predictable discontinuities 59, **59**
triangulation 266–7

uncertainty 7–8, 30, 35–6, **35**, 74, 189, 191–2, 264; assessment procedure **206**; broad planning perspective 24–5, *25*; and choice 40–1; classification 201–2; and complexity 39, 40, 44, 46–7, **48**; contextual 45–9, **46**, 48, 70, 74–5; costs and cost estimation 7–8, 49, 78, **79**, 216, 221–2, **221**, 267; in decisions 38–42, **40**, **41**, **42**, 54; definition 35; and estimates **246**; estimation of 49; event 49; factors 54;

uncertainty – *continued*
identifying 200–3, **201**; impact of 43; and information 43–5, **43**; mapping 164; operational 45, **46**, 48, 49; and opportunities 39–40, **40**; outcome space 40–1, **41**; outcomes 39; and progress 239–40, 242, **246**; and risk policy 42; Stad shipping tunnel project 198–9; systematic 49–50, 265; unsystematic 49–50
uncertainty analysis 200–3, **201**; assessment procedure **206**; low risk factors 204; opportunities 204–6; risk classification 202–3, 203–8, **203**, **205**; Stad shipping tunnel project example 203–8
uniqueness 3
United Nations (UN) 10, 99, 105, 189
United States Agency for International Development (USAID) 10
University Hospital project, Oslo 12, 14–5, 19, 147–8, 159–60, 249, 254, **255**, 256
University Hospital project, Trondheim 78
USAID 99
user analyses 25
user satisfaction 144, *144*
users 21, *21*, 22; perspective 23, *23*
utility 11, 21–2, 83–9, 203; definition 83–4; effect and impact 86–9, **87**; overestimation 84–6, **84**, **86**

viability 85, 103, 198, 206–7
water supplies, Zambia 73, 258–9
White Elephants 258–60
word usages, ambiguity 125–6
work, organization 3–4
World Bank 32, 66, 99
World Drinking Water Supply and Sanitation Decade 105–6
World Health Organization 86–7
Wright, George 136

Zambia, water supplies 73, 258–9
zero option, the 94, 101–3